Rhodes and the Dodecanese

Travellers' Guide

Rhodes and the Dodecanese

by Jean Currie

with 16 photographs by Cora Pongracz

Jonathan Cape London 1975

First published 1970
Revised edition 1975
Text and maps © Copyright Helga Greene 1970
Photographs © Copyright Cora Pongracz 1970
Maps by Janet Landau
General Editors: Judith Greene and Kenneth MacKinnon

Jonathan Cape Ltd
30 Bedford Square, London WCI
ISBN 0 224 01051 4

Printed in Great Britain
by Richard Clay (The Chaucer Press) Ltd, Bungay, Suffolk,
for Jonathan Cape Ltd, 30 Bedford Square, London WCI

CONTENTS

MAPS AND CHARTS

Acknowledgments

I am greatly indebted to the following publishers for permission to quote from works under their imprint:

Cassell & Company Ltd, *The Second World War* by Winston S. Churchill and *Journey to a Greek Island* by Elias Kulukundis.

Faber & Faber Ltd, *The Home Book of Greek Cookery* by Joyce M. Stubbs.

George Rainbird Ltd, *Gods, Men and Wine* by William Younger on behalf of The Wine and Food Society. Published by Michael Joseph Ltd.

Routledge & Kegan Paul Ltd, *Patmos* by Friedrich Hölderlin, translated by Michael Hamburger.

Many other works quoted are long since out of copyright but it would be ungrateful not to record the pleasure I feel in my debt to Thackeray, whose *Notes on a Journey from Cornhill to Grand Cairo* reveal him as a uniquely entertaining travel journalist; to the remarkable eighteenth-century lexicographer, Dr John Lemprière, D.D., whose *Classical Dictionary of Proper Names in Ancient Authors* has been likened to Johnson's *Dictionary* for sheer readability; to the two volumes of Charles Newton's *Travels and Discoveries in the Levant*, a vice-consul of the nineteenth century with an enviable ability to record and bring to life the stuff of his wanderings; and finally to Cecil Torr, the author of the nineteenth-century classics of reference *Rhodes in Ancient Times* and *Rhodes in Modern Times*.

Among the many people and organizations who have helped me gather the matter of this book I wish particularly to thank the staffs of the National Tourist Organization of Greece in Rhodes, London and Athens, the staff of the Archaeological Service of the Dodecanese in Rhodes, Miss Jane Taylor who read the manuscript in its various stages and even gave up holidays to travel some of the ground with me, Miss Mary Coleman who managed to read my writing and produce a model typescript, my husband for his help with this revised edition, and, not least, that most civilized of employers, the J. Walter Thompson Co. Ltd who gave me the sabbatical that enabled me to undertake the field-work of this book.

Finally, I must acknowledge the part played by all those authors and compilers of all nationalities who have covered the field before me. My views and facts are my responsibility, but it is inevitable that every work of this nature owes much to the discoveries of others. I only trust I have added some items of my own to the general store of knowledge.

Street well, Old Town, Rhodes

Turkish fountain, Old Town, Rhodes

Arch, Old Town, Rhodes

Wall, Old Town, Rhodes

Asklepieion, Kos

Ruined church converted to mosque, Old Town, Rhodes

Kamiros, Rhodes

Valley of the Butterflies, Rhodes

Street and Crusader arch, Lindos, Rhodes

Volcano, Nisyros

Donkey station, Lindos, Rhodes

View from Filerimos, Rhodes

Caves at Kefalos, Kos

Monastery of St John (interior), Patmos

Monastery of St John (rooftop), Patmos

Temple of Apollo, Monte Smith, Rhodes

INTRODUCTION

Some modern maps still call the Dodecanese by their old name of the Southern Sporades and, geographically, they are not incorrect. However, since 1908, custom has rechristened the group the '*dódeka nísos*': the Twelve Islands. Even this is a baker's dozen because it is generally allowed that there are thirteen islands in the Dodecanese (and one school of thought says fourteen). The essential Dodecanese, however, includes the following islands: Rhodes, Kos, Kalymnos, Leros, Patmos, Simi, Tilos, Nisyros, Karpathos, Kasos, Chalki, Astypalaia and Kastellorizzo.

The modern Dodecanese is not the first group to be so named. To the traveller of the eighth century A.D., the Dodecanese denoted a group of islands in the Cyclades. As late as the thirteenth century, Naxos was designated capital of the Duchy of the Dodecanese, and one of the Venetian Dukes who ruled Naxos held the title of Duke of the Dodecanese. Certainly it is clear that the Byzantines, when they talked or wrote of the Dodecanese, did not mean the present group; this they still knew as the Southern Sporades.

The name came to life again in 1908 when it proved a convenient label for the twelve islands which were protesting that the privileges accorded them in the sixteenth century by Suleiman the Magnificent were being withdrawn. (Neither Rhodes, now the senior island of the Dodecanese, nor Kos was among these original 'privileged islands'.) It is interesting to reflect that today the Dodecanese are still privileged: later in this book you can read how they came to be given special tax exemptions after the end of the Second World War.

Whatever the shifting political name of the group, geographically the islands of the Dodecanese are nearer to Asia Minor than to Greece. Most of them lie virtually off shore from Turkey and throughout history they have enjoyed or endured the spoils and toils of this position. Lying as they do on one of the main routes between east and west, the islands have held key positions in Aegean strategy; one moment triumphant, the next invaded and oppressed.

Today, the Dodecanese include some of the most attractive holiday islands in the Aegean.

To most people, a great part of the appeal of Greek islands is in their variety and individuality. Thus, the Dodecanese are not only entirely unlike the Cyclades (geographical structure, appearance and architecture are markedly different) but islands within each group can exhibit very dissimilar characteristics. For example, Kos is mostly green, gentle and floral and has been strongly influenced by the Knights of St John, the Turks and the Italians. An hour by boat from Kos is Kalymnos, which is spare, rocky and indomitably Greek. Kalymnos suffered the same invasions as Kos but she simply refused to absorb anything of her invaders' customs, culture or architecture. (A Kalymniot once bragged to me that everything the Italians built during the day the islanders pulled down overnight.)

There are of course many common denominators but which island or islands appeal to you most will depend on what you are looking for on your holiday.

The following list should help (see also the Chart of excursions opposite p. 29):

1. Islands best organized to receive tourists (i.e. hotels, transport, etc.): Rhodes, Kos.
2. Best beaches (accessibility, safety, sand, etc.): Rhodes, Kos, Patmos, Kalymnos.
3. Best bus service: Rhodes, Kos.
4. Wooded islands: Rhodes, Leros.
5. Bare islands: Kalymnos, Patmos, Simi, Tilos, Nisyros, Astypalaia, Kastellorizzo, Chalki.
6. Plentiful taxis: Rhodes, Kos, Kalymnos, Leros.
7. Best for Archaic, Classical and Hellenistic remains: Kos, Rhodes.
8. Byzantine churches, etc.: Rhodes, Patmos.
9. Castles, fortresses, etc., of the Knights of St John: Rhodes, Kos, plus some lesser examples on Kalymnos and other islands.
10. Turkish influences: Rhodes, Kos.
11. Best museums: Rhodes, Kos, Patmos.
12. Worth taking your car to (or car hire available): Rhodes, Kos.

GETTING TO THE DODECANESE

The following information is based on high-season timetables: in winter, frequency is reduced and special inquiries should be made. There are several British tour operators offering excellent tours by air and sea which include Rhodes. For further information refer to the National Tourist Organization of Greece (N.T.O.G. for short), 195–97 Regent Street, London WIR 8DL. In the U.S.A., apply to the National Tourist Organization of Greece, 601 Fifth Avenue, New York 10017, N.Y.

AIR

To Athens

From London: Daily flights to Athens by British Airways and Olympic Airways, connecting with flights to Rhodes (see below).

N.B. All Olympic flights land at Athens West Terminal, all other airlines land at Athens East. This means that if you fly Olympic and are flying onwards to Rhodes, Kos or other internal destinations, you simply transfer to the domestic departure lounge. If you arrive at Athens East you will need to take a taxi or airline bus to transport you to Athens West.

To Rhodes

From London: British Airways and Olympic flights once or twice weekly direct to Rhodes. Summer only.

From Athens: Daily. Up to six times a day during the season.

From Crete: Once daily during the season.

From Karpathos: Four times weekly during season.

To Kos

From Athens: Daily, once or twice a day.

To Karpathos

From Athens: Four times weekly during season via Mykonos, Rhodes. However, it is cheaper and quicker to fly to Rhodes and connect with the plane to Karpathos from here.

N.B. The Skyvans which fly this route are only 18-seaters, so you should book well ahead.

AIR TOURS

From Athens: Several tour operators, including C.H.A.T., Key Tours, A.B.C., organize short air tours from Athens of 3 to 4 days which include Rhodes.*

From Rhodes: C.H.A.T. also offer a short air tour, Rhodes–Crete–Rhodes.

N.B. A few other Dodecanese islands can now be reached by small charter or private aircraft or helicopters operated by Olympic Airways. For further information apply to Olympic Airways, 141 New Bond Street, London WI or to the N.T.O.G. (address above).

PACKAGED TOURS

From London, Gatwick, Manchester, etc.

There are a number of packaged tours which are either based on or include one or more islands of the Dodecanese. Apply to the N.T.O.G. for latest information.

RAIL

There are three main routes to Athens from London: via Calais, Paris, Milan, Belgrade, Thessaloniki; Ostend, Cologne, Munich, Thessaloniki. For information, refer to British Rail Travel Centre, Lower Regent Street, London SWI.

EUROPABUS

Mid June to September: London–Ostend–Munich–Belgrade–Skopje–Thessaloniki–Athens.

* *Individual Tours*

A number of firms specialize in supplying tours specially tailored to individual needs. Of these, personal experience leads me to recommend two: Olympic Air Cruises Ltd, 141 New Bond Street, London WIY OBB, an organization which can devise a 'personal package' using scheduled services of Olympic Airways, and Hayes and Jarvis (Travel) Ltd, 6 Harriet Street, London, SWIX 9JP. This company is at the more expensive end of the scale but you get full value for money in efficiency and unobtrusive personal attention throughout the journey. Moreover, virtually every hotel they list has been personally visited by at least one member of their staff.

SEA

To Athens

There are sea routes from Genoa, Venice, Ancona, Naples, Brindisi, Bari, Marseilles and Trieste. For further information refer to the N.T.O.G.

To Rhodes

All islands of the Dodecanese except one (Kastellorizzo) are served by regular scheduled steamers from Piraeus. Frequency varies according to the importance of the island. One or more vessels a day leave for Rhodes but smaller islands may be visited only once a week or less. (See p. 37 for further details.) It is well to realize that cargo is as important as passengers on many of these boats: they are the service links with the islands, bringing and collecting food, stores, post, etc., so timetables may run late if loading or unloading takes longer than expected.

From Piraeus: At least one, often two, sailings per day. No sailing Sunday.

From other ports in the Mediterranean and Adriatic: Several shipping lines have cruise boats or passenger-carrying cargo vessels that call at Rhodes from Venice, Cyprus, Haifa, etc. For advice, ask the National Tourist Organization in London.

From Crete (ports of Aghios Nikolaos or Sitia)*:* Up-to-date information from tourist agencies in Athens.

From Turkey: Rhodes has day-excursions links with the Turkish mainland. Inquire at the National Tourist Organization of Greece in London or Rhodes or the Turkish Tourist Office, 49 Conduit Street, London wi.

Cruises to Rhodes

Several shipping lines and tour organizations offer short cruises from Athens which include Rhodes and sometimes Kos. Air/Sea cruises ex-London are run by Wings, Gellatly Hankey, Olympic Holidays, Thomas Cook, etc. Details from N.T.O.G., London, or travel agencies in Athens.

To Kos

From Rhodes: Excursion trips once or twice a week (see p. 37).

From Turkey: There are excursion trips between Kos and Bodrum, on the coast of Asia Minor. These generally start from Kos and return the same day. Inquire Kos, Athens or Bodrum.

TO PATMOS, LEROS, KALYMNOS

From Piraeus: By scheduled inter-island vessels and some tour organizations.

From Rhodes and Kos: By scheduled inter-island boats from Rhodes; by day excursions from Kos.

From Turkey: No regular routes from Turkey but there are occasional *caïque* excursions between the mainland and Kalymnos and Leros during the summer.

N.B. *For up-to-date information about excursions to Turkey mentioned in this book, refer to the N.T.O.G. or Tourist Police.*

BOOKING

Most sea voyages must be booked from a travel agent or shipping agent in Athens or in Piraeus. Air flights and cruises can be booked through your travel agent in London.

Agents in Athens or on the various islands are the only people who can keep up to date with the day-to-day vagaries of island shipping, and you should always check vessel, time of departure and even day of departure with them. A helpful source of potted information about sailings from Piraeus is the free weekly booklet, *This Week in Athens*, available from Olympic Airways in London and Athens. Sailings are also published in some of the Athens dailies (in Greek) and, if you plan to do a fair amount of movement from island to island, I recommend the *Key Travel Guide*, published monthly and available in Athens from: Key Travel Guide, 6 Kriezotou Street, Athens 134 (street running alongside the King's Palace Hotel). Price: Drs 75. This is the Bradshaw of the Aegean but even it is not infallible.

TRAVEL CONCESSIONS

Children, groups of students, teachers, artists, etc., are sometimes eligible for special discounts, but as the rates and circumstances vary according to the company it is not possible to set these out in detail here. You should refer to the National Tourist Organizations in London, New York, Athens or Rhodes; best of all, apply to the shipping companies or Olympic Airways direct.

CAR FERRIES

It is worth while taking a car to only two islands in the group – Rhodes and Kos. There are car ferries from Piraeus to Rhodes and landing is easy. Most scheduled vessels on the Piraeus–Kos run can accommodate a few cars. Check landing facilities with your travel agent. The N.T.O.G., London, will provide up-to-date details on cost (size of car is the factor), how to book, etc.

CAR DOCUMENTS

These are identical to those you need to bring your car into Greece:
Either (*a*) A 'Carnet de passage en Douanes';
or   (*b*) If you arrive at the Greek frontier without this, you can obtain a 'Vehicle Free Entry Card' valid for four months.
   (*c*) Your national driving licence.

PASSPORT AND CUSTOMS

No visa is required by British nationals. Your passport enables you to stay in Greece for up to three months; if you wish to stay longer you must apply to the Aliens Department, 9 Halkokondyli Street, Athens, for renewal of permission (arm yourself with three extra passport photographs). Your passport does not authorize you to seek employment.

EXCHANGE

You are allowed to bring unlimited amounts of foreign currency into the country (subject, of course, to being allowed to take unlimited amounts out of your own country). Sums of over $500 or equivalent in sterling must be declared, however. You may not take out of Greece foreign currency exceeding the amount that you brought in. Nor may you import or export Greek currency exceeding Drs 750. For this reason, when applying to your bank for traveller's cheques it is worth asking for a few in small denominations as it saves you, at the end of your visit, having to change an unnecessarily large cheque and so being left with too much Greek money. When leaving Greece, you are charged a tax of about Drs 40, so leave yourself enough to pay this tax.

N.B. *Current world-wide inflation makes it necessary to utter a warning about the prices mentioned in this book. They are accurate at the time of writing but crystal-gazing is not among the attributes of the writer. Please, therefore, apply to the N.T.O.G. for up-to-date information on all major costs prior to departure.*

CUSTOMS

You can bring in personal effects of most kinds except articles for sale. Note: All Dodecanese islands have their own Customs which will examine your luggage when you leave.

ANTIQUITIES

You may not buy antiquities (i.e. anything dated earlier than 1830) of any sort or period – Byzantine icons, Classical marbles, etc. – from any source other than a genuine dealer. And you may export these purchases only if you possess a special permit to do so from the Archaeological Service at the Ministry of the Prime Minister in Athens.

Do not attempt to smuggle out antique pieces of any kind. The authorities are very rough indeed on offenders and, following some fairly flagrant instances in the last few years, the police everywhere now keep a sharp look-out for sinners. Fines and/or prison sentences have been imposed.

TRAVEL WITHIN THE DODECANESE

AIR

The only inter-island connection within the Dodecanese is between Rhodes and Karpathos. Note that you can also fly to Rhodes from Crete (see p. 31).

SEA

Inter-island Steamers

For the most part, it is on the scheduled inter-island steamers plying in and out of Piraeus that you can travel from island to island.

You will find that islands are linked together in groups on these Piraeus–Rhodes schedules. One route from Piraeus includes Patmos, Leros, Kalymnos, Kos and Rhodes. (Note that on some days Patmos or Leros may be excluded from the ports of call; Kalymnos, Kos and Rhodes are always included.) To this group can be added, once weekly, Nisyros, Tilos and Simi.

A second route from Piraeus goes to Astypalaia and thence to Kalymnos, Kos and Rhodes. A third route is the Piraeus, Crete, Karpathos, Kasos, Chalki, Rhodes run.

The same groupings and variations apply to return journeys to Piraeus.

Thus, while it is possible to hop from one island to another within a linked group (e.g. from Rhodes to Kos, Kos to Kalymnos, or Karpathos to Kasos, etc.) it is less easy to travel from an island in one group to an island in another. For example, you cannot go direct from Astypalaia to Patmos (or vice versa). You would have to use Kalymnos as a place to change boats.

Frequency presents other problems. Between Rhodes, Kos, Kalymnos and Leros calls are almost daily. Patmos gets fewer calls, and Nisyros, Tilos, Simi, Karpathos, Kasos and Chalki are visited by only one boat a week in either direction.

It will be appreciated that detailed timetables are impossible to give here, for schedules vary from season to season and from month to month, but during the high season boats from Piraeus call at Dodecanese islands approximately as follows:

Astypalaia: once weekly
Patmos: 4 sailings weekly
Leros: 7 sailings weekly
Kalymnos: 13 sailings weekly
Nisyros: once weekly
Tilos: once weekly
Simi: once weekly
Kos: 14 sailings weekly
Rhodes: 15 sailings

Karpathos: once weekly
Kasos: once weekly
Chalki: once weekly
Kastellorizzo: no scheduled boats from Piraeus

Both Rhodes and Kos are useful stepping-off islands. From Rhodes you can go south-west to Karpathos, Kasos or Crete, or north to Simi, Tilos, Nisyros, Kos, Kalymnos, Leros, Patmos and Astypalaia. The same islands are accessible from Kos. From Kalymnos you can get to Astypalaia, Patmos, Leros, Kos and Rhodes.

For up-to-date timetables please refer to shipping agents or travel agents in Athens or on the islands.

You can get to Crete from Rhodes and vice versa: approximately once a week in the peak tourist season an inter-island scheduled boat runs from Mykonos to Rhodes.

It is worth noting that the local day-cruises from Rhodes, Kos and Kalymnos provide additional means of travel between islands. If these cruises are not full you can often travel one way on them, as on an inter-island steamer.

LOCAL STEAMERS

The *Panormitis II* calls at most of the Dodecanese islands on its weekly journey. This is a small and quite comfortable local steamer. It is one of the few local vessels – other than *caïques* – to call at Kastellorizzo. Inquire at the Panormitis II office in Georgiou Kirmichalis Street, Rhodes, or shipping agents on other islands, for details of the current timetable. Note that the *Panormitis* is a good deal slower than inter-island scheduled boats.

The *Rodias* of Chandris Cruises sails regularly out of Rhodes to Simi, Kos and some other islands of the group.

DAY-TRIPS BY SEA

Some tourist companies on Rhodes and Kos own small coastal vessels and offer attractive day-trips – sightseeing and swimming – along the coast. From Rhodes there are also short trips to nearer islands (Simi, Kos, etc.) and from Kos you can take one-day trips to Patmos, Kalymnos, Leros, Nisyros and Rhodes. There are ferry-boat trips and regular day-excursions to Marmaris on the Turkish mainland from Rhodes and regular day trips from Kos to Bodrum.

(If you enjoy the castle the Knights built on the waterfront of Kos, you will probably enjoy even more their great Castle of St Peter at Bodrum.)

LOCAL BUSES

Rhodes and Kos have regular bus services. The smaller islands have only one or two buses at most.

TOURIST COACHES

Plentiful and excellent on Rhodes; less frequent on Kos; rare or non-existent on other islands.

GUIDED TOURS

Official guides can be engaged on both Rhodes and Kos. The training of a Greek guide is lengthy and thorough, and official guides are usually well-read and intelligent.

On Rhodes: Apply to the N.T.O.G. or
  Mr and Mrs Cottis (tel. 24.566)
  Mrs Despo Papathanissi (tel. 22.307)
  Mrs Efi Papathanissi (tel. 24.148)
  Miss Phyllis Mavraki, C.H.A.T. (tel. 24.986)
  Mr Agapios Karpathios (tel. 6.03)

On Kos: Mr George Soultanos can be contacted through the Tourist Police or at the Hotel Kos.

Of the other islands, only Patmos really requires a guide, and the monks of the Monastery of St John perform this function.

TAXIS

Greeks take taxis as we take buses and are much less class-conscious about it. Taxis are relatively cheap and, when the price is shared between five housewives or several fishermen, the cost per person is little more than a bus. One advantage of this casual use of taxis is that the tourist is saved that uneasy feeling of 'lording' it or taking the easy way out. Moreover, the taxi is often the only sensible means of transport. Local buses don't always go there and back in a day but a taxi will – and show you far more than you might see by bus. And taxi-drivers, even those with little or no English, are always delighted to show off their islands. On some islands (Kalymnos is an example) a taxi is the everyday means whereby housewives living on one side of the island can do their shopping over in the port.

In general, taxi rates are similar to those operating on Rhodes:

Drs 3·80 per km. for return journey.
Drs 6·50 per km. one way only.
Drs 36 per hour waiting time (first 15 minutes free).
Drs 5 minimum and for journeys less than 1 km.
In the city itself, the average cost of a journey is between 12 and 20 drachmas.

If rates per km. are not quoted, arrange an all-in rate there and back before you start. The taxi-driver will take into account the length of time you want to be out as well as the distance to be covered.

CAR HIRE

Rates vary according to the size of car, but, as an example, the daily rate for a Fiat 850 is about Drs 287. Fully comprehensive insurance costs approximately Drs 45 per day. (You would be wise to take out this insurance.) These figures vary slightly from firm to firm but average out much the same. Generally, you receive the car with a full tank and pay for the amount used on your return. You can make advance arrangements to hire a car through your travel agent in England. (Ask your British Airways Agent for information about the British Airways/Avis Freewheeler holidays.)

The above rates are average for Rhodes and Kos. On other islands there are no recognized car-hire firms.

BICYCLE AND SCOOTER HIRE

Bicycles and scooters are available for hire on Rhodes and Kos. The charge for a bicycle ranges from Drs 4–6 per hour and Drs 25 per day. The rate for a scooter is approximately Drs 120 per day with no extra charge for the first 150 km. and the first tank of petrol. A powered cycle costs approximately Drs 30 per day. You are *not* covered by insurance when driving a hired scooter.

MOTORING

Drive on the right, and observe speed limits in town and country-side where marked. Elsewhere, use your own judgment.

The Italians, with their talent for road-making, made a great contribution towards the development of the islands when they set to work to give both Rhodes and Kos the basis of a good system of roads. This road system is now being extensively overhauled and rerouted. See pp. 94 and 137 for further information.

Note that there are sheer drops alongside some stretches of Rhodian road and it is as well to be prepared for these as they often have no protecting wall or fence. Most sign-posts give destinations lettered in both Greek and English alphabets.

PETROL

Cheaper in the Dodecanese than elsewhere in Greece.

On Rhodes and Kos there are pumps at all the more important villages. There are also pumps on other islands, e.g. Kalymnos, Leros, Patmos.

MAPS

One hopes that, when the new road system is complete, Rhodes will take the opportunity to produce maps of comparable quality to those obtainable on Crete. However, since the first edition of this book appeared, Rhodian maps have improved and the best of the current ones is large-scale and a great deal more accurate and detailed than its predecessors.

Kos has an adequate map of the island, and Patmos and Karpathos have both recently produced useful maps with helpful additional information. To date, none of the other islands yet has a tourist map.

HOTELS AND RESTAURANTS

By about May of each year, the National Tourist Organization of Greece in London can supply you with the latest list of hotels, with categories and prices. (Note that this list does not include many hotels in the least expensive categories, i.e. D and E.) If you plan to visit the Dodecanese in July, August, September or even October, you should book well in advance if possible. During these months foreign tourism is at its height and Greek families are on holiday, too. Rhodes, Kos and Patmos are particularly busy at this time.

The following gives general information about the hotel system in Greece. A selection of hotels is listed in the Information section for each island. Bear in mind that the only islands with hotels as we understand them are Rhodes, Kos, Kalymnos, Leros and Patmos. On all other islands, accommodation is often very simple and limited to pensions, restaurants with rooms to let or, perhaps, a few rooms in private houses.

CATEGORIES AND PRICES

Standards of accommodation and prices are set by the Government. Hotels are classified as L, A, B, C, D and E. The system works very well for the tourist, though there are some inevitable anomalies. Thus, a brand-new C-class hotel will quite probably be better value in terms of amenities than an older A-class hotel – though it may lack the character of the older hotel. The system of pricing has recently been re-organized and simplified. The provisions of the new system are stated on the printed notice that the law requires shall be displayed in all hotel bedrooms (excluding luxury hotels). On the notice you will find the inclusive price of the room during the summer season (April 1st–October 31st) and for the winter season (November 1st–March 31st).

AVERAGE PRICES (DRS)

The following prices are high-season rates and include services and taxes. Breakfast is generally an optional extra (except, of course, where you choose full or demi-pension terms). A very few hotels are authorized to charge obligatory demi-pension rates but do not necessarily do so; inquire about this on the spot or in advance.

Type of accommodation	L	A	B	C	D
Single room					
Without bath	205	150–200	120–145	95–115	79–90
With bath	350	265–345	120–175	120–175	105–115
Double room					
Without bath	360	240–355	180–235	120–175	110–115
With bath	500	360–495	215–355	170–210	135–165

If a private bath or shower is not provided in the room, hotels, pensions and rooms may charge Drs 14 for a hot shower and Drs 7 for a cold one.

A single person occupying a double room is charged 80 per cent of the double rate. If an extra bed is put into a room the price is raised by 20 per cent.

Note: (*a*) There can be quite considerable reductions on out-of-season room rates, and visitors should inquire about winter terms.

(*b*) There is a surcharge of between Drs 35 and Drs 55 for air-conditioning.

You are expected to vacate your room by 2 p.m. on the day of departure. If you stay on till 6 p.m. you are charged for an extra half-day. Beyond 6 p.m. the charge is as for a full day.

XENIA HOTELS

Xenia is the Greek word for hospitality, and hotels of this name were originally built and managed by the National Tourist Organization. They offer A, B and C class accommodation. At the time of writing, the only Xenia in the Dodecanese is on Grikou Beach on Patmos.

PENSIONS AND ROOMS

On arrival at an island you will probably find owners of pensions and rooms waiting on the waterfront, and you can always agree to look at what they offer without committing yourself. Don't hesitate to say 'no' if you don't like the accommodation; they won't be offended. The other sources of information are the N.T.O.G. office, wherever there is one, or the Tourist Police.

Accommodation of this sort is officially classed into A, B and C categories. Owners who want their rooms to appear on Tourist Police lists must submit them for inspection and classification.

Prices range from Drs 150 for double room with bath in an A-class pension to Drs 45 per bed in a D-class pension. Prices are often charged on this 'per bed' basis especially in village guesthouses where a bed will cost about Drs 25–40. These prices include service.

If a pension provides a common bathroom or shower an extra charge of a few drachmas can be made.

Many pensions provide breakfast: it is usual, however, to wander into the village and breakfast at a café.

YOUTH HOSTELS

There is no Youth Hostel in the Dodecanese.

CAMPING

You can pitch camp more or less where you like, but don't choose military or archaeological sites. If you fancy an orchard or farm-land, seek out the farmer if possible – if only as a courtesy. The N.T.O.G. or Tourist Police will give advice if you need it. Provisions can be bought in Rhodes or the villages. You can buy Li-los, canvas buckets, spirit stoves, etc., in the town.

VILLAS AND HOUSES TO RENT

There are few villas built specially for this purpose, but you can rent houses on Rhodes, Kos, Kalymnos and Patmos. Write to:

Rhodes: National Tourist Organization of Greece.

Kos: The Tourist Police, Kos.

Kalymnos and Leros: The Mayor of Leros, or the following agencies: Argonautis, Olympia Express.

Patmos: Mr Capranis, Estate Agent, Patmos; or Tourist Police.

TAVERNAS AND RESTAURANTS

Greece has a confusion of different categories of eating establishments, and Rhodes possesses examples of nearly all of them. The restaurant or *estiatório* is a relatively formal eating-place, generally conveniently situated for the tourist. *Tavérnas* are native Greek restaurants, today often catering for the tourist trade. At a *tavérna* you can eat local dishes, sometimes to the accompaniment of an ancient horn gramophone. (More likely, your music will come from a radio that will blast *bouzoúki* music at you through loud-speakers. Greeks love noise, the more of it the better.) *Tavérnas* in Rhodes are more tourist-orientated than most, and are likely to be equipped with refrigerators and similar modern catering assets. This is not to be truly regretted: food stays fresh and you are offered a wider variety of menu. In the traditional *tavérna*, how-ever, you go into the kitchen and choose from any of a dozen dishes simmering on the range.

Then there is the pastry shop or *zacharoplasteíon* which provides cakes, ices and sometimes light meals. Meals at a *zacharoplasteíon* are generally rather expensive and you can eat light dishes more cheaply at a small *tavérna*. The smarter pastry shops serve coffee but the others are usually quite willing to send a boy down the road to a *galaktopoleíon* to get it for you. The *galaktopoleíon* is a kind of dairy which serves milk, butter, yoghourt, bread and honey, and is a good spot for breakfast. Sometimes the two types of shop merge into one and you will see GALAKTOZACHAROPLASTEION over the door. The word is formidable but the result convenient.

The *kafeneíon* is the Greek gossip-shop and you will find some good examples in the old town of Rhodes where young men and old idle the hot afternoon away playing backgammon (*távli*) and talking politics and people, drinking Turkish coffee and herbal teas. There are also '*ouzeríes*' where, as you can guess, the speciality is *oúzo*. Rhodes has lots of snack-bars, too, and a number of eating places which specialize in Scandinavian food for the numerous Scandinavian tourists whom Rhodes attracts as flowers attract bees.

Names of some restaurants and cafés are included in the sections on each island.

NIGHTLIFE

Little or none on the smaller islands. On Rhodes, however, you can drink wine, dance, visit the casino, go to the cinema, watch 'Son et Lumière' or attend folk-dance programmes at Rodini Park or in the 'Medieval Theatre' in the Old Town. You can also take an evening trip by sea down the coast or join a coach tour to an outlying village to dine and watch the folk-dancing.

Kos has cinemas, *tavérnas*, a night-club. On all the other islands nightlife is limited to the *tavérna* and, sometimes, the cinema.

However, you can always consider arranging with a *caïque*-owner to join his crew on an all-night fishing stint (a marvellous experience), or you may find yourself somewhere in the hills joining in a name-day festival at some tiny church: drinking under the moon, dancing to a fiddle.

On most islands, however small, there is also the nightly *vólta*. This generally takes place between 6 and 8 p.m., and it is the time of day when Greeks dress up in their best (particularly the women and children), and stroll up and down the waterfront, meeting friends, showing themselves off to each other. Unmarried girls walk with their parents or in little groups; the boys walk strictly apart. It is still a very formal and strictly regulated society.

Prices are fixed by law and vary according to the class of restaurant or café. All bills will add a 10 per cent service charge. Only on Rhodes is it really possible to spend a lot of money on evening entertainment, and then only if you patronize the casino, the grander hotels, the smarter restaurants. It would be misleading, in the present financial climate, to hazard prices but it seems fair to say that, in general, a good but unassuming meal will be an unassuming price and that a glass of *oúzo* or *retsína* is still not a wild indulgence.

PRACTICAL INFORMATION

TOURIST INFORMATION

The National Tourist Organization of Greece (*Ellenikós Organismós Tourismoú*), 195–97 Regent Street, London WIR 8DL, is well-informed and helpful. In New York the address of the National Tourist Organization of Greece is 601 Fifth Avenue, New York 10017, N.Y.

The N.T.O.G. offices in Athens are at 6 Karageorgi Servias Street and 4 Stadiou Street. There is also an office at the Hilton Hotel.

Olympic Airways have an office at 141 New Bond Street, London WIY OBB, and in New York at 647 Fifth Avenue, 10022, N.Y.

The Ticket Office of Olympic Airways is at 6 Othonos Street, Athens; the International Town Terminal is at 96 Syngrou Avenue and the Domestic Terminal is at 122 Syngrou Avenue.

The British Airways Ticket Office is at 10 Othonos Street, Athens. (Othonos Street forms one side of Syntagma Square.)

Tourist Police are on duty at all the more frequented tourist centres of Greece. They are a branch of the national police force and wear an olive-green uniform with a 'Tourist Police' flash on the sleeve. Officers who speak a foreign language also wear the flag of that nation. Tourist Police inspect all restaurants, cafés, shops and accommodation, and complaints should be taken to them.

CLIMATE AND CLOTHES

The Dodecanese have ever been wonderfully sunny islands. 'The astonishing brightness and clearness of the sky under which the island seemed to bask, struck me as surpassing anything I had seen ... every fig tree was gilded and bright ... the creepers on the walls quite dazzled with the brilliancy of their flowers and leaves ... the people ... only talked a very little, as if idleness and silence were a condition of the delightful shining atmosphere in which they lived.'

Thus Thackeray, who in *A Journey from Cornhill to Grand Cairo* wrote such vigorous sense and made such illuminating comment about Greece and the Greeks that no one has quite matched him since (though on this matter of climate he was only echoing the reactions of visitors as varied as Strabo, Lucian and Alexander the Great).

Recent Rhodian figures record 136 hours of sun in January, rising to 440 in July. Temperatures are mostly pleasant but can rise to the middle or upper eighties in July, August and September.

For many, the late spring is the perfect time to visit the Dodecanese: it is warm but not too hot, wild flowers are abundant (the anemone is the first to appear, in January) and the islands begin to put forth their many varieties of cistus or rock-rose, the pink and white oleander, scarlet hibiscus and dense banks of bougainvillea. The evenings will be cool or mild and the sea warming up.

September and October are also very tempting. Most of the vegetation has dried up but the sun has also released memorable herbal scents among the hills and you can gorge on autumn fruits – particularly melon and grapes. If you fancy a post-Christmas holiday, you could do worse than come to Rhodes. I once arrived there on December 30th, and, save for a torrential downpour on New Year's Day, spent the following fortnight in sunshine and content. You cannot, of course, be guaranteed such weather, and February and March are certainly to be avoided.

In spring, women should bring a woollen dress and sweater and a coat or anorak for the evening and light things for the day. A sweater and anorak plus a warm shirt are recommended for men. In high summer, everything should be light, cotton and washable and don't stint on plenty of comfortable shoes and easy sandals. Always bring a sweater and anorak if you plan to travel by sea. If you stay in one of the luxury or near-luxury hotels of Rhodes you will need smarter dresses for the evening. Men will find a lounge suit useful but even in these hotels a dinner jacket is quite unnecessary.

HEALTH AND DRINKING WATER

RHODES

Rhodes is probably better supplied with doctors than any other island in Greece. In the town itself, a recent count listed 18 G.P.s, 2 surgeons, 5 gynaecologists, 1 heart specialist, 5 pediatricians and a T.B. specialist. There were also 13 dentists, 3 X-ray specialists and 2 oculists, as well as numerous chemists.

There is an Institute of Common Health, and the main hospital is the Vassilissis Olgas in Helvetias Street.

Drinking water in the town is perfectly reliable. Don't risk well-water; if in doubt, stick to *retsína*, *oúzo*, orangeade, soda-water, etc.

KOS

As the birthplace of Hippocrates, Kos would be embarrassed to be less than well served medically and is, accordingly, the workplace of a number of doctors who enjoy their link with the father of them all. It has also a hospital that bears Hippocrates' name. There are several chemists in the town.

KALYMNOS

One hospital, several doctors.

OTHER ISLANDS

Some will have at least one doctor or nurse, others will share medical help.

MONEY-CHANGING AND BANKS

The drachma is the coin of the country. It is divided into 100 lepta. Denominations are: 5, 10, 20, 50 lepta; 1, 2, 5, 10, 20 and 30 drachmas. This last coin is analogous to the British crown piece and you are unlikely to come across it very often.

Notes are Drs 50, 100, 500 and 1,000.

The English £ is worth roughly Drs 70 and the U.S. $ roughly Drs 30; but you should check exchange rates with your bank, as they are subject to considerable fluctuation.

The major banks, including the National Bank of Greece, the Commercial Bank of Greece and the Ionian and Popular Bank, have branches in the town of Rhodes and on Kos. On most of the smaller islands there will either be a branch at the chief town or a small sub-agency with a desk in a stationer's or grocer's shop.

Banks are open seven days a week on Rhodes and the hours of opening of main branches are:

Weekdays	08.15–13.00
	14.30–22.00
Sundays and	09.00–13.00
holidays	16.00–21.00

Opening hours are shorter on the other islands.

On Rhodes, some banks operate exchange offices in the centre of town around Cyprus Square. Hotels, too, will cash travellers' cheques, though the banks and exchange offices generally give you a better rate.

Whenever you are changing money, you should have your passport with you.

If you want to travel to Turkey from Rhodes or other Dodecanese islands, remember that you cannot exchange Greek currency for Turkish. You should either arm yourself with some American dollars – which can be bought from the Greek banks – or wait to cash a travellers' cheque into Turkish currency on arrival. This last is another reason why it makes sense to ask your bank for a few small-denomination travellers' cheques, as you may need only a small amount of Turkish money if you are taking a day-trip.

SHOPPING

Purchasers of petrol and drinkers of whisky will not take long to discover that these items are much cheaper among the islands of the Dodecanese than elsewhere in Greece. So is English cloth. So are furs. In Athens, whisky costs not much less than at home. In the Dodecanese you can reckon it costs about a third less.

Why these concessions? It all started in 1947 when the islands were reunited with Greece – after 390 years of Turkish rule and 35 of Italian. The central government in Athens decided to bestow certain marks of honour and privilege upon the islands. The privileges included taxation at a rate markedly lower than the rest of Greece, and this applied to personal taxation as well as duty on goods.

The period of reduced taxation was originally limited to ten years, but the privileges were extended and remain in force today.

The tourist benefits in various ways. Goods and raw materials which the Dodecanese imports direct from foreign countries enter at the reduced rate (though they are subject to a municipal tax of 4 per cent). On the other hand, items imported from Athens or via Athens are likely to cost more than in the capital, as they have to bear the cost of transport as well as municipal tax.

You might, therefore, expect English and American cigarettes to be cheap; in fact they are very expensive: about Drs 30 for twenty. This high price is aimed at protecting the large Greek tobacco-growing industry as a whole, and also the local, Rhodian tobacco industry. But you can get good-quality Greek cigarettes for Drs 10–15 (try 'Papastratos No. 1'). Rhodian cigarettes are even cheaper; ask for 'Special' (strong) or 'Zenith' (mild).

On Rhodes shopping can be very sophisticated. Newspapers from Europe and the U.S.A. arrive daily; there are several book-shops. You can get Scotties and Kleenex face tissues, Palmolive shaving cream and branded tooth-pastes, and hairdressers are excellent and reasonably cheap. It is quite usual to see furriers doing good business with wealthier visitors at ten o'clock on a hot Rhodian night.

If you want to picnic there are plenty of imported branded goods available – Nescafé, Maxwell House, Kraft processed cheeses, Plumrose tinned meats, Nestlé's tinned milk, Rowntree's chocolate, and other popular brands. All these, in spite of Rhodian tax privileges, will cost more than at home.

Side by side with these familiar items are the Greek staples and delicacies. You can buy fresh bread and rolls from small bakeries, also *paximádi* – the hard, rusk-like slabs that Greeks dunk into coffee or glasses of milk. There are round bread rolls, scattered with seeds and pierced in the centre by a hole so large that the small boys who sell them sometimes wear them like a giant bracelet up their arms. Rolls, cakes and biscuits can also be bought, more hygienically, from the little glass cabinets set up at the entrance to the New Market.

Fruit and vegetables are superb; as good to look at as they are to eat. According to season, you can buy melons, peaches, pears, apples, grapes, figs, oranges, lemons, strawberries, pomegranates ... Cucumbers are often peeled and eaten by Greeks as we eat bananas. Greek cheeses are well worth sampling, especially the salty, white *féta* (literally 'slice'), *kaséri* (a yellow cheese) and the Gruyère-like *graviéra*.

There is a variety of canned and bottled soft drinks (cans of the excellent 'Sunfix' orange juice are part of the Greek tourist scene). You can also buy bottled orange squash (*portokaláda*) and lemonade (*lemonáda*). (For natural orange squash and lemon squash, ask for *mia portokaláda himó* and *mia lemonáda himó*.)

SOUVENIRS

RHODES

Gold and silverware, jewellery, ceramics, woven dresses, lace, embroidery, dishes and bowls of olive wood, Turkish utensils of copper and brass – these are the most common souvenirs of Rhodes. The quality varies; and certainly one would hesitate to say that modern Rhodes is producing much original contemporary design. But some modern copies of Lindos plates and bowls are pleasing and you can buy old pieces from any of the many shops in Sokratous Street in the old town. Sokratous Street has many shops selling Turkish copper, wooden spinning staves, shish-kebab skewers. At No. 163 is Bergidis, a jeweller who makes charming reproduction jewellery, including copies of the Patmian ship pendants which eighteenth-century Patmos shipmasters gave to their wives. These tend to be somewhat expensive, of course, but Bergidis also makes less costly pieces. His silver rings, for example, are pleasing and original.

Also in the old town, just after passing under the arch from Argyrokastrou Square, is a jeweller of international standing, Elias Lalaounis. Whether he is copying or adapting classical work or devising a series of gold rings and brooches based on a highly unconventional idea, the result is beautiful and wearable.

The soft Rhodian peasant boots are very desirable and if you go to 13 Pithagoras Street in the old town you will find the workshop of Artemis Panas who will make you a pair. There are also one or two bootmakers in the village of Archangelos who will make boots for visitors.

In Panetiou Street, near the Palace of the Grand Masters, is an old and beautiful Turkish house which serves as showroom and shop for the wares of Nikos and Takis. Here the jewellery includes necklaces and bracelets of elegant design and Athenian ceramics in rich, sultry colours quite unlike the clear, bright tones of Lindian work. Woven materials are made up into sophisticated frocks and suits.

In the top price-bracket of souvenirs a woman visitor might (on condition that she is to be the recipient) include furs. Skins come from Kastoria near Thessaloniki and from Canada, and some are both beautiful and unusual. All Greece promotes its furs; in Rhodes they are cheaper than elsewhere.

Outside the city of Rhodes, only Lindos can be called a shopping centre. Most of the items already mentioned can be bought here, too, but, of course, Lindian plates are the chief temptation. Lindos also has a modern boutique, which sells everything from dresses and capes to 'Nureyev' caps.

OTHER ISLANDS

Kalymnos for sponges and honey; Patmos for the best postcards and tourist literature in the Aegean (on sale in the Monastery only);

Kos for a locally bottled jam. You can buy *kombollói* (Greek 'worry beads') almost everywhere. Some of the most desirable of Greek souvenirs are the cheapest – fragments or off-cuts of marble, vari-coloured polished pebbles, tins of Turkish coffee, dried figs, etc.

TIPPING AND HAGGLING

The rules of tipping are reasonably simple though sometimes deli-cate. A taxi-driver will not demand a tip but on such a cosmopoli-tan island as Rhodes he has probably come to expect one. It need only be a few drachmas unless you have been on a long run. In restaurants and cafés there is a service charge but it is usual to tip over and above. Where you leave the tip is important: a coin for the waiter should be left on a plate with the bill; anything placed on the table is the property of the boy who brings the water and brushes the table.

Haggling? Yes, haggle – within reason and propriety. In the souvenir shops of the old town a little enjoyable fencing will cer-tainly be understood and appreciated. However, there's no point in trying to bargain over the price of branded goods, even though there is no retail price maintenance in Greece.

CINEMAS AND THEATRES

Rhodes is well supplied with cinemas and the more populated of the other islands have one or more cinemas. On the smaller islands, the cinema may be an occasional event only: once a week or less.

The most regular and popular entertainment is 'Son et Lumière', which takes place nightly under the walls of the old town. There is also a folk-dance group which performs daily, except on Sundays, in the 'Medieval City' Theatre in the old town (*Map* **30**).

For details, see the Information section for each island.

MUSEUMS AND MONUMENTS

The museums and monuments of the Dodecanese are administered by the Archaeological Service of the Dodecanese. Sites and museums are open throughout the year; summer and winter opening times differ slightly. The summer period begins March 16th and ends October 15th; the winter session begins October 16th and ends

March 15th. Nowadays, summer opening times can be very flexible, opening earlier in the day, sometimes not even closing for lunch. On the other hand, during the very hot weather the lunchtime closure may be observed. This book gives opening and closing times but suggests the reader should make inquiries on arrival.

Museums in Rhodes are closed on Mondays (except the Museum of Decorative Arts). Museum and archaeological sites are also closed on the following national holidays: January 1st, March 25th (Independence Day), Orthodox Good Friday till 12 noon, Easter Sunday, Christmas Day. Local museums on the smaller islands set their own times of opening; ask the police or hotel.

Entrance is free on Thursdays and Sundays, except to groups of more than five, or persons accompanied by an official guide. Sites, unless otherwise indicated, are free.

A free pass is obtainable by foreign students of archaeology and professors and teachers of archaeology, fine arts, etc. To obtain this pass, apply to the General Directorate of Antiquities and Restoration, Department of Museums, 14 Aristidou Street, Athens. You will need a passport photograph and your passport or a certificate issued by your school or college. The office is open on Monday, Wednesday and Friday each week between 11.00 and 11.30 for issue of these tickets. (If you belong to one of these categories and have no opportunity to get a card, you can enter museums, etc., at half price providing you can show documentary proof of your occupation.) Season tickets for three months cost Drs 200. Apply to the Archaeological Funds Service, 1 Tossizza Street, Athens. Office hours: daily except Sundays and holidays 08.00–14.00.

CAMERAS

You can use a still camera or an 8mm. or 16mm. cine camera on open sites and in museums on condition that you don't use a tripod and do pay a sum equivalent to the general admission charge. An extra charge is made for the use of a camera with tripod whether on sites or in museums. N.B. Special charges and rules apply if you want to undertake photography involving opening showcases, use of electric current, etc. These charges differ according to whether you are amateur or professional. For detailed information, refer to the N.T.O.G. or write direct to the Office of the Director General of Antiquities, 14 Aristidou Street, Athens.

HOLIDAYS AND FESTIVALS

PUBLIC HOLIDAYS

National holidays (when shops and banks stay closed) are:

January 1st.
January 6th (Epiphany).
March 25th (Independence Day).
The Monday before Lent.
Orthodox Good Friday.
Easter Monday (note that the Orthodox Easter rarely coincides with Easter elsewhere and you should check the date with the N.T.O.G. in London).
June 6th (Feast of the Holy Spirit).
June 29th (St Peter and St Paul Day).
August 15th (Feast of the Panaghia).
October 28th ('Okhi' Day – on this day in 1940 Greece rejected Mussolini's ultimatum and entered the war on the side of the Allies).
Christmas Day and the day after.

FESTIVALS*

The following list includes national festivals and a number of the more important Rhodian or Dodecanesian festivals. As most of these dates are in the Orthodox calendar you will find similar celebrations taking place in one village or another throughout the Dodecanese.

January 6th	In **Rhodes** a bishop tosses a silver cross into the harbour outside the Church of the Evangélismós. Children dive for it, the winner is ducked, and later he takes the cross from village to village and is rewarded with money, food and oil.
January 7th	Feast of St John the Baptist. Lawrence Durrell says that in some areas children go mumming and wear masks.

* Virtually all local celebrations of saints' days *begin the evening before the date stated*; indeed, this is often the liveliest part of the festival. The tourist authorities can provide up-to-date local news.

Easter	Midnight Mass on Easter Saturday: every worshipper lights a candle in the church and the air is bright with flame and dark with guttering smoke; the ancient cry goes up, *'Christós Anésti'* ('Christ is risen').
Sunday after Easter	Folk-dancing in **Messanagros** village.
April 23rd	St George's Day feast in the village of **Afantou**.
Whit Sunday	On the island of **Simi**, one of the noisiest, most popular, most exuberant festivals of the year. The great monastery of St Michael at **Panormitis** is the scene of the festival; excursion boats generally set out from Rhodes.
June 15th	Aghios Amos, near **Faliraki**.
June 17th	Festival of Aghia Marina at **Paradissi**, **Asgourou, Koskinou**.
Throughout July, August, September	Wine Festival, **Rodini Park**.
July 20th	Profitis Ilias.
July 30th	Festival of Aghios Soulas, a fellow-passenger of St Paul. This festival is held near **Soroni**. Great enthusiasm, donkey races, etc. Durrell gives a wonderful account of it, joyous, rowdy, tragic.
August 6th and throughout the month	This is the month when the expert village dance groups really show off. They appear at **Maritsa** on the 6th, also at **Kalithies**; they are at **Trianda** and **Kremasti** for the great national festival of the Panaghia on the 15th and 23rd, also at **Embona**. Dancers visit Rhodes from neighbouring Kos, Simi, Kasos and elsewhere to join in the August festivities.
August 26th	St Fanourios Church, Old Town, **Rhodes**.
August 29th	**Karpathos**. St John the Headless.
September 8th	Name-day of the Virgin Mary: on Rhodes, the day when barren women pray at the monastery high up on **Mount Tsambika**.

September 14th	Feast of the Cross at **Kalithies, Malona, Apollona, Damatria.**
September 26th	Feast of Agh. Demetrios at **Artamiti.**
October 28th	'Okhi' Day: generally celebrated with flags flying and a holiday.
November 7th–9th	**Simi.** Another festival at St Michael, **Panormitis.**

SPORTS

HUNTING

The shooting season is from August 15th to March 10th. Most birds and animals – but not deer – may be shot during this period, though hares, rabbits, woodcock and partridge are the most common. A licence is necessary; apply to the police.

SWIMMING

Swimming is, of course, the most popular and available outdoor sport on all the islands, however small. Details of beaches are given in the Information section for each island.

TENNIS

Several hotels on Rhodes now have their own courts: Rhodes is the only island with public tennis courts.

GOLF

There is a new 18-hole course at Afantou. Par is 72. (Tel. Afantou 255.)

WATER SPORTS

Sailing, canoeing, water-skiing, fishing. The N.O.R. Club in Rhodes offers all these. On other islands, you will usually find *caïque* owners willing to take you on fishing expeditions. The most memorable fishing expeditions are those by night when the boats go out with lights mounted at the prow in search of cuttlefish, octopus, moray, etc. Spear-fishing is popular among visitors but you should bring your own equipment as, except on Rhodes, you are unlikely to be able to buy it on the spot. Spear-fishing is not allowed within 100 metres of public bathing beaches.

POSTAL AND TELEPHONE INFORMATION

RHODES

Open seven days a week. Poste Restante desk is closed on Sunday afternoons.

The Cable Office (O.T.E.) is in the same building as the Post Office and is open 24 hours a day throughout the week.

There are very few call-boxes in the town; but phones are available at most of the newspaper kiosks. If you use a call-box you may need metal *kérmata* or jetons – these cost Dr 1 each and the nearest kiosk owner supplies them.

KOS

The Post Office is off Vass. Paulou Avenue (*Map* **10**).

The Cable Office (O.T.E.) is in Lord Byron Street.

OTHER ISLANDS

The Post Office is generally to be found on or near the harbour. Few islands are in 24-hour phone or cable communication with Athens, so you may have to book a call and be ready to take it later in the day.

POSTAL RATES

United Kingdom	*Air mail*	*Surface mail*
	Drs	Drs
Postcards	3·00	3·00
Letters	from 4·50	from 4·50
Air letters	from 4·00	

United States		
Postcards	5·00	from 3·00
Letters	from 6·50	from 4·50
Air letters	from 5·00	

WEIGHTS AND MEASURES

The metric system is general throughout Greece, though sometimes you may come across one or two old-fashioned measures – e.g. the *oká* (1·28 kg. or 2·82 lb.).

> 1 Kilo (1,000 gm.) = approx. 2·2 lb.
> ½ Kilo (*misó kiló*) = approx. 1·1 lb.
> ¼ Kilo (*éna tétarto*) = approx. 9 oz.

LIQUID MEASURES

In the *tavérnas* wine is often sold by the liquid kilogramme; milk is also sold by the kilo. The quantity differs according to the weight of the liquid but, as an example, a kilo of water is equivalent to one litre or 1¾ pints. Petrol is sold by the litre.

LENGTH

Metres and kilometres are the common measures, though a men's tailor may use the English yard.

> 1 metre = 39·37 inches
> 1 kilometre = ⅝ of a mile, roughly.

To convert kms. to miles, divide by 8 then multiply by 5.
To convert miles to kms., multiply by 8 then divide by 5.

TEMPERATURE

Temperatures are quoted in Centigrade and though, in theory, we should by now understand Centigrade values most of us don't.

To convert Centigrade to Fahrenheit, multiply by $\frac{9}{5}$ and add 32.

To convert Fahrenheit to Centigrade, deduct 32 and multiply by $\frac{5}{9}$.

ELECTRICITY

The current is AC or DC: voltage is either 220 or 110. Some of the smaller or more remote islands may cut off electricity around midnight; a few villages may have no electricity.

TIME

Two hours ahead of Greenwich Mean Time (i.e. 1 hour ahead of British Summer Time).

GEOGRAPHY AND GEOLOGY

Some of the islands were probably broken off from the mainland of Asia Minor by earthquakes occurring during the period of pre-history and these same earthquakes are believed to have raised other islands from the sea-bed. The narrow straits dividing island from island and separating the islands from the mainland are relatively shallow, probably because the upheavals created rifts and valleys, allowing the sea to run in and the high ground to become the present islands.

It is likely that Rhodes herself was submerged several times as a result of these seismic catastrophes and even that she was for a time rejoined to Asia. The final immersion was at the end of the tertiary era and when Rhodes reappeared it had the highly individual features now characteristic of the island – hills and mountains with sloping tops (notably Mt Paradissi), lower hills with humped and rounded summits, shallow valleys of soft soil much eroded by rain and coastlines unusually gentle.

The rock formation of the islands is primarily limestone with cores of crystalline rocks, and geographers and geologists report discoveries of shells and fossils not only at the foot of hills and mountains but also on the top – sure evidence that some at least of the islands once lay beneath the Aegean. (And an absorbing example of how myth is created, for the legend that Rhodes rose from the sea is almost certainly an ingenious invention by the ancients to account for the presence of these shells in such unlikely places.)

Minerals include clay and marble. Both are still found and worked on Rhodes and Kos; Nisyros provides pumice stone, and some iron and silver is produced on Karpathos.

One of the earliest geographers of the islands was Strabo, the Roman who was born in 54 B.C., became a Stoic and wrote a geography in 17 books. (His study of Greece appears in books 8, 9 and 10.) Lemprière, a vastly readable classical lexicographer of the eighteenth century, observed that 'Strabo travelled over a great part of the world in quest of information and to examine with the most critical inquiry not only the situation of places but also the manners of the inhabitants, whose history he meant to write.'

FLORA AND FAUNA

Mountainous and bare, island after island reveals its common parentage with Asia Minor. Nevertheless, much of the barren rockiness of the group is man-made: the Turks felled the forests without thought for the future, and erosion and degeneration took place very rapidly. Today, certain islands – Patmos is one – have barely a few inches of top-soil whereas in antiquity and for long after the islands produced enough pine, cypress and plane to sustain large and thriving boat-building yards.

At one time the islands were fertile enough to be able to export a surplus. Grapes, oranges, lemons, figs, pears, peaches, almonds – and, of course, olives – grew in abundance. Kos was famous as a garden island and the Kos lettuce still remains a standard variety throughout the Western world.

Flowers are among the signatures of Greece. Where they don't or won't grow in a wild state, they are nurtured in pots, old petrol tins, jugs, American processed-cheese cans and even rotting dinghies. The common flowers of the islands include the hibiscus, oleander, bougainvillea, jasmine, honeysuckle, cistus (rock rose), asphodel in its many forms, and hundreds of herbs and flowers that make up the low, scrubby growth of the *maquis* and *garigue*. (If the flowers of Greece begin to interest you I cannot do better than recommend an informative and entrancing book: *Flowers of the Mediterranean* by Oleg Polunin and Anthony Huxley.) The strange, tall agave is to be found on some islands, notably Kos, where the *agave americana* shoots up to about 30 feet.

Honey is a consequence of flowers, and perhaps nothing you can see, smell or taste in Greece today is so truly part of the past as honey. Fat bees lumbered from luxurious flower to luxurious flower then as they do now and the honey of the Dodecanese was reckoned to rival that of Hymettos. Strabo particularly praised the Kalymnian product; it is delicious still.

Productive animals include goats and some sheep and cattle: from these the islanders make a wide variety of cheeses, different types of yoghourt, goat milk and pale butter. Island wool is of high quality. The cat is the reigning domestic animal, often a sad, thin creature but with a standard of living today much higher than it was when I first visited Greece twenty years ago. The sharp, wedge-shaped faces and big ears of Greek cats seem to place them somewhere in lineage of the Abyssinian cat – although you will also find plenty of solidly muscled tabbies. Their favourite haunts are the tourist restaurants and sometimes one is tempted to think that they work on a union basis, so carefully do they observe their particular territories.

The deer is closely associated with Rhodes (but is probably not indigenous) and Karpathos is still stocked with hares. Both Aristotle and Pliny referred to the silkworms of Kos and the fine Koan silk was much desired by Roman women and much talked of among travellers (no doubt because it was virtually transparent).

The most famous natural product of the Dodecanese, however, is the sponge, though the modern sponge-fisherman is more likely to fish off the coast of North Africa than in the Aegean. It is a terrible trade and a cruel life, but men who stay on the islands often become divers because there are so few other occupations available. However, with the coming of synthetic sponges the bottom is falling out of the market and sheer lack of work is stepping up the pace of depopulation.

Crayfish and lobsters are found in the waters around the islands, but much of the fishing takes place in deep water, and this accounts for the anomaly that, in the Dodecanese as elsewhere in Greece, fish is one of the most expensive dishes that you can buy.

HISTORY

INTRODUCTION

From the invasions of prehistory in approximately 2500 B.C. to the arrival of the Italians in A.D. 1912 the history of the Dodecanese has been one of foreign influence.

Rome, Byzantium, the Knights of St John, Turks and Italians make up the greater part of the fabric of the past, though the Venetian Dukes and the Genoese also made their contributions.

Venice entered the picture in about 1204, when it was a party to the Treaty of Partition which led to attacks on Greece by the Crusaders, and the award of some of the Cycladic and Dodecanese islands to Venice. Besides appointing Leon Gavalas as Governor of Rhodes, Venice made no attempt to occupy these islands, contenting herself with encouraging her richer and more powerful citizens to settle among the islands and thus wield Venetian power through private hands. (This is why there is so much Venetian work to be seen on the Cycladic island of Naxos, for instance, where the Sanudo family settled. Similarly, the Quirini family made Asty-palaia their kingdom and the Stanco family went to Kos.)

One historical oddity is that Patmos was left untouched. But Patmos was the island of St John the Divine and so highly regarded for its religious stature and influence that Venice felt it politic to leave the island severely alone and even to establish good relations with it.

For the most part, the history of Rhodes is also the history of the Dodecanese, and the following pages trace the extraordinary past of this resilient island. Items of historical interest peculiar to other islands are dealt with in the appropriate sections.

The history of Rhodes was virtually determined by a simple accident of geography, lying as it does twelve miles from Asia Minor, on the direct route from and to Egypt, a stepping-stone to north, south, east and west. Consequently, from the first, dimly perceived days of prehistory down to modern times the island has suffered almost continuous invasion, acquisition, settlement and re-invasion. Practically no period of Aegean history or art passed Rhodes by; always in the mainstream, it suffered, grew rich, was famous, was plundered ... a history of remarkable ups and downs.

STONE AGES

(*a*) PRE-NEOLITHIC: TO 5500 B.C.
(*b*) NEOLITHIC: 5500 B.C. TO 2500 B.C.

The Stone Ages are clouded by much myth and little knowledge. All that one can assume is that the profusion of myth probably indicates the presence of some small embryonic settlements during these periods.

COPPER AND BRONZE AGES (2500 B.C. to 1150 B.C.)

(*a*) FIRST INVASIONS (ANCIENT AND MIDDLE HELLADIC – 2500 B.C. TO APPROXIMATELY 1550 B.C.)

According to Thucydides (and one cannot rely too much on him because he was writing some two thousand years after the event), the Kares, a no-account group of pirates from Asia Minor, were among the first to invade Rhodes. The next arrivals were better documented. They arrived from the east, from their land which lay between Lebanon and the Mediterranean, and they were the Phoenicians. They overran Rhodes and then moved west to Crete and beyond.

Fragmentary archaeological evidence begins to appear with the arrival of the next invaders because these newcomers did not move on. They came and they stayed, a band of immigrants dispatched to Rhodes by the Minoan thalassocracy of Crete. One of their settlements was at Ialysos, the present-day Filerimos.

(*b*) ACHAIAN RHODES (LATE HELLADIC OR MYCENAEAN PERIOD – 1550 B.C. TO 1150 B.C.)

However, the first invasions of real consequence did not take place till about the middle of the fifteenth century B.C., when Achaian Greeks conquered first Crete and later Rhodes. These Achaians came from the Peloponnese and Attica and they brought to Rhodes not only their native Achaian–Mycenaean skills but also the culture they had absorbed from Crete. (Crete at this time had passed through two major periods of civilization, the period of the early palaces and also the post-palatial period that followed the destruction of the palaces.) And it is around this time, between 1450 B.C. and 1400 B.C., that the vessels and vases of the period begin to show clear evidence of the growth of Mycenaean influences and the decline of the earlier, immigrant Minoan characteristics. The discoveries made at Ialysos and Kamiros can be seen in the museum at Rhodes and in museums around the world. These bowls, vases and vessels of all kinds bear unmistakable signs of Mycenaean culture – yet they were locally made in Rhodes and indicate that Mycenaean ways of life were now uppermost in Rhodes.

About this time the trading and voyaging characteristics of the islanders were emerging, too, and the discovery of an Egyptian scarab has provided one of those tiny but gigantic pieces of evidence upon which deductive history can be built – in this instance, evidence of communication with Egypt.

At the end of this period the descendants of the Achaian invaders stepped out of history and into literature. Homer includes among the great muster of those who sailed to Troy (a date still elusive, but 1183 B.C. meets with general agreement) the name of Tlepolemos, leader of the Achaians, son of Heracles. He and his fleet departed from the bay of Lindos, the third of the Achaian settlements and by then the biggest and most important of the three.

DORIAN INVASION (1150 to tenth century B.C.)

Somewhere about the middle of the twelfth century the period of Mycenaean influence came to an end on Rhodes and the whole of Greece suffered an upheaval so profound as to change the course of her history, habits and even the name of her people. The great Dorian invasion, driving across Greece from central Europe and Thrace, swept up Rhodes as well. The Dorians were probably the first of the invaders to have ideas beyond mere acquisition and settlement. They saw farther and did more. They were not absentee landlords: they stayed, they planned and organized, they put men and ideas into developing the island. Under the Dorian aegis Rhodes became both rich and powerful. Indeed, it was a period of change for the whole of Greece. Before the Dorians the people of Greece must be thought of as Achaians; after the Dorians they became Hellenes – true Greeks. Before the Dorians, Greek religion was maternal and feminine and centred upon earth-mothers and goddesses. The blond, masculine Dorians translated goddesses into gods or, more accurately, encouraged a masculine way of thought whereby gods gradually took precedence over goddesses.

ARCHAIC PERIOD (tenth to fifth centuries B.C.)

Lindos was a city even in Achaian times. But under Dorian influence Ialysos and Kamiros became cities, too, and the three cities expanded in vigour and riches. Often they took the initiative and instead of themselves being exploited and pillaged did some adventuring of their own, mostly constructive rather than destructive. Together, they were instrumental in forming the Dorian Hexapolis (the other members were Kos, Knidos and Halikarnassos).

Although Dorian rule was dictatorial at the outset, a form of democracy was well established by 700 B.C. It was a remarkably advanced society, with the three cities united but independent. For instance, there was apparently nothing but approval all round when, in 690 B.C., Lindos 'went it alone' and did some colonizing on her own account in Sicily, Italy (where she formed the settlement that later became Naples), Spain and France.

CLASSICAL PERIOD (fifth and fourth centuries B.C.)

Rhodian history in these centuries must be seen in the context of events in Greece and the Mediterranean generally. In 491 B.C. the Rhodians fought off the first Persian attempt to take the island but were forced to become a Persian ally in the years that followed. So when Xerxes invaded the Greek mainland in 480 B.C. forty of the ships that fought on the Persian side at Salamis were Rhodian.

The Greek victory in this great sea battle condemned Rhodes to a period of subjugation to Athens. Later, this developed into an alliance to which the island was reasonably faithful. However, the outbreak of the Peloponnesian War in 431 B.C. found Rhodes seesawing between Sparta and Athens with an inconstancy only surprising to those who imagine that political duplicity and opportunism are a relatively modern phenomenon. Read Thucydides and learn otherwise.

There then came, almost at the dawn of the fourth century, an event of profound importance to the island and, indeed, to the whole eastern Aegean. In 408 B.C., the city of Rhodes was founded, a direct outcome of consultation among the three ancient cities who probably judged that the future of the island lay in consolidation rather than decentralization – the more so since none of their harbours was capable of handling the volume of trade and shipping that was finding its way to the island.

The site of the new city, on the north-east point of the island, provided three admirable harbours and at least two more of lesser value. The three founder cities thereafter gradually – but only gradually – began to decline, and though Lindos retained power and position for some centuries after the foundation of Rhodes, the time came when all three cities became little more than religious centres.

One of the manifestations of the more sophisticated trading methods that followed the creation of Rhodes was an extension in the use of coins. Lindos had minted her own as far back as the sixth century and Kamiros and Ialysos followed suit in the fifth century. Many of these coins are of great beauty, particularly the fig-leaf and double rectangle of Kamiros. Now, in the fourth century, Rhodes produced her own coinage: the tetradrachm with the head of Helios on the obverse and the 'rose' of Rhodes on the reverse is an authoritative piece, befitting a city of wealth and prestige.

During this period, too, the island began to produce the stream of poets, philosophers, painters and sculptors that was to continue until the deterioration of the Roman era.

With all these blessings came problems, of course. It was vital for the island to remain politically flexible so that trade should not be threatened. So, for many years, throughout the reigns of Philip II of Macedon and his son, Alexander the Great, Rhodes trimmed and adjusted her policies with considerable deftness. Only when Alexander's victories clearly stamped him 'the Great' did Rhodes cease to be neutral. The island then came to a friendly agreement with the conqueror, who left her free to make her own political decisions and to pursue trade with Egypt. (Rhodians were doing a roaring wine trade with Egypt at this time, as the countless double-handled Rhodian amphorae found in Egypt indicate.) The extent of Alexander's regard can be guessed from his decision to name a small island off Alexandria 'Antirodos'. (If it was not regard, it was certainly tact.)

HELLENISTIC PERIOD (late fourth century to 31 B.C.)

Alexander died in 323 B.C. and it was natural, the ties being strong, that Rhodes – fully aware of the envious eyes and sharpened swords that surrounded her – should elect to side with Egypt. She had an opportunity to publicize this decision when Antigonos of Macedon set out to make war upon Egypt. Demetrios Poliorkitis, son of

Antigonos, demanded the support of Rhodes. Rhodes refused, whereupon Demetrios launched his great siege of Rhodes (305 B.C.). This was the siege made famous by the introduction into it of an enormous helepolis – a remarkable, nine-storeyed assault tower calculated to bring the Rhodians into submission. It failed, and the story of how it was used and how it failed receives thorough and extremely enjoyable treatment in Lawrence Durrell's *Reflections on a Marine Venus*.

The victory over Demetrios sent Rhodian prestige soaring. Demetrios, a gentleman, had left the ruined helepolis behind him as a token of his admiration for the Rhodian defence. The Rhodians sold the remains and used the money to commission Chares of Lindos to fashion and erect a giant statue to celebrate the victory. Begun in 302 B.C., the Colossus of Rhodes took twelve years to complete, but once the job was done Rhodes had yet another claim on fame and the history books. She now possessed one of the Seven Wonders of the World.

But not for long. The Colossus, about 100 feet high, dedicated to Apollo (or Helios), was destroyed by an earthquake about 227 or 222 B.C. The great bronze figure had stood for barely seventy years. When in A.D. 654 the shattered remains were sold and transported to Syria it took, says report, nine hundred camels to bear away the debris. (A much more recent estimate points out, in dampening tones, that the twenty tons of metal would not have required anything like that number of camels. More like ninety, says Torr, writing in the mid-1880s.)

The Rhodians of the third century B.C. were at the peak of their supremacy and success. The population of the city is estimated to have been between 60,000 and 80,000, two or three times larger than modern Rhodes. The contributions of the island to the arts, trade and law of the time were tremendous; Rhodian commercial and marine law, in particular, gained such wide acceptance that a full three centuries later Augustus applied it to the entire Roman Empire.

In 164 B.C. Rhodes signed a treaty with Rome, a petulant and dangerous ally. For, alarmed by the increasing power and prestige of the island, displeased by an earlier Rhodian offer of an alliance with the king of Macedonia, Rome decided to clip the wings of this too rich and too independent partner. This it did simply by proclaiming Delos a free port. It was a fatal blow to Rhodian trade, which declined with dramatic rapidity. Probably the last straw in the break-up of Rhodian power was an unheralded attack in 42 B.C. by Cassius. After the assassination of Caesar, Rhodes had refused to join Cassius against his enemies. Cassius thereupon sacked the island, stripped the city of its three thousand works of art and sent them to Rome, confiscated public and private money, allowed the citizens to be butchered and finally set fire to what was left.

COMING OF CHRISTENDOM (A.D. 51 to early-fourteenth-century Byzantium)

Christianity did not bring much hope of either revival or peace. At the end of the fourth century A.D. Rhodes exchanged the rule of Rome for that of Byzantium. She was plunder for any hungry attacker and was so vulnerable at this time that the fortresses at Lindos, Kamiros, Skala, Feraclos, Filerimos and elsewhere were the direct result of Byzantium's attempts to fend off these constant attacks. The number of assaults upon the island is bewildering. There were smash-and-grab raids by pirates and corsairs, the Goths came in the third century A.D., there were Arab invasions in the seventh and ninth centuries A.D. Then Saracens, Venetians, Franks and Genoese all laid hands on the island between the early Byzantine period and the fourteenth century.

RHODES UNDER THE KNIGHTS OF ST JOHN (1309–1522)

The twelfth and thirteenth centuries seem a preparation for the coming of the Knights of St John. The Crusaders appeared in Rhodes in 1097, then Richard Cœur de Lion and Philippe of France came to the island in 1191 in an attempt to gather a mercenary army. When the Franks seized Constantinople at the beginning of the thirteenth century, Rhodes remained independent under a Greek governor, Leon Gavalas. By 1248 the Genoese had gained control and, nominally at least, held the island till the Knights arrived and requested that they might settle on Rhodes. The Genoese refused and the Knights took the island by force (1309). The Knights had been forced out of Jerusalem after the loss of their previous stronghold at Acre. They first went to Cyprus and then settled on Rhodes. During the 213 years of their stay they built the great walls and bastions and moats of the medieval town, developed Rhodian trading with great success and led the island back into the reckoning of Europe once more.

These Knights, to whom we owe this most splendid of medieval fortified towns, dominated Rhodes for over two centuries – and dominate it still. The two Orders, the Knights Templar and the Knights of St John of Jerusalem, are frequently confused. The Knights Templar, though they were the most powerful of the Orders that sprang from the richly fertile ground of the Crusaders, were suppressed early in the fourteenth century, leaving the Knights of St John to inherit their wealth and power.

By the time the Knights of St John appeared on Rhodes, the Order had settled into clear and workable forms. There were three main classes of member: military knights or Knights of Justice, recruited only from noble families; serving brothers who might act as soldiers or nurses and who did not need to be of noble birth; and the chaplains who served in the churches and chapels of the Order as members of separate 'Tongues'. These were named after the language of origin of the Knights – hence the 'Tongue of France', 'Tongue of Auvergne', 'Tongue of Provence' (these were all independent states at the time), and the Tongues of Italy, Aragon, Germany, Castile and England. (The English Tongue died out completely after the Reformation.*)

Each of the eight 'Tongues' had its appointed leader – a prior or *pilier*. The Order was ruled by a Grand Master, appointed for life. The French so outnumbered other nationalities that during the 213 years of their stay on Rhodes, no less than fourteen out of nineteen Grand Masters were French. You can see this from their names and their coats of arms.

* The Order was revived in England in 1831 and became active again during the Franco–Prussian War when it was formed into a first-aid and ambulance organization. (The Order also exists today in Germany, the Netherlands and Sweden, and the Sovereign Order of Malta has its headquarters in Rome.)

The original twelfth-century home of the English Order was the Priory of Clerkenwell, near the Well of the Clerks in the City of London. Young English recruits came to Clerkenwell before they were posted to Rhodes. The Priory was rebuilt in 1504 and part still survives – the Gate House or St John's Gate in St John's Lane. This is the only monastic gate left in the City.

COATS OF ARMS OF THE GRAND MASTERS OF THE ORDER OF ST. JOHN

Arms of the Order

Foulques de Villaret
1310-1319

Hélion de Villeneuve
1319-1346

Dieudonné de Gozon
1346-1353

Pierre de Corneillan
1354-1355

Roger de Pins
1355-1365

Raymond Béranger
1365-1374

Robert de Juilly
1374-1377

Ferdinand d'Hérédia
1377-1396

Philibert de Naillac
1396-1421

Antoine Fluvian
1421-1437

Jean de Lastic
1437-1454

Jacques de Milly
1454-1461

Raymond Zacosta
1461-1467

G. B. degl'Orsini
1467-1476

Pierre d'Aubusson
1476-1505

Aimerie d'Amboise
1505-1512

Guy de Blanchefort
1512-1513

Fabrizio del Carretto
1513-1521

Ph. Villiers de l'Isle Adam
1521-1522

From the outset, the Hospitallers of the Order of St John of Jerusalem were a nursing Order. They were founded by a group of merchants in Amalfi in the early eleventh century; their first home was a Benedictine hospital of St John the Baptist in Jerusalem. This hospital was dedicated to the care of pilgrims and it is interesting that the first patron saint of the Hospitallers was not John the Baptist but a sixth-century Cypriot bishop, St John the Almsgiver. The Order was enjoined to build hospitals, treat the sick, train doctors, even to undertake research. But two related factors encouraged the development of their military function. First, a part o the original duty was to protect pilgrims and 'to reduce to silence the enemies of Christ'. At the time of the Crusades, protection meant assault upon the non-Christian enemy – so the nurse must also be a soldier. Thus, after the First Crusade, the Hospitallers became a body of military, armour-bearing Nightingales who were formidable men in every way.

They were aristocrats, for a start. Most Tongues required that a potential military knight should spring from at least four generations of unbroken noble lineage and the German Tongue required eight. Then they had a 'call'. As Catholic champions of Christianity, the young Knights could carry a cross in one hand and a sword in the other. That the Order also demanded absolute discipline and self-denial only made the attraction greater and the career purer. Though these vows were abused or ignored by some, the majority of Knights adhered fervently to the promises of chastity, poverty and obedience that they made when they entered the Order.

All the same, it is easy to understand why the Knights were regarded in their day more as military zealots than gentle healers. Every battle they fought was an act of Christian championship. They were courageous and staunch in defence of the Cross and if this brought down much trouble on the heads of those they were protecting – well, that was the will of God.

Thackeray provides a dash of caustic as counter to over-romantic imaginations: 'In the Crusades my wicked sympathies have always been with the Turks. They seem to me the better Christians of the two ... As far as I can get at the authentic story, Saladin is a pearl of refinement compared to the brutal beef-eating Richard – about whom Sir Walter Scott has led all the world astray ...'

Their knightly title and the great walls they flung up in Rhodes and elsewhere make one think of them as land-based warriors. But they were islanders and had to venture at sea in defence of Christendom and they became, in effect, corsairs, the most feared and daring fighting seamen in the Aegean. When the Turks interfered – as they often did – with the passage of trade and pilgrims, the galleys of the Knights patrolled the straits, hi-jacking shipping and engaging and sinking Turkish vessels.

Yet all this aggressiveness did not lead them to neglect their nursing duties. Rhodes possessed two great hospitals, both built by the Knights. The first now houses the Archaeological Service of the Dodecanese and the other and greater building has for many years been the Museum of Rhodes.

Though the fortifications that one sees today have suffered various mistreatments and structural alterations since the Knights departed in 1522, substantially they are still the same. The immense thickness of the walls – 40 feet in some parts – dates from the last fifty years of the regime. The Order found that the wars it had to fight and the increasing efficiency of weapons demanded much reinforcement of the original structure. The number of entrances was a weak link, too, so these were reduced and the curved surfaces of the later towers and turrets gave greater protection against cannon fire than the earlier square ones.

These outer walls with their beautiful swallow-tail battlements and chessman turrets are a traveller's first sight of Rhodes: golden in the sun (almost all the stone is from Rhodian quarries), flushed red in sunset or elephant-grey in twilight, their power and grandeur pronounce the absolutism, the moral certainty of these rigid, arrogant and brave soldier-knights.

During their stay the Knights had to fight off a number of attacks. In the very early years they took the precautionary step of protecting themselves from the east by capturing islands which might serve as enemy bases – so there are walls and castles of their building on Simi and Nisyros, Tilos and Kos, Kalymnos and Leros and, to the west, Chalki.

They survived two major sieges, the first in 1444 by the Sultan of Egypt and the second in 1480 by Mehemet II. It was after this last siege and the damage it caused that most of the strengthening work was done – carried out by the Grand Masters of the day, Pierre d'Aubusson and Aimerie d'Amboise.

In 1522 came the crunch. The success of the Knights at sea was a serious threat to Turkish trade, so Suleiman the Magnificent made a determined effort to reduce the garrison at Rhodes. He was thrown back repeatedly and after some six months was about to admit defeat when the Knights were betrayed by one of their own number. The Chancellor Amaral (in revenge, it is thought, for not having been appointed Grand Master) got a message through to Suleiman and revealed that the Knights were almost at the end of their resources. Suleiman took new heart, launched a series of attacks in October and November, and the shattered city eventually broke open and let the Turks in. On January 1st, 1523, led by Grand Master Villiers de l'Isle Adam, the Knights left Rhodes for ever. It was estimated that they had withstood a Turkish force of at least 100,000 with no more than 650 members of the Order, supported by 200 Genoese, 400 men from Crete (Candians), 50 Venetians and the 6,000 Greek and other inhabitants of the town.

TURKISH RULE (1522–1912)

On the face of it, it is curious that nearly four centuries of Turkish rule should have left so small a mark upon the island. In the walled town there are a few mosques and minarets, some Byzantine churches were converted to mosques (and sadly damaged in the process), there are Turkish fountains and carvings and Turkish courtyards – yet these are all externals. There was no fundamental change, no assimilation of the Greek by the Turks, and no absorption of the Turkish way of life by the Greeks.

This becomes less surprising if one looks a little below the surface. Consider the characteristic Turkish indolence, for a start. As a nineteenth-century French writer, Charles Cottu, noted, 'the Turk destroyed nothing, built nothing: he was content to squat on his carpet, puffing at his pipe throughout the centuries ...'

But perhaps the Turks were not always so. Thackeray, seeing the Rhodian Turks in their last century of inertia, wrote:

The Turks, who battered down chivalry, seem to be waiting their turn of destruction now ... one is strangely affected by witnessing the signs of this double decay ... When this superb fraternity [the Knights] was obliged to yield to courage as great as theirs, faith as sincere, and to robbers even more dexterous and audacious than the noblest Knight who ever sang a canticle to the Virgin, these halls were filled by magnificent Pashas and Agas ... Now the famous house is let to a shabby merchant ...

to a small officer, who ekes out his wretched pension by swindling ... The lords of the world have run to seed.

This terminal unconcern produced effects of a negative, wasting kind. The island was there to be milked and that was about the measure of it. Thus the great forests were allowed to be despoiled till little was left. Sluttishness on a grand scale is indicated in the tendency to let things lie, to leave them as they were throughout the centuries. One eye-witness records how guns and weapons dating from the 1522 siege were still scattered *in situ* in the mid nineteenth century. In the early years of the same century visitors to the Grand Master's Palace were horrified to find the chapel used as a cattle shed.

But perhaps the strongest factor in the survival of the Greek way of life – for Greek religion, thought, traditions, songs, superstitions and habits all survived and even flourished – was the Turkish attitude to the islanders. Any real contact between Turk and Greek was rigidly suppressed. Only Turks and Jews were allowed to live in the walled town. Nightly, a bell rang and the Greeks who worked in the town by day made their way out to homes in the villages and the new settlement of Nea Chori ('New Town') which they had established outside the walls. (Nea Chori is now part of the modern new town and retains its original name.)

Thus, by so deliberately cutting themselves off from Greek influence the Turks in fact ensured that the Greek characteristics should endure and survive.

ITALIAN OCCUPATION (1912–45)

The Italians came to Rhodes in the course of their expansionist war of 1912. The objective was to unseat Turkey from her bases in North Africa and the southern Aegean. Naturally, Rhodes applauded Italian aims and welcomed the new arrivals with some warmth. However, it became all too clear all too quickly that the Italians intended to stay put and so protect their new sphere of interest. Though a good deal of international argument took place in the next few years, the Italians could not be dislodged.

As you might expect, it is extraordinarily difficult to obtain objective, unbiased information from the Rhodians about either Turk or Italian. Too many emotions and memories muddy the water. Deduction must really be based on one's own observation.

Certainly, there is no argument that the Fascist years of Italian occupation brought great hardship to the island, oppression much more painful and harrowing than anything suffered under the Turks. But at least the island is benefiting now from some of the works of their past rulers. The Italians built roads (of course), they exercised their great skill with gardens, they built a number of public buildings and a great many private villas; they laid down the groundwork of the present flourishing tourist trade. Their academic interests were directed into archaeology – notably the compilation of the nine-volume conspectus of Rhodes and Kos entitled *Clara Rhodos* (Institute of Archaeology of Rhodes, 1929–38). They rebuilt the Palace of the Grand Masters and the row is still echoing: you either accept it or hate it. They did a good deal of restoration on classical sites: not all of it enduring, for quite a lot of what they re-erected has since fallen down again (the portico at Kamiros is an example).

Time passes and the Turkish and Greek communities on Rhodes appear to coexist amicably; many of the old Turkish laws are now part of Rhodian law, the Mufti lives in his house hard by the Mosque of Murad Reis. But perhaps the Italians are still too recent to be other than a bitter memory.

SECOND WORLD WAR AND AFTER

After the fall of Italy, Rhodes was occupied by German troops until 1945 when Greek and British forces recaptured the island. It was reunited with Greece in 1947.

GOVERNMENT

Administratively, the group is in the Nomarchy (prefecture) of the Dodecanese and the Nomarch's seat of government is on Rhodes. Rhodes and Kos also have an Eparch (sub-prefect). All islands have their own Demarch or mayor. The Demarchs are locally elected; the other officers, also the ministers of education, finance, etc., have always been appointed by Athens. The police belong to the national force; Tourist Police are appointed to the busier tourist islands.

RELIGION

The Orthodox Church is the established church of Greece. Included in the diocese of the Metropolitan of Rhodes are the islands of Tilos, Nisyros, Chalki and Simi. Three other Metropolitans share responsibility for the rest of the Dodecanese with the exception of Patmos, which in most matters is administered by the Patriarch of Constantinople. Priests of the Orthodox Church may marry but married clergy are prohibited from holding high office and may not enter a monastery.

There are small Turkish minorities on Rhodes and Kos. Rhodes even has her own Mufti, of whom you can read in Durrell's *Reflections on a Marine Venus*. He still smokes his cigarettes in an ebony holder and remains meek-mannered. But fame has reached into his sleepy mosque and pebbled courtyard, so he is likely to bid you wait while he fetches a cardboard box full of photos of himself and Durrell and a sifting of newspaper cuttings.

The refinements and detail of Greek Orthodox practice are complex. Some of the outward signs of Orthodox worship are, however, interesting and relatively easy to explain. The iconostasis is the wooden or stone rood-screen that divides nave from sanctuary; it generally bears several tiers of icons. Another form of iconostasis is the free-standing shrine which also bears an icon – probably of the Virgin or the patron saint of the church.

The double door in the centre of the screen frequently bears a portrait of the Annunciation: the angel on one door, Mary on the other. Only the priest may pass through this door.

In almost every Greek church or chapel you will find silver and gold *támata* hanging from icons. These are comparable to pre-Christian votive offerings. They are embossed or engraved with the likeness of various parts of the body: a leg, an arm, a heart, even a child in its cradle; and they are prayers for recovery or thank-offerings made after recovery.

During a service, men and women worshippers are separated: the men stand in the nave, the women occupy the porch (or a gallery if there is one).

LANGUAGE

Today's Greek is Greek in transition, experimental and fluid. Just as Shakespearian English was open to new usages and influences, so is the Greek of today. It is in this interesting if confusing state largely because there are two, if not three, forms of Greek in current use. The literary language or *katharévousa glóssa* is the form of Greek used for legal documents, for academic treatises and for government administration. It is formal Greek. Demotic (*dimotikí*) is the vulgar language in its true sense: it is the everyday spoken language of the people and it is this form which is most receptive to new ideas, words and influences. Demotic is now regarded as the most flexible and expressive vehicle by modern Greek writers and a modified form of it is used even for presentations of classical drama. Readers who have seen Greek plays performed by the National Theatre of Greece during Peter Daubeny's 'World Theatre' season in London have heard Aristophanes and Sophocles translated into this form of demotic.

The 'third' language exists in a perverse way: the Press has been undecided which form to use and while the more adventurous use demotic others sit on the fence and add to the confusion by adopting a mixture called *kathomilouméni*.

Pity the poor schoolchildren, therefore. For generations they have had to learn both *katharévousa* and demotic and though at the moment moves are being made to settle for one form or the other, it is not without vigorous protest from adherents of both forms.

No one can pretend that modern Greek is easy to learn; the grammar is extremely complex and even highly educated Greeks admit to having troubles with it. Nevertheless it is much easier to communicate in Greece than one imagines and even an indifferent linguist can make surprising headway once the alphabet is mastered. It is the apparent difficulty of the alphabet that makes so many people give up before they start, yet an hour or two of application will acquaint you with it and once you have broken through this 'alphabet barrier' the frequent sight of Greek words on shop fronts, posters, menus, etc., speeds up recognition very quickly.

It is an accented language: emphasize the accented syllable and you won't go far wrong. But make sure you do hit the right syllable, for some words are virtually identical except for the accent. The writer once stopped a passer-by and asked a question: 'Poú eínai to trapéza?' The passer-by looked baffled. 'Trapéza ... drachmés,' the writer insisted. 'Ah, i trápeza,' said the passer-by, light dawning, and courteously set me on my way. There is, you understand, a difference between asking the whereabouts of a table (*to trapézi*) and the whereabouts of a bank (*i trápeza*). (See index for the correct stress accents of the place-names used throughout the book.)

You will also realize that there is considerable variation and latitude in Greek spelling. Much of this is, of course, due to grammatical endings and agreements, but much is due to the free and flexible nature of the language. This is why, in this book, there is some flexibility in the spelling of Greek words. I have, for instance, generally used 'K', which is a letter of the Greek alphabet, rather than 'C', which is not (thus Kos, Kalymnos) but have preferred 'C' wherever 'K' seems to me pedantic to English eyes (e.g. Hippocrates rather than Hippokrates). Yet what am I to do about Socrates Street and Hippocrates Square in Rhodes? If I use 'C' I make it more difficult for you to read them off the street signs. So, as street names, they become Sokratous and Hippokratous. There are problems of translating Greek sounds into English, too, notably 'X' which is pronounced like 'Ch' in 'loch' before 'a', 'o' or 'oo' and 'h' before 'i' or 'e'.

For all this, you can quickly acquire enough knowledge and a sufficient vocabulary to help you on your way and delight the Greeks. You need never feel that embarrassed Anglo-Saxon fear of making a fool of yourself in a foreign language when you essay modern Greek. After all, no one *expects* you to speak Greek, no one looks down on you because your grammar is minimal – and the Greeks you meet will be enchanted that you attempt to use their language, however hesitantly.

In the Dodecanese, occupied by the Italians for over thirty years, some of the older generation will offer Italian as an alternative language and many educated islanders speak French. High-school children everywhere, learning English at school and set upon getting jobs in America, will pounce upon you and try out their English on you, while staffs of hotels and restaurants have sensibly made great strides with their English.

There is, inevitably, some variation of dialect in the islands but only in the very isolated ones are you likely to come across incomprehensible Greek.

There are a number of excellent phrase-books. The following are recommended: *Travellers' Greek* (Jonathan Cape, 1972); Collins' *Greek Phrase-Book* (1964); and *Say it in Modern Greek* (Dover Publications of New York, distributed in England by Constable & Co. Ltd).

MYTH

CREATION OF RHODES

It is fair to assume that myth is simply the best explanation available for something that is inexplicable at the time. Certainly myth is often strongest where knowledge is least.

The beginnings of Rhodes are a paradox: so lost in mists of antiquity yet so illumined by the blinding rays of Apollo that we have had little luck in piercing the bright, hazy curtain to see what are the facts that lie beyond.

Tradition has it that the first inhabitants of the island were the Bronze Age Telhines, a people who settled first on Crete and then on Cyprus before coming to Rhodes in the middle of the third millennium. Their successors were said to be the Heliades, but whether the Heliades existed or are simple legendary creations – for legend asserts that they were the descendants of the marriage between Helios and Rodon – is an example of how hard it is to distinguish fact from myth when one tumbles over the other, borrows from the other, anticipates and explains the other.

Best, perhaps, to sit back and rejoice that at least there is always robust legend to fall back on when the feebler trail of knowledge peters out. The most popular of these legends attributes the creation of Rhodes to the moment when Zeus divided the earth among his fellow gods on Olympus. While the distribution was taking place, the Sun God, Helios, was traversing the sky on his daily journey. He returned and found that Zeus had forgotten to allot him a share. Zeus behaved with uncharacteristic fairness and offered to reapportion the shares but Helios, searching the world below, suddenly saw Rhodes glittering beneath the surface of the sea. He concealed his discovery and persuaded the gods to agree that he should be given any part of the world not yet allotted. Obligingly, Rhodes then rose from the sea and Helios showered upon it all his powers of light and luxuriance and made it his bride.

Clearly associated with the metaphor of this marriage is the legend that Helios fell in love with and married the nymph Rodon, daughter of Poseidon and Amphitrite, and that it was she who gave her name to the island. The fruits of this marriage were seven sons; one of these sons had three sons, Ialysos, Kamiros and Lindos. These three, says legend, founded the three cities of Rhodes which bear their names – almost certainly a myth created to explain away the perhaps unpalatable fact that the cities were, in fact, founded by Dorian invaders.

The legend that Helios caused Rhodes to arise from the sea probably has its origin in fact, too. We know that earthquakes caused the islands to rise from the sea and to deposit fossils and shells high up on the hills. Lacking geology, the ancients created a myth.

Custom has named Rhodes Apollo's island, but myth sees it as the island of Helios. Here real confusion has arisen, an overlapping of myth with myth. Apollo was a sungod only – the god of sunlight – but Helios was the god personifying the sun itself. In Rhodian legend the two have become one, and you can see, on fourth-century coins, how Helios has been given some of the attributes of Apollo; the head of the Sun God in the museum also shares the two identities.

ISLAND OF ROSES?

There has always been speculation about how the island got its name. It is pleasant to pander to fancy rather than fact and assume that the legendary marriage of Rodon to Helios was the origin. However, it is generally accepted that *ródon* refers to a rose rather than the nymph. But here again, opinions vary. A rose is a rose is a rose ... but what kind of 'rose'? One school of thought believes it is the pomegranate flower, another that it is the hibiscus, another the oleander; and my own contribution to this confusion is the wish that perhaps the cistus, the rock-rose that grows so profusely about the island in spring, was the true rose of Rhodes. However, it is hard to argue with the claims of the pomegranate flower that appears on Rhodian coins of the fourth, fifth and sixth centuries B.C. On this evidence it does seem likely that the flower which gave the island its name – if any flower did – was the pomegranate.

Rhodes possessed numerous other names, too. Pliny gives several, including Ophiussa, Asteria, Corymbia and Atabria, and Strabo submits that Stadia and Telhines were also early names.

CUSTOM AND LEGEND

Island peoples, to some extent insulated from change, cling very strongly to their legends and their customs. When, in addition, you have a people who have been oppressed and occupied for over four hundred years, these customs and legends and even styles of dress stay alive because they are a means – perhaps the only means – of self-expression.

So, although the constant depopulation of the Dodecanese is reducing the number of participants in ancient customs, island life still has a nodding acquaintance with memories. Some of these are exclusive to Rhodes and are related elsewhere, but others are worth recording here. Leros, for example, has a carnival which is believed to stem from the Dionysian celebrations at Eleusis. Satirical verses are specially composed and children dressed as monks – though no one now knows why – recite them at the homes of newly weds. Unusual in this very masculine land, Leriot law ensures that property passes through the female line, so that today most houses and much property belong to women.

Legends associated with the names of the islands are innumerable. One of the most attractive relates to Simi and tells how Prometheus fled to the island to escape Zeus and there created man from clay. The enraged Zeus promptly transformed Prometheus into a monkey (*simia*) and kept him on the island till his death. This legend lived long and in the Middle Ages sailors were still calling the island Simia.

There are some startling (and mostly unhygienic) superstitions and customs surrounding birth: Charmian Clift, in her book *Mermaid Singing*, described how, even today, these are commonly adhered to on the island of Kalymnos. Marriage is sometimes preceded by an elaborate, formal furnishing of the house which is undertaken by processions of friends in the days before the wedding. (Skyros, in the Northern Sporades, has a delightful variant of this.) The *spervéri* or bed-curtain of the newly married is part of the folk-furnishing of Rhodes. New boats are always blessed: you may find a brightly painted new dinghy hauled up on a shore and around it the owner and many friends. An icon is perched on a seat, candles flicker in the prow, the priest, black robes fluttering, pronounces his blessing upon the boat and those who go to sea in her, and the gathering breaks up into a cheerful beach party enjoying a great deal of *oúzo*.

Costume is part of custom and the many and beautiful costumes of the islands are quite commonly worn still, though the more elaborate versions appear only on high days and holidays. On Patmos women wear necklaces of the kind found at Troy. Each is differently shaped from the next and each is said to have a magic ability to ward off a particular ill or evil. Patmian traditional dress is elaborate and the gold and gauze headdress has a Byzantine air. The Koan tradition of transparent fabric, so famous in classical times, still lives on in modern Kos; a part of the native dress is a very fine veil, white for every day and red with gold embroidery for a bride. On Karpathos, the strong, gaunt, village women stride out in island costumes.

It is, of course, only the middle-aged or old who wear local costume daily and though one may regret the inevitable, ultimate disappearance of the habit it is possible to get a great deal of pleasure from the contrast presented by the young, who manage to make and wear modern dress in the most unpromising circumstances. I remember being helped and befriended by a wildly beautiful sixteen-year-old in a country district of Kos. She wore her modern clothes with an elegance that would have done Athens or Bond Street proud, yet her home was a tiny, primitive cottage and her mother and grandmother wore local peasant dress. The Greeks retain an immense sense of personal style.

ART AND CULTURE

The earliest artists of Rhodes were those unknown men who fashioned the beads, seals, vases, etc., which have been found at various sites around the island. Many of these finds are in the museum at Rhodes; a considerable number are in the British Museum.

They are, perhaps, less interesting as works of art than for the strong foreign overtones they reveal: the pre-Mycenaean and Egyptian influences absorbed by a seafaring and trading people who were also much subject to invasion.

Recorded culture begins to take the shape of conscious art around the ninth and eighth centuries B.C. with protogeometric and geometric vases. By the seventh century B.C. we start to find personalities and names. Peisander of Rhodes, an epic poet, was one of these.

When Rhodes entered the Classical and Hellenistic periods, the same phenomenon occurred as elsewhere in Greece – an extraordinary outpouring of talent in all the arts and sciences. It was a many-sided society: the poets, artists, sculptors, architects, historians, doctors, philosophers, scientists and athletes of this marvellously civilized world found argument and occupation in Rhodes, and the island itself and some of its sisters produced their own share of great men.

Time and earthquakes have destroyed most of their work, but their names and reputations resound. There was Timocreon of Ialysos, whose lyric verse was penned during the Persian Wars. From the island of Tilos came the sad Erinna, a greatly talented pupil of Sappho. She wrote some three hundred verses and then, condemned to domesticity and forbidden to exercise her gifts, she died, aged nineteen. Apollonius of Rhodes was not a native of the island but its people liked him and his work so well that he reciprocated by styling himself a Rhodian. His story of Jason's voyage, *The Voyage of Argo*, is alive today in a Penguin paperback (tr. E. V. Rieu, 1971).

Theocritus, who spent some period of his life on Kos though he was a native of Syracuse, sang his country songs there, and these idylls are as fresh now as they were to the ear of his patron, Alexander the Great.

Among the scientists was Hipparchus, who, says Lemprière, 'worked in an observatory at Rhodes, and is known as the greatest astronomer of antiquity'.

There is little argument, however, that the most significant figure produced by any island of the Dodecanese was born on Kos about 460 B.C. Hippocrates, father of medicine, studied at the Koan temple of Asklepios, travelled about the Mediterranean learning and teaching, and then returned to Kos to practise his art.

It seems that Rhodians had a natural bent for rhetoric and when Aeschines of Athens settled on the island, a group of scholars gathered about him and developed the Rhodian school of rhetoric. Even Cicero came to Rhodes to attend the school, as did Caesar, Brutus, Cassius, Tiberius and others. It was said, perhaps truly, perhaps a trifle bitchily, that the Rhodian school excelled at teaching clarity of expression but was shaky as to content and thought.

Law and the expression of it was another Rhodian talent and the maritime law of Rhodes was adopted by both Rome and Byzantium.

For the most part, the work of the painters has long since vanished (though there are lovely traces to be seen on some Roman houses in Kos). Apelles, whom Pliny called the greatest painter of antiquity, worked on Rhodes and on Kos. It is Pliny who reports that when Apelles fell in love with the model for his *Aphrodite Anadyomene* (she was a concubine of Alexander), Alexander presented her to the painter.

Such knowledge as exists about the early Rhodian sculptors of the period we owe to Pindar. When the city was at its peak, there were at least three thousand statues, many of them colossi. Today very few remain. According to Pindar, when the Rhodians discovered that neighbouring Kos had commissioned an Aphrodite from the great Praxiteles, they promptly ordered five statues of deities from Bryaxis. The Koans were not so very clever, however, for Praxiteles had offered them a choice of a draped Aphrodite or a nude. The Koans selected the draped goddess and let Knidos, in Asia Minor, buy the nude and were much chagrined in later years when it became clear that the nude Knidian Aphrodite was a great deal more popular than their own more puritan choice.

At about the same time (350 B.C.) another of the great sculptors of the day, Lysippos, received a commission from Rhodes. This was for the great quadriga or chariot of the Sun God.

It was a pupil of Lysippos, Chares, who made the vast bronze statue the world knows as the Colossus of Rhodes. Chares was as unlucky as the statue itself, for after he had worked on the commission for twelve years he discovered an error in his arithmetic and, in despair, killed himself. The work was completed by Laches who reaped all the honour, including the inscribed 'credit' on the finished Colossus.

The Colossus was one of the most famous statues of all time yet we have no reliable verbal or visual record of it and do not even know for certain where it stood (current thought rates as unlikely the old belief that it straddled the entrance to Mandraki Harbour). All we can tell is that it was approximately 100 feet high, that it was in the likeness of the Sun God and, presumably, bore some of the characteristics of coins of the period – the head surrounded by the sun's rays, for instance – and that an earthquake destroyed it after it had been standing for less than seventy years. (The best-known guess at the likeness of the Colossus is based upon a drawing in a book dated 1826 by the French traveller Colonel Rottiers. It shows a smooth, muscular Colossus straddling the harbour entrance. His head is crowned with metal rays and his right hand bears a fiery vessel above his head.)

The only important extant works of Rhodian sculpture are the *Laoköon* and the *Farnese Bull*, both of them famous but neither of them representative of the finest period of Classical work. They are too exuberant, turbulent and dramatic to have the ring of truth common to the great Classical pieces. The Laoköon, of the first century B.C., is now in the Vatican and was the work of Aghesandros, Polydoros and Athenodoros; the Farnese Bull is in the Neapolitan Museum.

Sport in Classical times has a claim to be placed among the arts: it sprang so clearly from the view that the body should express the golden mean, harmonious and balanced. One man and one family tower above the rest: Diagoras and the Diagoridae. Pindar's seventh Olympian Ode celebrated the victory of Diagoras in the boxing matches of 464 B.C. Thereafter, the sons of Diagoras also became Olympic champions, and their sons, too. Pausanias says that when Diagoras' two sons won their laurels, they bore their father on their shoulders through the crowds. He tells, too, how a daughter of Diagoras managed to attend the Olympics disguised as a trainer. Women were strictly forbidden access to the Games and when Pherenike was discovered she would almost certainly have been condemned to death if she had not been the daughter of Diagoras. However, the scandal was not without consequence: thereafter, trainers as well as competitors had to appear naked at the Games.

The medieval and Byzantine periods on Rhodes produced some excellent frescoes and some good but small-scale Byzantine church-building. A school of pottery and ceramics in Kos, Rhodes and Patmos followed Byzantine traditions but was also genuinely individual.

During the Byzantine period a primarily domestic form of decoration was developed. This was the use of pebbles, generally black and white with red, to make a paving for the interior of a house or the floor of a courtyard. This technique is called *chochláki* and was first introduced during the Hellenistic period when the pebbles were used without any formal patterns being made. During the Byzantine period the pebbles were laid in abstract, formal and stylized designs, and today, particularly in Lindos, you can see some delightful examples of this work. Circles, stars, formalized flowers, cypress and other designs are common. The technique was not merely decorative: it was also practical because the pebbles, when they have been washed down, glitter and throw off coolness on a hot day. There is a bastard use of the technique in Venizelou Street in the new town of Rhodes. Here a wealthy Turk chose to face two walls of his large house with *chochláki* – and rather splendid it looks, too.

In more modern times the arts have continued to centre around the home. (See p. 154 for a history of Lindian plates.)

In general, the islands today display a folk-culture rather than sophisticated art forms. Work songs – particularly the songs of the sponge-fishermen – are very much part of the living folk-culture and there is still an impulse to express emotions in dance. This is as true of the Dodecanese as of the rest of Greece, as any visitor to a *tavérna* who has watched a villager rise to his feet and, alone and absorbed, dance for himself to the music of a horn gramophone will realize. Sometimes both songs and dance are dressed up a little and presented as tourist attractions. On Rhodes you can make an evening visit to a village to dine and wine and watch the dancing and there are theatrical performances of the songs and dances of the islands. But this kind of presentation should not obscure the continuing vitality of folk-dance and song in the life of the islands. This is no folk-art which has been exhumed; it remains a necessary, normal part of village life.

FOOD AND DRINK

There is a considerable paradox in Greek cooking. Basically it is
simple. Frequently it is rendered exotic by the use of herbs or
particular methods of cooking. Moreover, as most meals are eaten
out of doors, even the simplest food is invested with one's own
heightened awareness of flavour.

The predominant influence on Greek cooking is Turkish, particularly in the creation of sweetmeats and cakes. In the Dodecanese
this influence is even stronger than elsewhere, for obvious reasons.
A number of Turkish dishes or Turkish glosses on Greek dishes are
to be found. These include such pleasures as a yoghourt 'dip' called
tzatzíki (pronounce this 'jadjíki' and you will be understood).
There is, too, a Turkish variant of *baklavá*: this is called 'Ladies'
Lips' and is a tiny *baklavá* soaked in rose-water as well as honey.

However, much of the island food is similar to that of Greece
as a whole. The common denominators are *souvlákia* (morsels of
veal, lamb or pork grilled on a *soúvla* or skewer, preferably over a
red-hot charcoal fire), steak, chops, *moussaká*, *keftédes* (delicious
meat-balls, deep-fried in oil), *dolmádes* (vine leaves or cabbage leaves
stuffed with meat and rice), chicken, rice, spaghetti (called macaroni
on most menus), excellent omelettes and salads of all kinds according to season. The ingredient least used in a salad is the lettuce (even
on Kos), a local decision which I applaud. Instead, there are sliced
green peppers, white *féta* cheese, *maïntanós* (coarse parsley), sliced
onions, tomatoes, cucumbers. You can have most of these ingredients as a mixed salad or singly, with or without oil. Another
favourite dish is the *pítta*. This is the word for pies of all sorts. The
most popular is a cheese pie of pastry and cream cheese called
tirópitta.

Less common dishes include *skordaliá*, a garlic sauce which goes
well with fish and is made with oil, garlic and potatoes; Smyrna
sausages (*soutzoukákia*) which are highly spiced and often known as
'scorching sausages'; *donér kebáb* (outside some restaurants you will
see a large cut of meat revolving on an upright spit – this is carved
into slices as the meat cooks).

Of the soups, the best known is *ávgolémono*, a soup thickened with
egg and flavoured with lemon. Another dish found on the islands
is chicken boiled in its own soup, *kottópoulo vrastó*. This arrives

garnished with pasta and with a piece of boiled chicken sitting in the middle. It sounds bleak but it is very appetizing and comforting.

Fish (*psári*) dishes are usually the most expensive on the menu. Fish is served and sold by the kilo, so it is as well to go into the kitchen, select the fish you want and have it weighed before ordering. The most popular fish are red mullet (*barboúni*), bream (*sinaghrída*) and *ghlóssa*, a kind of sole. Shellfish include prawns (*gharídes*), small, sprat-like fish (*marídes*) and lobster (*astakós*). Other popular sea-foods are octopus (*oktapódi*) and squid (*kalamarákia*), usually fried.

Sweet things are numerous. Several sweet cakes are made from the tissue-thin pastry called *fílo* (leaf). You may happen to look in at a pastrycook's when this is being made and rolled out. If not, there is a superb description by Thackeray of the bakers in the Constantinople Seraglio whom he saw making a variant of this pastry for the delectation of the 'sultanas'. He heads the passage 'The Sultana's Puffs' and continues:

> How those sweet lips must shine after eating these puffs! First, huge sheets of dough are rolled out till the paste is about as thin as silver paper; then an artist forms the dough-muslin into a sort of drapery, curling it round and round in many fanciful and pretty shapes, till it is all got into the circumference of a round metal tray in which it is baked. Then the cake is drenched in grease ... and, finally, a quantity of syrup is poured over it, when the delectable mixture is complete. The moon-faced ones are said to devour immense quantities of this wholesome food ...

Baklavá is one of the sweet cakes made from *fílo*, with nuts in layers and the whole soaked in honey. *Kataïfi* is another and looks disappointingly like shredded wheat but is also a concoction of *fílo* and honey. Ice-cream is popular everywhere in Greece among all ages; most good cafés offer a variety of sundaes and concoctions. Of the branded ice-creams 'Evga' is excellent – try the vanilla cornet topped with hard chocolate and nuts. Greek yoghourt (*yiaoúrti*) is unbeatable; try it with honey trickled on top or sugar or simply neat. There is also a delicious dish called *rizógalo* which it is cruel to call cold rice pudding for though, basically, this is what it is, it also contains lemon and egg yolk and is sprinkled with cinnamon (*kanélla*).

Bread (*psomí*) can be white, brown or 'country' bread. This latter is a wholemeal variety and must be eaten the same day.

RECIPES

Recipe-collecting is an occupation that goes well with leisure. Many restaurants or friendly Greeks will be willing to tell you how a dish is made (though they may be short of time during the height of the tourist season). A few recipes follow; all these dishes have been presented to my guests and thought well of by them.

MOUSSAKÁ

This is a Rhodian variant of the well-known Greek dish, using cloves as an important feature.

Ingredients

1 lb. minced steak or lamb; 1 large pepper; 1 large or 2 small aubergines; 2 cloves garlic; 1 large onion; small tin tomato purée; 15 cloves.

Slice aubergine and leave to soak for half hour. Dry, fry, drain. Line casserole dish with aubergine slices. Fry chopped peppers, onion, garlic, cloves and tomato purée in oil until all soft. Add half pint of water, then the meat, and cook gently for about 20 mins. If more water is needed add just enough to keep mixture soft and moist. Put into lined casserole. Top with rich white sauce (Béchamel) to which you have added, when cooling, a beaten egg. Scatter top with grated cheese and cook for 1–1½ hrs. Begin at Gas No. 3 (350–375° F) then reduce slightly. Serves 4.

TZATZÍKI

You can use this as a side-dish with meat as the Greeks do or present it as a party dip.

Ingredients

4 cartons natural yoghourt; 3 cloves garlic; some finely chopped cucumber.

Drain the yoghourt for 2–3 hours (overnight if possible). This eliminates as much liquid as possible and produces a thicker, creamier mixture. To drain, use fine muslin or nylon and hang up with dish underneath. Then squeeze garlic into yoghourt and add about a 2-in. length of cucumber, finely chopped. Place the chopped cucumber between absorbent kitchen paper to reduce the water content before adding to the mixture. Mix yoghourt, garlic and cucumber well, put in dish and chill thoroughly before serving. Serves 3. Increase ingredients proportionately for larger numbers.

Rizógalo

Most Greek cooks have their own favourite ideas about how best to make this dish; certainly, they all agree that the slowness of the cooking is vital. The version that follows is, basically, that given by Joyce M. Stubbs in *The Home Book of Greek Cookery*.

Ingredients

1½ pts milk; 2 lb. sugar; 1½ tablespoonfuls rice; lemon peel; 1 egg yolk; cinnamon; pinch of salt.

Boil milk, sugar, rice and lemon peel together – using a double saucepan if possible. Add salt, and cook very slowly. When the rice has absorbed all the milk, remove from the fire and cool a little. Then mix in egg yolk already beaten up in a little cold milk. Cook for a few minutes longer and pour on to individual plates or into small dishes. When cold, sprinkle generously with cinnamon.

WHAT TO DRINK

Thackeray had tart views on Greek wine: 'Think of "filling high a cup of Samian wine",' he scoffed. 'Small beer is nectar compared to it, and Byron himself always drank gin' – not entirely fair, as in the passage quoted Thackeray was as much absorbed with attacking Byron as Greek wine.

In the past, Rhodian and Koan wines were famous throughout the Greek world. Cato gave instructions on the making of them and William Younger in *Gods, Men and Wine** notes that 'among the seventeen to eighteen wines ranked by the Romans as the finest in the world was the Koan'. He adds that the wine of Kos was sometimes flavoured with sea-water and quotes Athaneus on the subject: 'Wine is sweet when sea-water is poured into it.' Mr Younger comments that Greeks tolerated this peculiar mixture and even had

* W. Younger, *Gods, Men and Wine* (Michael Joseph for Wine and Food Society, London, 1966).

a name for it: *oínos thalassinós*. The taste probably grew because the wine jars were sluiced in sea-water.

Today, *retsína* is the wine of the country. It is flavoured with resin from pine-trees and has a sharp flavour that takes some acquiring. Once addicted, always addicted, however, and it is an excellent foil to the character of Greek food. *Retsína* is available white or red, bottled, draught or by the glass. For white *retsína* ask for *áspro*, for red, *kokkinélli*. Drawn from the barrel, your *retsína* will be served in a bright orange or blue tin measure – and remember that draught *retsína* is liable to be stronger than bottled. It rarely produces a hangover, however. *Retsína* costs about Drs 12–15 a bottle.

White wines are sometimes slightly resinated but ask for un-resinated wine and you will get it. *Demestica* is a popular, cheap white wine and there are many of the famous Greek wines to sample if you wish. *Mavrodaphne* is more attractively named than attractive to drink but *Palini 'A'* is a very pleasant white wine; so is *Santa Helena*. Fortunately, the taste for wine flavoured with sea-water has vanished and there are several pleasant modern Rhodian wines: *Lindos Blanc Sec* and the red *Chevalier de Rhodes* are both enjoyable. Rhodian wine producers are C.A.I.R. and S.F. Fokialis. Beer is relatively expensive though it should be remembered that the Greek beer-bottle is a fairly large one. 'Fix' is the best Greek brand from about Drs 12 and there are now several imported lagers, notably Tuborg, Amstel and Carlsberg from approximately Drs 20 per bottle.

Ouzo and brandy are the most popular aperitifs. A glass of ouzo can vary between Drs 3 and Drs 8; a bottle of Fokialis 'Colossus' ouzo will be around Drs 30 to 40. Greek brandy is sweeter than French and does not pretend to be in the same class but is, on its own terms, very acceptable. 'Metaxa' is the famous brand (you can get it in three-, five- or seven-star quality). With your pre-dinner ouzo or brandy you get *mezédes*. These are titbits served on a saucer and include almost anything: from neat squares of fried bread to cold fried octopus, tomato, cheese, olives, nuts, *taramasaláta*, tiny fried sprats, etc.

Should you prefer soft drinks, you can get orangeade and lemon-ade, both bottled and fresh, fizzy or still. A can of ice-cold 'Sunfix' orange juice is very popular. Soda-water is drunk quite a lot (ask for the brand 'Sáriza'). Try *vissinátha*, too. This is a non-alcoholic cherry drink and generally comes bottled, but the best way to have it is to find a café where they serve it as a little dish of black cherry jam which you spoon up and dip into a glass of clear, cold water.

Greek (or Turkish) coffee comes in tiny cups and costs from about Drs 2·50 to Drs 8 depending on the class of café. Some of the smart hotels won't descend to serving Greek coffee – or *retsína*, come to that. You can have it *glikó* (very sweet), *métrio* (medium) or *pikró* (bitter). Stipulate which of the three you want – *métrio* suits most people best. You can also get what the Greeks tend to call 'Nes'. This is straight black Nescafé. In the better restaurants and hotels you can sometimes obtain French coffee, and a number of the snack bars provide Espresso. Tea is available, too, and lemon tea is especially good. If you want to emphasize that the water *must* be boiling, try *tó neró na vraízi, parakaló*. A glass of water (*neró*) always accompanies a cup of Turkish coffee.

N.B. The prices quoted here were correct at the time of writing.

INTRODUCTION TO ISLANDS AND ROUTES

Of the thirteen islands of the Dodecanese, this book provides detailed information about five: Rhodes, Kos, Kalymnos, Leros and Patmos. The remainder are looked at more briefly, not because they have less appeal – several are extremely attractive – but because communications tend to be infrequent and accommodation is minimal.

The five main islands each have a section setting out routes round the island or, if the road system is sketchy or distances too short to be called routes, a number of excursions. *During 1974/75 the round-the-island roads on Rhodes are being remade, in some areas by-passing villages and greatly shortening a route (e.g., that part of Route 1 between Rhodes and Lindos). However, because the final course of these remade roads is not complete and possible access roads from the villages not even decided, the Routes recommended in the book follow the original road system unless stated otherwise.* (See p. 137 for further information.) *To a lesser extent, similar road-works are taking place on Kos.*

Distances are given in kilometres and are one-way. They are marked cumulatively from the main centre (excluding detours). In the route directions at the beginning of each route, detours are shown in brackets, and on the Route Diagram maps they are marked as Optional Detours. Distances on Link Routes are marked cumulatively from the starting-point on one main route to the destination on another.

There is a comprehensive Chart of Excursions (facing p. 29) covering all the islands; distances on this are also one-way.

RHODES

The island is 78 km. (49 miles) long as the crow flies (the local term is 'by bee-flight'), 38 km. (24 miles) wide, and covers 540 square miles. The distance from Piraeus is 260 nautical miles. The city of Rhodes occupies the northern tip of the island and is divided into two parts, the New Town and the old walled town. The New Town encloses the old on all sides except the seaward. The largest village is Trianda, with a population of 3,150. The total island population is 64,000; 27,000 live in Rhodes itself.

INFORMATION FOR VISITORS

All map references are to Rhodes New Town Map (pp. 132–33).

Getting to Rhodes For information about sea connections with other islands see pp. 33–34, 38–39.

Air Maritsa Airport lies 15 km. south-west of the city of Rhodes. Airport buses and taxis wait to take you into the city. For frequency of flights, etc., see p. 31. N.B. A large new airport is being constructed near Paradissi but the opening date is unknown.

Airlines *British Airways Office/TWA, Vass Marias* 28–30; *Olympic Airways* Terminal, Ierou Lochou Street, *British Airways* Terminal, Ierou Lochou Street.

Shipping lines *Epirotiki Line,* at Geo. Frarakis Tours, 41 Vass. Sofias Street; *Kavounides Line,* 25 Martiou Street; *Nomikos Line* at Kronos Tours, Cyprus Square; *'Panormitis II' Office,* Georgiou Kirmichalis Street (off N. Plastira Street).

Boat trips Some tour companies operate small coastal vessels for day-trips down the coast and make regular day-return visits to the island of Simi and to Marmaris in Turkey. There is also a day-return excursion to Kos.

Public transport Almost all local buses and taxis depart from the New Market area. Two companies, K.T.E.L. and R.O.D.A., provide the local bus services. K.T.E.L. operates along the east coast (venturing inland here and there) while the west coast is R.O.D.A. territory. The two lines meet only rarely, so there is little '*correspondance*'. Buses include smart, long-range 'Pullmans' and a few rattling, beat-up hulks — which, nevertheless, get you there.

The two bus stations are within a hundred yards or so of each other at the back of the New Market. The K.T.E.L. concourse (*Map* **17**) is beside the 'Son et Lumière' park, under the walls of the Palace of the Grand Masters. R.O.D.A. departures are from Averof Street, immediately behind the New Market (*Map* **15**).

Timetables are designed to meet local needs rather than those of tourists. An exception is the K.T.E.L. route to Lindos, which is frequent and reasonably fast.

Taxis These gather at the old town end of the New Market (*Map* **16**). Rates: see p. 40.

Coach tours Coach tours are plentiful, good and reasonably cheap. They are operated by international and local companies and offer half-day and full-day tours.

These tours go to all the main sights and there is one specialist tour of the island by Triton Tours, which visits many of the Byzantine churches referred to in this book. All tours are by comfortable Pullman. Coach and guide service is included. The N.T.O.G. or hotels will make bookings or you can book direct through the agencies.

Travel agencies *A.B.C. Tours*, Archbishop Makarios Street; *Argo Tours*, Vass. Marias 28–30; *C.H.A.T. Tours*, Vass. Konstantinou 14; *Elias*, Archbishop Makarios Street; *Geo. Frarakis*, Vass. Sofias 41; *Helios*, Archbishop Makarios Street; *Hermes en Grèce*, Vass. Konstantinou 14; *Karyanides, Kronos*, Cyprus Square; *Triton*, 25 N. Plastira Street.

Car hire, motor-cycles, bicycles A sample of reliable car-hire firms includes: *Hertz, Avis, Camiros, Heart, Hobby, Rhodos, Rent-a-Car*.

Motor-cycles can be hired from a number of cycle shops in the new town of Rhodes, also from the Square of the Jewish Martyrs in the old town.

Information The *National Tourist Office* of Greece is on the corner of Archbishop Makarios Street and Papagou Street (*Map* **13**).

British Consulate Sokratous Street, Old Town.

Banks See p. 49 for opening hours. *Old Town:* Commercial Bank, Museum Square; Ionian and Popular, Simi Square; National Bank of Greece, Museum Square. *New Town:* National Bank of Greece, Cyprus Square; Bank of Greece, Mandraki Harbour.

Exchange offices Commercial Bank, Cyprus Square; National Bank, corner Cyprus Square and Plastira Street; Ionian and Popular Bank, Gallias Street (off Cyprus Square).

Post office Mandraki (*Map* **9**).

Public Toilets Near taxi rank and 'Son et Lumière'.

Hospital Helvetias Street.

Catholic churches St Maria, near the now-closed Hôtel des Roses; St Francis, Athinon Street (where road from town meets right turn to Lindos; *Map* **24**).

Early closing Thursday.

Festivals See pp. 55–57.

HOTELS

Though the last few years have seen the arrival of several hotels in areas outside the town of Rhodes, it is still true that the greater proportion of the island accommodation is in Rhodes itself. Most of these hotels are within a matter of minutes from harbour or open sea.

As the town occupies the entire northern tip of the island, there are two coastlines, one to the east, the other to the west. On these shores many of the large beach hotels are sited and in the past few years there has grown up along the west coast a new group of luxury and first-class hotels.

The number of hotels in Rhodes is considerable and has been growing yearly; the proportion with up-to-date facilities is therefore high. A selection only is given here; refer to the N.T.O.G. for more complete information. Note that (*a*) several of the hotels close during the winter, (*b*) some will quote special prices for children and (*c*) the out-of-town west coast hotels are served by a good bus service to and from Rhodes.

Rhodes City and environs

L Class (de luxe)   *Grand Hotel Summer Palace* facing sea on west coast of town. Very smart, very expensive; beautiful sunset views. The Casino of Rhodes is attached to the hotel (roulette, baccarat). Two seawater swimming pools, two night-clubs, tennis, etc.

Miramare Beach Hotel about 6 km. out of town on west coast. This is one of the bungalow hotels that are now a common feature of the Greek holiday scene. The attractive Miramare bungalows lie in a green and scented private garden and give directly on to the shore. Greek and international food at the restaurant; swimming pool, golf, tennis. Shops, hair-dresser. Night-club April to October. You can hire a little 'Miramarette' car to get you into Rhodes and around the sights.

A Class   *Blue Sky* on west coast about 7 minutes' walk from centre of Rhodes. Built 1969. Pleasing interior. All rooms have phone, private bath-room, balcony. Pool, beach, restaurant, lifts. Sunset views across to Turkey.

Oceanis Hotel 5 km. along west coast, a short distance before the Miramare. At night, a spectacular hotel – long and low and glittering with lights, like a ship at sea. Built 1965. All rooms have private bath, phone, radio. Air-conditioning optional. Restaurant, night-club, snack-bar, mini-golf, pool, private beach, etc.

Hotel Bel-Air about 4 km. from town centre. Completed in 1967. On the beach, swimming pool, bar, hairdressing salon, etc.

Golden Beach Bungalow Hotel west coast approx-imately 8 km. out of town. Built 1966. Each bungalow has two verandas, one looking out to sea, the other inland to Mt Filerimos. Private grounds, bar, night-club, tennis, swimming pool, restaurant, etc.

Rhodos Bay. One of the latest of Rhodes' new-style hotels. On west coast approximately 6 km. from town. Sea-water swimming pool, private beach, tennis, mini-golf, sauna.

Avra Beach 6 km. along west coast next to Miramare. Opened 1973. Main building and bungalows, beach, heated pool, garden, discotheque.

Dionysos. Approximately 5 km. from town on west coast. Built 1971. Set back in the hills, about 300 yards from the sea. Two swimming pools, two tennis courts.

Belvedere on west coast at entrance to town. Modern, comfortable, private beach, tennis court, restaurant.

Metropolitan Capsis on west coast, 5 km. from town. A very large hotel, opened 1972. Swimming pool, tennis, mini-golf, *tavérna*, night-club, hairdresser.

Rodos Palace. A large new resort complex of rooms and chalets, two Olympic-sized swimming pools, restaurants and snack-bars, tennis, mini-golf, sauna and Health Club, night-club and discotheque beach, special facilities for children.

By the time this revised edition is published, the new *Electra Palace*, Trianda, should be open. Approximately 9 km. from town, the hotel will stand well off the main road and directly on the shores of the Bay of Trianda. A heated pool and sun-terrace is planned, also a discotheque. Views across the bay and inland to Filerimos.

Other A Class hotels in or near the centre of town

Ibiscus, Vassileos Pavlou Square, east coast, private beach.

Mediterranean, Kos Street, east coast, private beach.

Plaza, Ierou Lochou Street.

Cairo Palace, Archbishop Makarios Street.

Kamiros, Archbishop Makarios Street.

Park, Riga Ferraiou Street. (Dancing, swimming pool.)

Thermai, Athinon Street. (Tennis courts.)

Regina, Archbishop Makarios Street.

Siravast, Vassileos Pavlou Square. East coast. Private beach.

Cactos, Kos Street.

Of these, the *Park* and *Thermai* are pleasantly situated among trees, just outside the walls of the old town. All have their own restaurants.

B Class

Posseidon on west coast at Kritika, near entrance to town. Private beach. Built 1963.

Solemar on west coast at Ixia. Approximately 4 km. from town. All rooms shower or bath. Restaurant, bar, swimming pool, garden.

Other B Class hotels in or near centre of town

All these are modern or restored, and most have restaurants.

Coral, Vass. Konstantinou Street.

Despo, Vass. Sofias Street.

Delfini, Archbishop Makarios Street.

Spartalis, North Plastira Street.

Angela, 28 Oktovriou Street.

C Class

Vellois Hotel approximately 6 km. out of town on the west coast. Faces Miramare. Modern. Bar, snack-bar, terrace.

Savoy, Ethelondon Street. Another modern hotel, medium size, comfortable and in centre of town.

Tilos, Archbishop Makarios Street. Central and up to date.

Moschos, Ethelondon Street.

Irene, 25 Martiou Street.

Achillon, Vassileos Pavlou Square.

Acropole, Archbishop Makarios Street.

Afrika, Alex. Diakou Street.

Afroditi, Patmos–Chalkis Street.

Arion, Archbishop Makarios Street.

Château Fleuri, Amerikis Street.
Colossos, Haile Selassie Street.
Diana, Griva Street.
El Greco, Efstathiou Street.
Flora, 28 Oktovriou Street.
Karpathos, Vassilissis Sofias Street.
Laokoon, Archbishop Makarios Street.
Mimosa, Efstathiou Street.
Royal, Vassilissis Sofias Street.
Victoria, 25 Martiou Street.
Few of these hotels have restaurants but most serve breakfast and some have their own bars.

D and E Class   A selection of D Class hotels includes:
Agh. Antonios, Ionos Dragoumi Street.
Amaryllis, 5 Griva Street.
Australia, 29 Lohagou Fanovraki Street.
Belmar, 3 Nikolaou Sava Street.
Helena, 30 Griva Street.
Rodiakon, 20 Apollonos and Amerikis Street.
For up-to-date information about other D Class hotels and recommended E Class hotels, ask the N.T.O.G.

Hotels in the rest of the island

At Mt Profitis Elias
A Class, *Elafos* and *Elafina*. Genuine Swiss-style Greek mountain hotels. Very curious. Over 2,500 feet up in the mountains; pine trees all about you, wonderful views. Deer graze – in wire enclosures. Open only for the two key months of summer: July 1st to August 31st.

At Kremasti
E Class, *Haravaghi*. Simple, village hotel.

Near Kallithea Spa
A Class, *Eden Rock*, approximately 8 km. from Rhodes. Hotel and bungalow accommodation. Built 1970. Beach, large swimming pool, tennis, mini-golf, etc. Hotel shops. Buses to and from Rhodes.

At Faliraki Beach
17 km. from Rhodes, the large, A Class *Faliraki Beach Hotel* opened in 1973. It aims to make a

holiday outside the city as well catered for as possible; hence there is a large swimming pool, two tennis courts, an extensive beach, hairdresser, hotel shops, a car-hire desk, lifts, etc. The hotel is fully air-conditioned.

There are also several much more modest small establishments of the 'restaurant with rooms' type being built at Faliraki. At the southern end of the beach there is the *Lito*, a small, attractive pension which recent opinion rates as very good value and which offers the quieter end of the beach to sunbathe upon. However, one cannot call Faliraki noisy and it is a very pleasant place to stay for a period of sunshine and swimming with the added advantage that the beach is excellent for children.

Pensions and rooms

Rhodes City

Your best informants are the N.T.O.G. and the Tourist Police; Map **13**. Most pensions and rooms are in the new town though there are a few in the old city too: the *Pension Elektra* in Panetiou Street is one, and there is another at 42–45 Aghios Fanourios Street. There are rooms to let at *Castello* also in Panetiou Street (near Nikis and Takis' shop). Many of the pensions of the new town are in the ornate, cool villas built during the Italian period.

Outside Rhodes City

There are a number of rooms to let in private houses in Lindos; for on-the-spot information, ask the policeman on duty at the bus square or any villager.

There are no other listed rooms in other villages on the island.

RESTAURANTS AND ENTERTAINMENT

Restaurants and cafés, New Town

Kon-Tiki	A floating restaurant in Mandraki Harbour. Rather smart. Expensive but good.
Astoria	At the taxi rank end of the New Market arcade.

	Very popular with tourists and Rhodians. Average prices. Good value.
Nireus	At the other end of the New Market arcade.
Panhellinon	Café and pastry shop in New Market arcade.
Demetriades	Also a café and pastry-shop. Probably the most popular café on the water-front. Try their crème caramel or *rizógalo* (chilled rice pudding dusted with cinnamon).
Aktaion	A luxe-class, open-air café between the New Market and Post Office.
Nautical Club (N.O.R.)	A restaurant on the point near the Elli Club.
Deloukas	19 Kos Street.
Kali Kardia	Inside New Market. Popular restaurant with Scandinavian tourists.
Nouri's	2 Komninon Street, a short taxi-ride or about 20 minutes' walk from town centre. Turkish restaurant. Walled courtyard is roofed with dense vine. Jasmine scents the air and jasmine flowers fall about your feet. A meal at Nouri's costs a little more than the average but it's worth every drachma. Ask for *tzatzíki* (yoghourt, garlic and cucumber), *soutzoukákia* (seasoned sausages), 'Ladies' Lips' (*baklavá* soaked in rose-water), etc.
Piccolo	Kastellorizou Street. Greek and international dishes. Greek music.
Hermes	Below Hermes Hotel, bottom of N. Plastira Street. New snack-bar/restaurant, clean, pleasant. Average prices.
Olympia	Pleasant café-bar, light meals. Archbishop Makarios Street, overlooking harbour.

Old Town

Alexis Moustafa Taverna	On right, looking up Sokratous Street. Fish a speciality. Not expensive.

Also in the old town, there is a group of three restaurants at the top of Apellou Street, just beyond the museum. Here are the Café Bar *Omonia*, the Café Bar *International* and the famous and pleasant *Café des Roses* (which until recently carried a board ⊙n its wall proclaiming 'Come on [sic]! Come all! Most sanitary and un-expensive.') Reasonable prices at all three.

Cinemas

Rhodes has several open-air cinemas including the *Rodon, Titania, Esperos, Orfeus* and *Rex*. The *Pallas* is indoor and air-conditioned.

Theatres

In the '*Medieval Theatre*' in the Old Town a Greek dance group performs nightly (except Sunday) (*Old Town Map* **30**). Folk-dance performances are also given at Rodini Park. In the summer months, classical plays are sometimes performed at the ancient theatre on Monte Smith.

Son et Lumière

From April 1st to October 31st or later. Two or three performances nightly, each in a different language; in the Municipal Gardens on the old city side of the New Market and near the taxi rank.

Night-clubs

Elli, Koundouriotou Square; *Isabella*, Grand Hotel; *Miramare*, Miramare Beach Hotel; *Step by Step*, Papalouka Street (near Belve-dere Hotel); *Dionysos Taverna*, off Sokratous Street, Old Town; *Bel Paso*, on Monte Smith (popular among Rhodians and tourists); *Aquarius Discotheque*, also on Monte Smith.

Casino

Grand Hotel. Jacket and tie; passport required.

Sport

See p. 57.

BEACHES

Other than the little enclaves of the luxury and first-class beach hotels, Rhodes has no seaside resorts in the usual sense of the term.

However, *Faliraki* beach with its small restaurants makes an attractive day by the sea away from the sightseeing of Rhodes, and, as discussed earlier, a very pleasant spot for a longer holiday.

Beaches on the island are fair to excellent. In Rhodes itself the most popular bathing place is the 'Elli' Club beach (*Map* 2); for a few drachmas a time (and a small tip to the umbrella man) you have the use of cabins, umbrellas, diving-boards, etc. There is a café for light refreshment. The west coast beaches in the environs of the town have already been referred to in the Hotels section; they lie on the Bay of Trianda for the most part, and the beaches nearest the town are the *Akti Miaouli* and the *Akti Kanari* just round the northern point.

The east coast beaches are the more sheltered and the sandy stretches of *Faliraki*, *Kolimbia* and *Tsambikos* are splendid. But the pride of place on this coast – and it is probably the finest beach on the island – must go to the stretch curving round the *Bay of Lindos*. Overlooked by the acropolis and temple of Athene, the shore is wide and sandy, and the sea, unless turbulent winds churn up the sea-bed, is invariably clear and still and safe. The beauty of this bay to some extent must be weighed against the appeal of the village and the acropolis that makes the beach rather over-popular at some times of the day.

Just before Lindos, a rough track turns left down to Vlicha Beach, 1·5 km. from the road. This attractive beach has a small restaurant and is relatively isolated as yet.

Also on the east coast is *Kallithea Spa*, 10 km. from Rhodes. (Kallithea Spa is not to be confused with the inland village of *Kalithies*.) This is a small, pretty bay, which the Italians caused to blossom with grottoes, pleasances and a pink-and-white confection of spa buildings. The spa is of the past and the buildings in bad repair but there is a restaurant in the season and the swimming is pleasant.

There are other beaches farther south on both coasts. At *Kamiros* and several other places down the west coast there are reasonably accessible beaches. South of Lindos, the long shallow *Bay of Lardos* is fringed with sand-dunes and almost deserted.

RHODES CITY

If possible, let your first sight of Rhodes be from the sea. The walled, medieval town rises from the sea: bastions of honey-coloured stone, turrets and towers, swallow-tail battlements.

Essentially a romantic spectacle, Rhodes is, nevertheless, no pretti-fied Camelot. It is a squat, solid citadel, designed for defence and war. It bears the signature of the Knights of St John who built it and lived in it – and of their successors, too, for amid the medieval trappings there also rise the minarets and domes of Turkish mosques.

Crowding the medieval walls is the New Town, as old as the Turkish occupation and as new as today. The map on pp. 132–33 shows the relationship between Old Town, New Town and Harbours, which together make up the city of Rhodes.

The mole leading to St Nicholas Fort is on ancient Greek founda-tions. The three windmills along the mole were there at least as early as 1480. Tradition has it that the Colossus of Rhodes straddled the entrance to Mandraki Harbour, one foot on this mole and the other on the old site of a lazaret, where today the N.O.R. Club stands (see p. 85, Art and Culture, and p. 68, History).

The ancient city, which extended inland as far as Monte Smith, was planned in 408 B.C. by Hippodamos of Militos in Asia Minor. He was the great architect of his time (he also produced the plans for ancient Piraeus). One of the streets in the walled town of Rhodes still bears his name. While it was no doubt child's play to find your way about his mathematically organized streets and squares when they were first built, today the geography of the city is confusing in the extreme. The visitor is in real need of helpful aids and land-marks. This book tries to provide these by dividing the old town into three sections: Northern, South-Western, South-Eastern (see Rhodes Old Town map on p. 107). The Northern Section includes the area called the Collachium, which was a city within the old city. Here the Knights built the Grand Masters' Palace, the Street of the Knights, the Hospital of the Knights (now the museum), etc. South of Sokratous Street (the wide shopping street running downhill to the sea from the Mosque of Suleiman) is the South-Western Section. It is bounded on west and south by the walls of the city and on the east by Pithagoras Street. To the east of the South-Western Section is the South-Eastern Section. This borders the Commercial Harbour and includes the old Jewish quarter and many winding alleys and medieval buildings.

Description of the Old Town sights is organized as follows. First, a general exploration taking in the sights of the Northern, South-Western and South-Eastern sections of the Old Town is described for each of these sections. As only a brief mention can be made of the various sights encountered on these explorations, the reader is usually referred, when a museum or mosque is mentioned, to a later page where a fuller description of that museum or mosque can be found. After the three walking tours, there are the fuller discussions of individual museums and mosques of the Old Town under the appropriate headings. Finally there is a description of towers, gates and ramparts to complete the information on sights of the Old Town.

It is only recently that, during the season, traffic in the Old Town has been banned after 11 a.m. Previously, visitors and locals alike were to be seen nervously flattening themselves against walls or shop fronts as young lions on motor-bikes and scooters gunned their way round corners and wide American taxis drove through narrow Rhodian streets.

OLD TOWN: NORTHERN SECTION

All map references are to the Old Town map (opposite).

On entering the old town through the *Liberty Gate* you arrive in *Simi Square*. Behind the policeman in his blue-and-white-striped traffic box is a ruined *temple of Aphrodite* (*Map* 1) of the third century B.C. To the left is the *sea wall* of the Commercial Harbour and also the *Arsenal Gate*. Facing you, and beyond the temple of Aphrodite, is one of the Inns of the Knights, the *Inn of Auvergne* (*Map* 5). An outside staircase leads to a gallery and first floor. The Inn now houses a local government office.

The road slopes up on your right; here there is a branch of Greece's most charmingly named bank, the Ionian and Popular. Note also the *ship's chandler* – very appropriately situated, for it is believed that behind here were the ancient dockyards. A flight of steps in this building leads to an *art gallery* housed on the first floor.

At the top of the slope is *Argyrokastrou Square* (*Map* 4). In the centre of the square is a *fountain*: the base is a Byzantine font. Font and fountain were discovered by Italian archaeologists in the Church of St Irene near Arnitha. The Greek archaeologists of today incline to regard Argyrokastrou Square as quite the wrong place for the font and fountain, but the result is so attractive and the fountain looks so pleasant and sounds so cool and idle that not many holiday-makers will agree with them.

Rhodes: Old Town

1 Temple of Aphrodite
2 Palace of the Grand Masters
3 First Infirmary (Armeria Palace)
4 Argyrokastrou Square
5 Inn of Auvergne
6 Museum of Decorative Arts
7 Enderoum
8 Hospital (Archaeological Museum)
9 Inn of England
10 Clock Tower
11 Chourmali Medresse
12 Mosque of Suleiman
13 Ste Marie de la Victoire
14 Agh. Panteleimon
15 Chadrevan Mosque
16 Agha Mosque
17 Hippokratous Square
18 Tribune of Commerce
19 Turkish Library
20 Archbishop's Palace
21 Takkedji Mosque
22 Square of the Jewish Martyrs
23 Ste Marie du Bourg
24 Ibrahim Mosque
25 Demerli Mosque
26 Public Baths
27 Mosque of Moustafa
28 Kavakly Mosque
29 Hamza Bey Mosque
30 'Medieval Theatre'
31 Abdul Djelil Mosque
32 Retjep Pasha Mosque
33 Pial-el-Din (Agh. Fanourios)
34 Dolaplee Mosque
35 Ilk Mihrab Mosque
36 Bourouzan Mosque

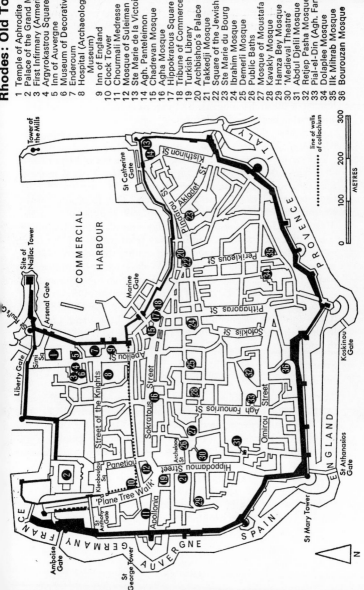

The *Palace of the Armeria* (*Map* 3), which is believed to have been the first infirmary of the Order, looks out on to Argyrokastrou Square. It was built in the fourteenth century – probably during the time of Grand Master Roger de Pins, whose coat of arms you can see on the wall.

The building (note the fine double stairway, arches and gargoyles) now houses the Archaeological Service of the Dodecanese. It is not open to the public but inside there is a splendid refectory, now the library of the archaeologists. The garden contains numerous stone and marble herms and sculptures.

At right-angles to the Armeria and facing down the slope is the *Museum of Decorative Arts* (*Map* 6; see p. 122).

You now pass under an archway, alongside the old *Enderoum* or *Orthodox Cathedral of St Mary* on your left (*Map* 7). It is intended that the Enderoum should shortly open as a museum of Early Christian and Byzantine art and artifacts. This faces into a small square in which are the *Inn of England* (*Map* 9) and the *Archaeological Museum of Rhodes* (*Map* 8; p. 115). The Inn of England is on the corner of a narrow street leading away from the square and down to the harbour. In the mid nineteenth century the original building was entirely destroyed and the Inn on show today is a restoration dating from 1919. A plaque relates its history up to the present day. Also in the square is the *shop* of Ikaros, the maker of ceramics.

To the right as you enter the square is the *Street of the Knights* (Odós Ippotón). It is cobbled for its whole length and terminates in the *Palace of the Grand Masters* (*Map* 2; see p. 119) at the top of the slope.

Street of the Knights

All map references are to the plan of the Street of the Knights

The Knights, as builders and architects, were strongly influenced by the Gothic buildings they left behind in their native lands. The city they built reflects the dual role of the Order, for though the buildings of Rhodes are for the most part superb examples of un-compromising military architecture, there are many ecclesiastical references which temper the military function.

The Street of the Knights was the main street of the medieval Collachium and it represents the most remarkable survival of a medieval street one is likely to see today. Stripped of the ram-shackle balconies and jalousies of the Turkish era and discreetly

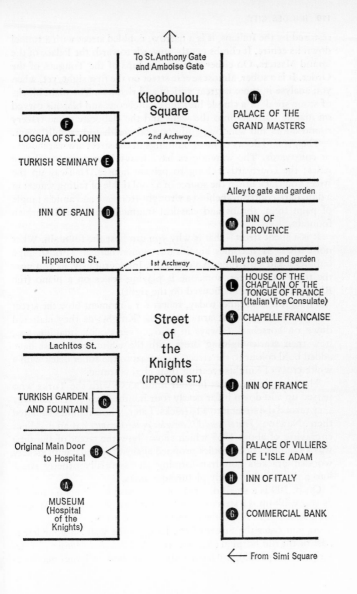

Kleoboulou Square

To St. Anthony Gate
and Amboise Gate

2nd Archway

N PALACE OF THE GRAND MASTERS

F LOGGIA OF ST. JOHN

E TURKISH SEMINARY

Alley to gate and garden

D INN OF SPAIN

M INN OF PROVENCE

Hipparchou St.

1st Archway

Alley to gate and garden

L HOUSE OF THE CHAPLAIN OF THE TONGUE OF FRANCE (Italian Vice Consulate)

K CHAPELLE FRANCAISE

Street of the Knights
(IPPOTON ST.)

Lachitos St.

J INN OF FRANCE

G TURKISH GARDEN AND FOUNTAIN

B Original Main Door to Hospital

I PALACE OF VILLIERS DE L'ISLE ADAM

H INN OF ITALY

A MUSEUM (Hospital of the Knights)

G COMMERCIAL BANK

← From Simi Square

restored by the Italians, it is a narrow, cobbled street with a runnel down its centre. It climbs gently upwards towards the Palace of the Grand Masters. On either side are the Inns of the Tongues of the Order. It is a sober, almost severe street on the first sight, yet, when you analyse it, there is great variety and richness. The plain blocks of stone speak of a simple life; the escutcheons and blazons carved on marble slabs set into the walls and the elaborate stone tracery round doors and windows add notes of wealth and establishment.

The ground floors of most buildings in the street are warehouses or courtyards. The warehouses have heavy iron doors or slatted gates; the courtyards belong to private houses. Halfway up the street you track down the source of a cool tinkle of falling water: in a dim, dark courtyard behind a wrought-iron gate and amid a tangle of palm trees, shrubs and classical fragments is a small Turkish fountain.

It is a silent street – that is why you can hear the fountain. What noise there is becomes significant. Somewhere a Turkish pipe bubbles a sad slow tune. A voice calls. Incongruously, as you near the top of the street, someone is playing scales on a piano (the Rhodian music club is housed on the right).

Though it is so quiet today, reflect for a moment how the street must have rung to the armour of the Knights as they clattered down on horseback (always in pairs, never alone). Imagine, too, how their scarlet fighting dress with the white cross must have added bold colour to the street, a contrast to the sober black with a white cross of knights wearing their civil costume.

Then people the street in your mind's eye with the Turks who passed up and down it for nearly four hundred years. At one stage they turned the street into a barracks. Later, whole families squatted there. Newton (*Travels and Discoveries in the Levant*) has an excellent engraving of about 1865 which shows how the street of the time was a shambles of balconies propped against the walls with rickety wooden brackets and transforming an essentially orderly street into a slovenly but vastly picturesque mess.

On p. 109 is a small diagram of the street; buildings on the left as you walk up the street towards the Palace of the Grand Masters are marked **A** to **F** and those on the right **G** to **N**.

As you enter the Street of the Knights the wall on your left is part of the old hospital (**A**), now the *Archaeological Museum* (for description see p. 115), and farther up you will find the large ogee doorway used by the Knights as the main entrance to the hospital (**B**).

On your right is a medieval building now occupied by the *Commercial Bank of Greece* (**G**). It has the characteristic windows and shutters of the idiom. Next comes the *Inn of Italy* (**H**). This bears a marble escutcheon of the arms of the Order quartered with the diagonal arms of Fabrizio del Carretto, Grand Master of Italy. The little *palace of Villiers de l'Isle Adam* comes next (**I**); he was the Grand Master who performed the melancholy ceremony of leading the Knights out of Rhodes after the final victory of the Turks. Almost opposite is the door to the old hospital already mentioned above.

De l'Isle Adam's palace virtually runs into the *Inn of France* (**J**). This large Inn is the most handsome of all and is enormously satisfying to look at. In this world of brilliant sunshine the relationship of basically severe, flat stonework and bold carving produces dramatic contrasts of light and shadow. The use of strong horizontals for the string-courses; the opposition of curves to flat surfaces as in the little pair of turrets; the outward thrust of gargoyles and merlons – all this skilful juggling of planes and surfaces is highly satisfying. So is the fenestration of the first floor, four superb windows with deeply carved half-frames which act as a balance to the horizontals of string-course and street. The whole is surmounted by the characteristic Rhodian swallow-tail battlements.

Various coats of arms embellish the front of the Inn of France. Beginning at the point where the string-course starts, just below the first turret, they include:

(*a*) The arms of Aimerie d'Amboise and the Order and below it those of Villiers de l'Isle Adam.

(*b*) Above the doorway is the date 1492, and on either side are the arms of the Order and of Aimerie d'Amboise. The Inn, though begun in 1492 during the Grand Master-ship of Pierre d'Aubusson, was completed while d'Amboise was Grand Master; probably in 1509.

(*c*) Next, the arms of de l'Isle Adam are repeated. Above them and between the final pair of first-floor windows, you will find the fleur-de-lis and crown of France alongside the arms of Pierre d'Aubusson (note that as these are surmounted by a cardinal's hat and hung with tassels on either side this escutcheon must have been set up after he became a cardinal in 1495).

(*d*) At the far end of the Inn of France a marble plaque records
that the façade of the Inn of France was restored by Maurice
Bompard, the French Ambassador to Turkey in 1913.

Almost opposite (*c*) above is the wrought-iron gate of a small
Turkish garden and fountain (**C**). A few yards higher up is a narrow
street, *Lachitos Street*.

Beyond Lachitos Street to the right is the small *Chapelle Française*
(**K**). This was the chapel of the Tongue of France. A Virgin and
Child stand in a niche below a carved stone canopy. Among the
escutcheons are the arms of Raymond Béranger who was Grand
Master between 1365 and 1374; this indicates that the chapel was
probably built during his term and makes it one of the oldest buildings in the street.

Abutting the chapel is the *house of the Chaplain of the Tongue of
France* (**L**). This is now occupied by the Italian Vice-Consul.

At this point an archway crosses the street and a narrow alley to
the right leads to a gateway and garden (sometimes the gate is open
and you can get in).

On the far side of the arch the *Inn of Provence* is on the right (**M**)
and Hipparchou Street on the left. The façade of the Inn of Provence is without any decoration save the date (1418) and an assembly of blazons including those of the Order, of France and of
Fabrizio del Carretto quartered with those of the Order.

Flanking Hipparchou Street is the *Inn of Spain* (**D**). The escutcheons applied to the façade are its only adornment: above the door
the arms of the Order are quartered with those of Antoine Fluvian,
the Spanish Grand Master from 1421 to 1437.

Beyond the Inn of Provence is another alley and on the left,
before you pass under a second arch, is the garden (**E**) of an old
Turkish seminary.

Beyond the arch is a restoration of part of the *Loggia of St John* (**F**).
This vaulted loggia originally connected the Palace of the Grand
Masters (**N**) with the Church of St John. The church and greater
part of the loggia were blown up in the great explosion of 1856.
The Church of Evangelismos down on the waterfront is a fair copy
of the Church of St John.

You are now in *Kleoboulou Square* (*Plateia Kleoboulou*) and virtually
everything here, including the palace, was rebuilt or restored by the
Italians. However, the 'strap' design on the multiple piers of the

loggia is original. To the right is the rebuilt *Palace of the Grand Masters* (**N**) (for description see p. 119).

Upon leaving the palace, turn right as you emerge into Kleoboulou Square. On your right and set back is another postwar restoration: a *Fine Art Institute* which acts as a hostel for visiting art students. Beyond this you enter a shady walk of plane trees which runs parallel with the ramparts. Turn right, and you come first to the *St Anthony Gate* and then to the *Amboise Gate*: turn left, and the street curves round to the *Clock Tower* (*Old Town Map* **10**). A miniature of 1480 clearly shows the wall which once ran from the Clock Tower downhill to the sea. This wall separated the Collachium or enclave of the Knights from the residential part of the old city. The line of this vanished wall is marked on the Old Town map. Now carry on past the Clock Tower to the *Mosque of Suleiman* at the head of Sokratous Street. This latter part marks the start of the South-Western Section.

OLD TOWN: SOUTH-WESTERN SECTION

All map references are to the Old Town map (p. 107).

Standing at the top of Sokratous Street, the *Mosque of Suleiman* (*Map* **12**; p. 126) is on your left and the *Turkish Library* (*Map* **19**) on your right. This eighteenth-century building contains a Koran of 1412 and there is another, richly decorated, which dates from 1540. The library also runs to a half-hearted reading-room (a collection of faded Turkish magazines, a cookery book and, if it is still there, a delightful book on Karagoz, the traditional Turkish–Greek character of punchinello bawdy).

The seaward side of the Turkish Library is on Hippodamou Street. Follow this street, turn left into Archelaou Street and you come to a square in which are the *Public Baths* (*Map* **26**). If you fancy luxuriating in a real Turkish bath, now is your chance, for this is the old Turkish *hammam* of the city, destroyed in the last war and now restored and in daily use. The *Mosque of Moustafa* (*Map* **27**; p. 126) is also in this square. A narrow lane off the square leads to the '*Medieval City*' *Theatre* (*Map* **30**), scene of the nightly folk-dance performances.

The area west of Hippodamou Street is relatively sparsely populated but it contains the *Mosque of Chourmali Medresse* (*Map* **11**; p. 124), the *Hamza Bey Mosque* (*Map* **29**; p. 124) and the *Takkedji*

Mosque (Map 21; p. 126). Facing you as you approach the Chourmali Medresse along Apollonia Street is the blocked-up *St George Gate*, one of the medieval gates into the city. Another gateway in this section is the old *St Athanasios Gate* at the southern limit of the section. Near by is the ruined *Church of St Athanasios*.

Within this Section, a confusion of streets and alleys wind and tangle. The most thriving area is the old *Bazaar district* of Sokratous Street, a wide ribbon that runs from the Mosque of Suleiman (*Map* 12; p. 126) downhill to *Hippokratous Square* (see below). Halfway down this street the *Agha Mosque (Map* 16; p. 123) juts out into the road.

OLD TOWN: SOUTH-EASTERN SECTION

All map references are to the Old Town map (p. 107).

Hippokratous Square (Map 17) is a large square at the foot of Sokratous Street. It is graced by an attractive fountain set with Turkish tiles and surmounted by a minaret. The most important feature of the square is the medieval *Tribune of Commerce (Map* 18), with its wide external staircase and horizontal string-courses. The Tribunal served as the court-house of the Knights; it was at one time known as the Palace of Castellania. Above the doorway is an outstandingly fine group of carved escutcheons. The centrepiece is an angel supporting the arms of the Order and the blazon of Aimerie d'Amboise. The entire lintel and jambs of this door are of marble.

Note also the decorative carving in an ogee frame above the head of the stairs. Just to the right, at the top of the ogee, is an empty stone socket. This is a banner socket and the Tribunal must have looked both brave and gay when the banner was flying. The window to the right of this has an unusual marble cross-bar and upright, both decorated with the fleur-de-lis.

Hippokratous Square leads into Aristotelous Street and so to the old *Jewish Quarter* and the *Square of the Jewish Martyrs (Map* 22). This square (the name dates from the last war) possesses a delightful *fountain*, faced with a series of carved shells, starfish, octopus, etc., and topped with bronze sea-horses. The fountain stands in front of the *Archbishop's Palace (Map* 20), another fifteenth-century building with characteristic period embellishments. It was the residence of the Latin Archbishop.

The street leading from the Square of the Jewish Martyrs takes you through the ruins of the *Church of Ste Marie du Bourg* (*Map* **23**). Part of this is on one side of the street, part on the other – the road appears to have been driven through the apse of the church. Beyond here is the *Church of Aghios Panteleimon* (*Map* **14**), near *St Catherine Gate*, and beyond this church are the ruins of *Ste Marie de la Victoire* (*Map* **13**).

From the Church of the Victory you can turn right into Kisthiniou Street and hugging the great walls, walk round the perimeter till you reach the *Koskinou Gate*. Alternatively, you can plunge into the maze and enjoy yourself among its quietness, its strange lanes, arched for protection against earthquakes, its talk from within dark courtyards, its glimpses and vistas. Mosques in the area include the *Dolaplee Mosque* (*Map* **34**; p. 124) and the *Ilk Mihrab Mosque* (*Map* **35**; p. 125).

MUSEUMS

All map references are to the Old Town map (p. 107).

Archaeological Museum of Rhodes: originally Hospital of the Knights
Map **8**.

Open Daily 08.00–18.00 (Pottery Dept. closed 12.00–16.00).
Sundays and holidays 10.00–13.00.
14.20–17.00.
N.B. Closed on Mondays.
Entrance Drs 10.

The museum faces Museum Square and one side of it runs up the Street of the Knights. In almost every way this is the most important medieval building in the old town. It is in fine condition and is the prime statement of the original function of the Order – to succour and care for the ill and the needy. Building began in 1440 under Grand Master de Lastic and was completed in 1489 by Pierre d'Aubusson.

Today, the building should be looked at in two ways: as a medieval hospital and a modern museum. The most important features of the hospital are the courtyard and infirmary. Almost every other room, gallery or cell now serves as a home for some of the treasures of Rhodes.

Before entering, look up at the first floor of the building from Museum Square. Running the length of this frontage is the Great

Infirmary. Above the main entrance is a three-sided bay with windows, which is part of the chapel of the infirmary. Over the entrance is a bas-relief of two angels bearing the arms of the order.

Ground-floor courtyard

On entering the museum through a Gothic archway you come immediately to the ground-floor courtyard. This is enclosed on all four sides by a two-storeyed arcade; note that the arches are not all the same size. The ground floor was used for storage and stabling and the upper floor housed the hospital and administrative offices.

In the courtyard is a *Rhodian lion* of the first century A.D. and a collection of stone and iron cannon-balls. Some of the larger ones are believed to have been used by Demetrios Poliorkitis during the siege of Rhodes in 305 B.C.; of the other, smaller missiles, some are Turkish-made, others were used by the Knights. The *mosaic* in front of the lion is from Karpathos.

First-floor gallery: Side A

The flight of steps from the courtyard takes you to the first-floor gallery. Turn left at the top and about halfway down the gallery is the carved stone doorway to the *Infirmary*. This huge, lofty stone hall (bats flit about the timbered roof) is divided down its length by seven pillars. The pillars each bear the arms of the Order and of Pierre d'Aubusson and support the roof. Some sections of the stone floor are original. Immediately opposite the main entrance is a shallow chapel framed in an elaborate arch. The ceiling is vaulted and the wall is pierced by tall windows. This chapel forms the bay that can be seen from Museum Square. It is not in the absolute centre of the hall; four of the pillars are to its left and three to the right.

Up to a hundred patients were cared for in the infirmary and along one wall are fourteen windowless cells, each with two doors. It is not known exactly how these were used. It is possible that they were merely cells for the use of monks or nursing members of the Order, but it is also possible they were small isolation wards or simply additional support for the long wall and gallery.

Around the walls are a number of funeral stones and carved coats of arms. One large stone carries the escutcheon of Grand Master d'Hérédia, while de Pins, Aimerie d'Amboise and Villiers de l'Isle Adam are also represented. Within a fireplace at the far end is a

marble relief of the lion of St Mark and the arms of one of the
Italian knights.

First-floor gallery: Side B

On leaving the infirmary, return to the top of the steps. Along the
side of the gallery facing you now are Rooms 1, 2 and 3.

N.B. *The contents of this museum are liable to be removed from one room to
another as part of the process of reorganization. For this reason, you may
find that items which at the time of going to press are located as follows have
been moved elsewhere or that some rooms have been closed and others opened.*

Room 1   Contains pots, votive figures and other small objects
           found in burial places at Tsambikos, Kremasti, Ancient
           Ialysos, etc. Most are dated between the ninth and sixth
           centuries B.C.

Room 2   Glass cases of pottery, vases, oil and perfume containers.
           There is a fine black-and-orange *krater* (jar in which wine
           was mixed) and a number of *kylixes* – those shallow cups
           with handles that are perhaps the most elegant of all the
           vessels created by the Greeks.

Room 3   Probably the best collection in the museum of black-on-
           red jars, *kraters* and dishes. The room also contains a
           charming group of four birds gathered round a bowl,
           and an endearing tortoise. Both are in clay.

First-floor gallery: Side C

           From Room 3 turn into Side C, facing the infirmary
           entrance.

Room 4   (leads into Room 5): Small room with chimney-piece.
           The outer surface of one *Attic kylix* portrays a chariot
           race and Hercules struggling with the lion of Nemea.
           Inside, there is a formidable Gorgon's head. Room 4
           also contains protogeometric vases from a grave at
           Kremasti discovered in 1949.

Room 5   (entered from Room 4): Note a black-figured *hydria*
           decorated with dancing youths and a horseman. Also, an
           Attic black-figured *amphora* of warriors and a chariot
           and Dionysos and two satyrs. This amphora is of the
           mid sixteenth century B.C., and is in particularly good
           condition.

Room 6   (entered from Room 5): Has a chimney-piece and contains red-on-black vases, a large and very beautiful *kylix*
and a number of votive figures. Also houses a heavy,
possibly ceremonial, necklace of fourteen rows of semi-
precious stones and a case of fine silver coins, mostly in
good condition. Look for the vigorous treatments of the
head of Apollo.

First-floor gallery: Side D

All the rooms on this side are closed at the time of writing. At the
end of Side D you turn right into Side A again, passing the infirmary. At the far end of Side A there is a narrow passage into
Room 7.

Room 7   This was the refectory of the hospital. It was badly
damaged during the Second World War and has been
restored. On the walls are a number of bas-reliefs of the
third century A.D.: most of them are from the island of
Nisyros. Note the use of '*Chaîre*' ('be happy') carved into
the stone. There is a particularly affecting relief of a
mother and child, bold and simple.

Room 8   This is a small, narrow room off the refectory to the left.
Contains some first- and second-century B.C. heads.

Room 9   Here there is a small Aphrodite of Rhodes, caught dry-
ing her hair after the bath. Dated about 90 B.C. Tech-
nically adroit, much-admired and wholly saccharine.

Room 10   Contains the best-known treasure of the Museum, the
Marine Venus. This is the nude which Durrell celebrated
in *Reflections on a Marine Venus*. She is life-size and probably dates from the third century B.C. There is also a
vigorous, dramatic head of the Sun God which possibly
comes from a second-century B.C. pediment.

Garden (11)

From Room 9 you can enter the pretty garden. There is
an open courtyard with a large lightwell in the centre.
Urns, plinths and altars are set about this garden and
many of them are planted with flowers, sage, mint and
other herbs. Don't miss the large black dolphin of the
Hellenistic period (and the baby dolphin alongside), the
Byzantine mosaic pavement from Karpathos behind

them, or the small stone boxes with sloping lids. These last were containers for the bones of Classical and Hellenistic citizens of Rhodes (you can see a name carved into one of the lids).

A flight of stairs (not open to the public) links the garden to the paved yard at the bottom of the lightwell. This was the original stairway used by the Knights to get from the ground floor to the first floor (the stairs in the main courtyard are recent).

On the side opposite the dolphins a door leads from the garden to Room 12.

Room 12 Here is the rightly famous funerary *stele* of Krito and Tamarista. Found at Kamiros, it is a Classical bas-relief of a daughter taking farewell of her dead mother. It is of the last quarter of the fifth century B.C. The cropped head of the daughter was a mark of grief.

Also in this room are two archaic *kouroi*. These male figures were both made during the sixth century B.C. but one is slightly later than the other. While each demonstrates the strong Egyptian influence at work during the period, the later figure is less stylized and reveals very clearly that the sculptor was more aware of bone and muscle and modelling than his predecessor.

From Room 12 return to the ground-floor courtyard by way of the main stairs. A door off this courtyard leads to the lightwell from where you can look up to the garden on the first floor. The lightwell is paved with mosaics. Adjacent to it are new lavatories; at the time of writing among the best-kept public lavatories in the Dodecanese.

Palace of the Grand Masters
Map 2.

Open Summer   09.30–13.00.
                                 15.30–19.00.
        Sundays and holidays 10.00–13.00.
                                 15.00–18.00.
        Winter   09.30–13.00.
                                 15.30–19.00.
        Sundays and holidays 10.00–13.00.
                                 14.30–17.00.
        N.B. Closed on Mondays.
Entrance Drs 5.

The first, fourteenth-century palace was built by the Knights to double as a fortress in war and a peacetime residence for the Grand Master and meeting-place for senior knights. It was so solid that even during the final siege of 1522 it suffered remarkably little damage. After the departure of the Knights, the Turks used it for a prison for a time, and thereafter, in their indolent fashion, were content to let it crumble. Destruction came as late as 1856 with an appalling explosion of gunpowder believed to have been left in the palace vaults since the siege. The explosion was probably set off by lightning; it destroyed the palace, wrecked the Loggia of St John and killed approximately eight hundred people.

The rebuilt exterior of the palace is a reconstruction of the fourteenth-century building as far as possible and was completed by the Italians before the last war. As they intended that the palace should be used by Victor Emmanuel III and Mussolini on state visits the interior is some way removed from the original and contains some grandiose flights of fancy.

The palace today is much visited on account of its mosaics; many of these were removed from Kos by the Italians. There is a lot of scholarly argument about the rights and wrongs of this, but it cannot be denied that the result has been the preservation of some extremely delightful mosaics.

You enter the outer courtyard of the palace from Kleoboulou Square. Ahead are two enormous crenellated towers. From here you pass through a covered hall to an inner courtyard. On the wall opposite the entrance is the cardinal's-hat *escutcheon of Pierre d'Aubusson*. In archways set about this courtyard are figures of the Hellenistic period, most of them from Kos. To the left, note a plinth and steps. On the plinth is a gateway of two pillars and a lintel; the pillars are from the Church of Aghia Irene at Arnitha and are similar to some found in Istanbul. Also at this spot is a *sarcophagus* found at Monolithos with handsome Christian crosses on it.

To enter the palace you turn back from the courtyard into the hall. On the right, at the bottom of the grand staircase, is a small *chapel* containing a Roman altar and some early Christian pieces. Almost everything else is modern. Under the stairway is a refectory.

At the head of the stairs you enter the first of a series of rooms which take you round the palace. *The rooms of the palace are untitled, so the following alphabetic guide is the author's. Room A leads into Room B, Room B into Room C, etc.*

Room A   This is a very large room, divided by three arches and two pillars down its length. The walls are of large blocks of multicoloured stone. There is a fine view across Kleoboulou Square to the Clock Tower and the Mosque of Suleiman. The room contains Roman and early-Christian mosaics; also Roman and early-Christian capitals.

Room B   Narrowish, with smaller, early-Christian mosaics.

Room C   In the centre is a *head of Medusa* (second century B.C.). Chinese and Rhodian vases.

Room D   Fan-vaulted ceiling and early-Christian mosaics.

Room E   A very large room which was used during the period of the Knights as a meeting-place of senior members of the Order. There is a large Roman *mosaic* in the centre and six pillars.

Room F   Runs off Room E to the left and contains an agreeable Roman *mosaic* of ducks, drinking goblets and formal designs.

Room G   Rhodian *mosaic* of the second century B.C., a simple design of a wavy border with a sceptre in the centre.

Room H   In the centre, a first-century B.C. *mosaic* of Europa and the bull – the bull here translated into a kind of spotted sea-monster. Around the outer edge is a fluent, ivy-leaf design.

       A long, narrow passage connects this room with the next; the doors on either side give on to offices once used by the Italian governor as private apartments.

Room I   The corridor widens and becomes this room: contains a *mosaic* of formal design and some carved wooden seats.

Room J   A room with pleasant views over the roofs of the Old Town.

Room K   A *mosaic* with dolphins sporting.

Of the remaining rooms, there is little to note except, repeatedly, the Roman and early-Christian mosaics. Only one room requires specific mention. This contains a magnificent *mosaic* of the Nine Muses (first century A.D.). In the order they appear in the mosaic they are: Klio (History), Euterpe (Music), Thalia (Comic and Idyllic

Poetry), Melpomene (Tragic Poetry), Terpsichore (Dance), Erato (Lyric and Erotic Poetry), Polyhymnia (Mimic), Urania (Astronomy), Kalliope (Epic Poetry).

Museum of Decorative Arts
Map 6.

Open Monday, Wednesday and Friday 09.00–13.00.
Entrance Drs 5.

This building is believed to have been the Arsenal. As a museum it is delightful and intimate, full of beautifully preserved and presented furniture, costumes, ceramics and other items of folk-art. The name of the museum draws proper attention to the strong decorative element that is emphasized throughout.

The contents have been so admirably arranged that it seems particularly unfortunate that almost nothing is labelled. Main features are (turning left after you enter):

(a) A small cubicle containing Rhodian embroidery; note the use of red and green, a Rhodian signature.

(b) On the end wall to the left, a *spervéri* curtain, a traditional feature of the bridal bed.

(c) Set into the end wall; two carved, olive-wood doors. These are the doors of a Lindian china cupboard.

(d) A glass case on the right side of the end wall contains a handsome collection of old Lindian plates and jugs. Note the freedom with which the flower and leaf designs are presented within the confines of the plates. Some plates reveal the later Turkish influence: there are variations on a delightful figure wearing trousers and bearing flowers, and also a spirited, elegant horse.

(e) On the long wall is a large glass case of costumes from Crete, Karpathos, Kasos and other islands.

(f) The far end of the long wall demonstrates how effective Lindian plates are as large-scale wall decoration.

(g) At right-angles to the wall, the tower of a *spervéri* spills down from the high ceiling. Next is a traditional platform bed some 3 ft. 6 in. to 4 ft. high, approached by a short flight of steps. A curtained doorway, carpets and rugs hung on the walls and laid on the floor complete this family bed.

(h) The final section of the museum is a reconstruction of a domestic interior. Featured are a loom and spinning wheel, a cradle and, on the wall, a woven 'baby carrier' which the mother would sling over her shoulder, thus carrying her baby on her back. The fireplace has a cooking shelf set into it and on this are earthenware pitchers and other utensils. Hanging from the ceiling is a rush carrier to enable cheese to be kept well above floor level.

When you leave the museum take a look at the cannon-balls piled up in the square, also the wrought-iron lamps clamped into the walls. The cannon-balls are left-overs from the last, great siege of 1522; the lamps cast dramatic and mysterious shadows at night.

MOSQUES OF THE OLD TOWN

All map references are to the Old Town map (p. 107).

The mosques are of two kinds. First there are those built as mosques from scratch, i.e. new buildings erected by the Turks. These include the Mosques of Suleiman, Hamza Bey, Chadrevan, Sultan Moustafa, Ibrahim Pasha, Retjep Pasha and the Agha Mosque. The second group are Byzantine churches which the Turks converted into mosques. Some of these have since been translated back into Christian churches.

Many of the mosques are in such decay that they are closed to visitors, some are occupied by squatters and hung about with washing and fishing nets. You will be expected to remove your shoes before entering a mosque which is in current use as a place of worship.

Abdul Djelil Mosque
Map **31**.

Originally Byzantine, badly damaged in the last war.

Agha Mosque
Corner of Sokratous Street and Aghios Fanourios Street; Map **16**.

This was the mosque of the Agha or Turkish Garrison Commander. It juts out into Sokratous Street and is the reason why you cannot see quite clear up the street from top to bottom.

Bourouzan Mosque
Map **36**.

Of no great note, but there is a private garden near by through which, if the gate in the wall is open, you get a very attractive view of the mosque and its minaret.

Chadrevan Mosque
Sokratous Street; Map **15**.

This lies almost in front of you as you enter the old town through the Marine Gate and is on your right as you begin to walk up Sokratous Street. Only occasionally open to the public.

Chourmali Medresse
Map **11**.

This is one of the Byzantine churches which were converted to mosques. It is the third of the tetragonal – i.e., four-apsed – churches of Rhodes; the others are St Nikolaos at Fountoucli and the church at Salakos. The Chourmali Medresse is in a bad state of repair and is not open to the public. Amid the battered, dusty, garden-slum in which it is set there rises a pleasing Byzantine dome (common to most of these churches-cum-mosques). It was once a Turkish theological school.

Demerli Mosque
Map **25**.

This was a fairly large Byzantine church of the early fourteenth century. Now ruined.

Dolaplee Mosque
Map **34**.

This is a small white church which stands in a ramshackle, deserted square, almost North African in appearance by virtue of its palm tree and tattered appearance. The Dolaplee is a very old Byzantine church, curious in that the two arms of the crossing are so long that their total length exceeds that of the nave and apse together.

Hamza Bey Mosque
Map **29**.

Occupied by squatters.

Ibrahim Pasha Mosque
In the middle of the old bazaar area; Map **24**.

A few years later (1531) than the Mosque of Suleiman, this is a large freshly painted mosque with a portico and a handsome plane tree that stands outside. It is open to the public and has a resident caretaker. He will probably indicate – with grace and dignity – that any tip should be placed into his palm and not into the waiting box. The mosque has a beautiful interior gallery and the minaret is modern, built by the Italians in 1928 to replace the original. Well worth a visit.

Ilk Mihrab Mosque
Map **35**.

All you can see is the ruined apse, open to the sky. Byzantine, 1300, converted. Some traces of frescoes in the apse.

Kavakly Mosque
Map **28**.

Hidden away behind locked doors; derelict.

Pial-el-din Mosque or Aghios Fanourios
Tucked away down the little street of Aghios Fanourios; Map **33**.

This was once the Pial-el-din Mosque, restored in this century and returned to Orthodox Christian use. Today, it no longer bears any reminders of its days as a mosque; it is a neat, small Byzantine church closely crowded on either side with dwellings. From its courtyard you step into the gloom and the candles and, peering upwards, you can see the only surviving frescoes of its Byzantine origin. The Turks used the church as stabling in the early days of their occupation and the frescoes were daubed over and gradually rotted away. The church was only restored in this century. It is now in constant use and there is a special service held on August 27th, the name-day of the saint.

Retjep Pasha Mosque
Map **32**.

Totally neglected and abandoned, Retjep Pasha was, in its day, the most splendid of all the mosques in Rhodes. It was built in 1588 with material from Christian churches. If you peer inside, there is little trace of all the immense richness of decoration of its prime. Instead, all you are likely to observe is the detritus of decay and the dank smell of it, too. There is a double gallery and a minaret; a fountain is in the square in which the mosque sits.

Mosque of Suleiman
Map 12.

After Suleiman captured Rhodes in 1522, the Turks immediately began building a mosque to be named after the conqueror himself. Nearly four centuries later, in the first decade of the nineteenth century, it was rebuilt. Today the rose-pink plaster, the tall minaret and the trees set about it remain extremely inviting. Most of the mosque was constructed with materials of an earlier period: the outer arcade, for instance, is supported by pillars from a Christian church (probably from the Church of the Apostles which stood on or near this site). Inside, there is a pleasing sense of uncluttered space. The pulpit is Byzantine, the air smells faintly of the dozens of carpets laid and overlaid on the floor. The ceiling is cool white and blue and all the hum of life which throbs outside in the old town seems far away in the contemplative quiet of this pleasant place.

Sultan Moustafa Mosque
Plateia tou Loutrou; Map 27.

This is in the same square (the Plateia tou Loutrou or Square of the Baths) as the public *hammam*. The two buildings are of the same date – 1765 – and both suffered heavy damage in the last war. The mosque is now closed and rotting; the baths have been restored to usefulness. Look for the graceful decorative notes on the exterior of the mosque – the green, yellow and ochre used to emphasize the capital of a pillar and similarly coloured detail above the door.

Takkedji Mosque or the Mosque of the Dervishes
Map 21.

Locked and ruined.

TOWERS, GATES AND RAMPARTS

Open Every Tuesday and Saturday at 15.00. Foregather in the courtyard in the Palace of the Grand Masters just before 15.00.
Entrance Drs 5.

The walls and gates of the old town of Rhodes are examples of great military architecture. This medieval, fortified city was built, for the most part, upon the remains of Greek and Byzantine walls. We know little about the Byzantine fortifications but they must have presented some challenge, otherwise the Knights would have found it easier to occupy Rhodes in 1309 than in fact they did. What is certain is that once the Knights took command they found it essential to set about strengthening and rebuilding. For they were extremely vulnerable, a small body of men on a small island. A few miles across the water lay not just a country or even a continent but a whole religion, bitterly opposed to Christendom. On Rhodes there now flourished possibly the most notable and formidable champions of Christendom that Islam had ever faced. Religion, spurred on by the needs of trade, makes for war, and Rhodes stood as a threat to the free passage of Turkish vessels. There was bound to be conflict.

So the Knights set about defending Rhodes. Here and there in the walls you will find the Hellenistic and Byzantine stones and sculptured marbles which they put to good use, but for the most part the walls and bastions are of limestone, a stone which hardens on exposure to air but, if the saline content is already high, does not stand up very well to sea air. This is why many of these lovely honey-coloured blocks of stone are today pitted and eaten away.

The two and a half miles of fortifications as they now appear are the result of centuries of constant building and reshaping. The final and greatest phase came after the Turkish siege of 1480 and is almost entirely the work of Pierre d'Aubusson (a great number of the escutcheons in the walls bear testimony to his energy and foresight). He greatly increased the thickness of the curtain walls and the width of the moats (at some points the moat is over 70 feet wide and the curtain wall nearly 40 feet thick), he reduced the number of gates into the city and strengthened those that remained, he altered the defensive towers. He compounded a most elaborate military fortification of curtain walls, the parapets surmounting these, the escarpment, the inner towers, the fosse or moat, a contrescarp and glacis. Your best view of this complex fortress is obtained by a walk along the ramparts.

The walls were manned by the eight Tongues of the Order: each Tongue was responsible for a certain section of the wall (the Bulwark of France, the Bulwark of England, etc.). The gates often bear the names of their builders and you can, in part, trace the history of the walls by studying the escutcheons placed upon them and over the gates.

The gate through which you are most likely to enter the old town is the modern *Liberty Gate* built in 1924 and at that time simply called the New Gate. As soon as Rhodes was reunited with Greece in 1947 it was given its present name. (With such a history of oppression it is understandable that the Greeks have a tremendous sense of the value of freedom, so the word *eleftheria* – liberty – is applied in almost every possible context. Wherever you find it – as a Christian name, the name of a street or square – it stands as a reminder of some great breaking of shackles: the War of Independence in 1821, freedom from Italian rule and so on.

To the left of Liberty Gate, before you cross the moat into the old town, is the *Gate of St Paul*. On this site was once the Tower of Trebuc. It was renamed in the last quarter of the fifteenth century when Pierre d'Aubusson reconstructed it and made it into a gate. At the far end of the mole on which St Paul's Gate stands was the distinctive *Tower of Naillac*, turreted at each corner, with an inner turret rising in the centre. This tower was destroyed in the nineteenth century but you can get an excellent idea of what it looked like from prints of that period and earlier.

The Gate of St Paul leads directly through to the Commercial Harbour. Here the waterfront is a wide roadway and the walls of the old town dominate the entire harbour. It is a long stretch of massive, formidable wall, pierced by three main gates – the *Arsenal Gate*, *Marine Gate* and *St Catherine Gate*.

The *Arsenal Gate* originally gave on to a dry dock used by the Knights. Today, an archway connects the two towers of the gateway and together they form a vehicle and foot entrance to the old town.

The *Marine Gate* is halfway round the Commercial Harbour and is very handsome indeed. (In the past the Marine Gate has often been called the St Catherine Gate and some real confusion exists. Even Torr fell into the trap. But modern authorities are firm that the Marine Gate is the one in the middle of the wall facing the Commercial Harbour and that St Catherine Gate is the one opposite the modern quay.) Two large machicolated round towers rise on either side of it. Before you pass through into the old town, look up and you will see a bas-relief in white marble under a carved canopy. The relief illustrates a Virgin Mary between St Peter and St Paul and below them are the arms of the Order and of Pierre d'Aubusson with the arms of France between them. The towers and gate were badly damaged during the last war; the skill of the archaeologists has brought about some discreet restoration.

Farther along and almost opposite the modern quay where the larger inter-island and ocean-going vessels dock is the *St Catherine Gate*. This was once known as the Gate of the Mills because the contemporary quay is on the site of one which, during the fifteenth and sixteenth centuries, had a long rank of thirteen mills striding down its length. (Part of the original mole runs along the southern side of the existing quay.)

The next sector of the wall skirts the Gulf of Arcadia. First you come to the modern *Gate of Italy* (1924) and then to the Tower of Italy.

The *Koskinou Gate* is also known as the *St John Gate*. You approach it by an arched footbridge over the moat. A pointed frame above the gate encloses a badly damaged bas-relief of St John. Below are the arms of Pierre d'Aubusson as they appeared prior to his elevation to cardinal.

The Italians entered the city through this gate in 1912 and an empty frame to the left of the gate once contained an inscription commemorating the event.

The *St Mary Tower* stands guard over this entrance to the city. The gate was the weakest link in the medieval fortifications and was the one through which Sultan Suleiman was able to force his way in 1522. There is a plaque to Victor Emmanuel over the gateway, replacing the escutcheon of Pierre d'Aubusson. The section of wall between the *Koskinou Gate* and the *St Athanasios Gate* was the Bulwark of England.

There next follows a long stretch of wall, the first part belonging to the Tongue of Spain, the second to the Tongue of Auvergne.

The *Gate of St George* (now blocked) is the combined gate and tower which separates this section of wall from the Bulwark of Germany. There is a relief of St George above the entrance, together with the arms of Grand Master Fluvian on the left and Pope Martin V on the right. The arms of the Order are enclosed by these two.

The *Amboise Gate*, the most impressive of the gates, was built in 1512 by Aimerie d'Amboise. It is approached by a triple-arched bridge across the moat and has two squat round towers on either side of it. Over the gate is the relief of an angel bearing the arms of the Order and of Aimerie d'Amboise. When you enter this gate you pass under the immense thickness of the wall and emerge on to a bridge over the second, inner moat. From here you enter the wide walk of plane trees below the walls of the Palace of the Grand Masters and this brings you to the *St Anthony Gate*. This was the grand entrance to the palace for visitors approaching from the countryside.

NEW TOWN

All map references are to the New Town map (pp. 132–33).

When the Turks held Rhodes they would not permit the Greeks working in the old town to stay within the walls at night, so a settlement grew up outside and was called Nea Chori or New Town. It retains this name today. The fabric of the modern New Town is primarily Italian; many villas, hospitals, public buildings – including the Town Hall, Government House and the New Market – were built between 1912 and the last war.

The town spreads north, west and south of the walled city. The segment in the north contains most of the hotels, shops and restaurants, the southern part has the densest suburban population. To the west are Monte Smith and the ancient stadium, theatre and temple to Apollo. These last are the only significant Classical and Hellenistic ruins to be found in the environs of the city but below the hotels and shops of central Rhodes lie innumerable silent sites. Every so often one of these comes to light as yet another foundation is sunk. As all work has to be suspended until the archaeological authorities have examined the new discovery, property development is a hazardous business; you never know whether the site for your new hotel might not turn out to reveal some new treasure.

The social centre of the new town is among the cafés and restaurants within the *New Market* (Map **14**). This polygonal arcaded building faces *Mandraki Harbour* and has an open market in the centre. The waterfront runs from the New Market right along the stretch that includes the *Post Office* (Map **9**), the *Town Hall* (Map **7**) and *Government House* (Map **4**), the 'Elli' Club and beach (Map **2**). Here it bends and continues past the *Mosque of Murad Reis* (Map **3**).

Mosque of Murad Reis
Map 3.

The shimmering white minaret of the Mosque of Murad Reis is certainly the most elegant on the island. You approach the mosque through a door in a wall on the left just past the 'Elli' Club and find yourself in a shady yard paved with black and white *chochláki* patterns. The mosque is to the left, the tomb of Murad Reis lies within a small circular building on your right. Murad Reis was one of Suleiman's admirals and was killed during the final assault on Rhodes in 1521–22. Surrounding this pretty and romantic courtyard – try visiting it by moonlight – is the cemetery, built in 1523. It is planted with a multitude of fluttering eucalyptus trees and crowded with Turkish headstones. (A man's grave is crowned with a turban, or a kind of 'pineapple'; a woman's is generally pointed and fairly plain.) A number of larger tombs contain the dust of viziers and even a Shah of Persia sleeps here.

Aquarium
Map 1.

Open 09.00–19.00.
Entrance Drs 10.

Follow the shore road north from the Mosque of Murad Reis and you come to the Aquarium. This was built by the Italians and also houses the Hydrobiological Institute. The aquarium is unique in Greece and down among the vast subterranean tanks you can gaze eye-to-eye at swordfish, giant rays and octopods.

HARBOURS

Today, the city has three working harbours, all on the east coast. The most northerly is the little *Mandraki*, or 'sheepfold', where *caiques* and yachts tie up. Next is the *Commercial Harbour*, the haven for inter-island and large ocean-going vessels. The third is *Acandia*, less important than the other two.

On either side of Mandraki Harbour are two pillars bearing a stag and a doe, the traditional deer of Rhodes. These are relatively modern (the she-wolf of Rome stood on one of the pillars during the Italian regime).

The bulky fort that commands the entrance to Mandraki is *St*

METRES

0 200 400 600

MANDRAKI

windmills

N

Kassou
Kos
Vass.
Kos
Kazouli
Konstantinou
Sava
Koundouriotou
Square
Eleftherias
Amerikis
Iossou
25 Martiou
Fanouraki
Vass. Marias
Eleftherdos
Makriotis
Plastira
Bissa
Gallias
28 Oktovriou
Alexandrou Diakou
Akti Miqouli
Akti Kanari
Taxiarchou Markou
Helvetias
Arhbishop
Kelassie
Aklani

1 2 3 4 5 6 7 8 9 10 11 12 13 14 15 16 17

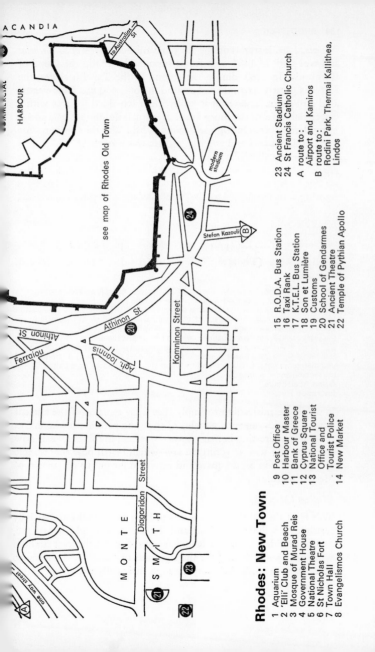

Rhodes: New Town

1 Aquarium
2 'Elli' Club and Beach
3 Mosque of Murad Reis
4 Government House
5 National Theatre
6 St Nicholas Fort
7 Town Hall
8 Evangelismos Church

9 Post Office
10 Harbour Master
11 Bank of Greece
12 Cyprus Square
13 National Tourist Office and Tourist Police
14 New Market

15 R.O.D.A. Bus Station
16 Taxi Rank
17 K.T.E.L. Bus Station
18 Son et Lumière
19 Customs
20 School of Gendarmes
21 Ancient Theatre
22 Temple of Pythian Apollo

23 Ancient Stadium
24 St Francis Catholic Church

A route to:
Airport and Kamiros

B route to:
Rodini Park, Thermai Kallithea, Lindos

Nicholas Fort. It stands on the site of a vanished *Chapel of St Nicholas* and was built in 1464 with funds supplied by Philip the Good of Burgundy. In 1480, during the second of the Turkish sieges, the fort was greatly strengthened around the base and was later elaborated still more. The result is an irregular ten-sided fortress with a tower rising from the inner keep. The small lighthouse was added in modern times. During the Second World War the fort sprouted gun emplacements and you can still see traces of these. Inside, it is rather forlorn, dilapidated and smelly. There is a sad little Orthodox chapel within the walls, all American cloth and plastic flowers. But no one today seems to care very much for the fort which has been fighting wars from 1464 to 1947 and hasn't really been dusted since.

ENVIRONS

All map references are to the New Town map (pp. 132–33).

Ancient City (Theatre, Temple of Apollo, Stadium, Monte Smith)

Route 2·5 km. approximately from Mandraki Harbour. An easy and pleasant walk at the end of the day; take a taxi when the sun is high.
  To reach the site you can take either of two routes. The first begins in Archbishop Makarios Street and continues past the Thermai Hotel, where you turn right up Venizelou Street and climb steadily until you come out on to the heights overlooking the west coast. From here you look down on the temple, theatre, etc. The other route also starts in Archbishop Makarios Street but passes Venizelou Street, taking a right fork into Agh. Ioannis Street (just before the School of Gendarmes). From this road you then turn right into Diagoridon Street and approach the area from below. This is the recommended approach.
Open At all hours.
Entrance Free.

It would be misleading to imply that what remains of the ancient city of Rhodes can rival remains of the same period elsewhere. But the site is interesting in many ways – not least in that it reveals how large the city was, covering an area which began near the Temple of Aphrodite in Simi Square and extended far out to the crown of Monte Smith.

Stadium (Map 23)

This is of the third century B.C. and is in fair condition, partially restored. It is 200 metres long and 35 metres wide and you may see, as I once did, a couple of Rhodian boys alone in the vast stadium who, with some feeling for the rightness of things, had chosen to come here to work their way through their daily exercises.

Theatre (*Map* 21)

This is adjacent to and a little above the stadium. Only the orchestra and three seats in the front row are original; the rest has been rebuilt in a blinding white marble which time will mellow, one hopes.

Temple of Pythian Apollo (*Map* 22)

Above the theatre is a wide platform, a broad flight of steps and a massive retaining wall of rusticated stone. The steps lead to another terrace and the area of the temple. This temple – like the one at Sounion on the mainland near Athens – was designed to be a landmark for ships at sea and even though only a few of the Doric pillars have been re-erected you can still discern Apollo's house as you approach the island from the sea. From the temple you get a fine view of the two cities of Rhodes. The area immediately around the temple has little to show.

Monte Smith

If possible you should make this expedition to the ancient city in the latter part of the day, for it is from the summit of the hill above the temple that you can experience a memorable moment that is made even finer when the sun is setting. Suddenly, you crest the hill and look down on the village of Kritika far below. The western sea glitters and Simi and part of Asia Minor lie in the distance. Stand here at sunset and watch the reluctant sun dragged slowly down beyond the horizon. The height on which you stand is Mt Aghios Stephanos, also called Monte Smith after the British Admiral Smith who, during Napoleon's war with the Turks, set up an observatory in 1802. From here he kept watch on the French fleet and guarded the Sea of Marmara.

If you now walk to the right along the metalled road you will find, scattered around a house and a palm tree, some tumbled and massive drums of the pillars of a temple of Athene Polias. Near here there was also an ancient nymphaeum.

Rodini Park and Tomb of the Ptolemies

Route Leave Rhodes by Route Exit B following Route 1 (p. 138). The park is approximately 3 km. from Rhodes.
Bus The Lindos bus passes the park gate and there are frequent town buses to and from the park.

Rodini Park is a pretty wooded area on either side of a ravine, with winding paths, streams and pools, water lilies and grottoes. There are some remains of a Roman aqueduct and a restaurant during the season.

From Rodini you can walk to the near-by rock tomb called, probably inaccurately, the Tomb of the Ptolemies. This is of the Hellenistic period and has a façade of blank pillars hewn from the rock. Restored 1924.

Koskinou

Route Leave Rhodes by Route Exit B following Route 1 (p. 138). Beyond Asgourou at 7 km. take left turn (sign-posted) to Koskinou. A further 2 km. along this road brings you to the village.
Bus Local buses : K.T.E.L. line.

If the local Rhodian authority were to offer prizes for the village with the most floral courtyards or the neatest painted gates and houses Koskinou (pop. 1,200) would walk away with the honours. Vines and rampant shrubs swarm up and over the courtyards, the scent of flowers drifts through wrought-iron gateways that are painted pink, blue, peacock and scarlet and are tricked out with bright silver. Maybe it is all a bit suburban and smug but the people who live there are delighted if you admire their neatness and will respond immediately with an offer of coffee or, if you are lucky, an invitation to enter their houses. The interiors are charming. In one I visited, Lindian plates and bowls looked down from the walls, wondrous period paintings of King Constantine I and his queen Sophia (looking rather like Queen Alexandra) faced one another from opposite corners, there was a handsome platform bed laid with carpets and rugs, an old piano and a *chochláki* floor. Another had a particularly pleasing *chochláki* courtyard and, inside, a vast drawn-thread cotton-and-lace curtain hanging from the high ceiling over the bed, so fine it looked like old lawn. There was a sofa, too, spread with an exquisitely laundered cotton cover.

Thermai Kallithea

Route From Rhodes via Route 1 along Route Exit B follow Stefan Kazouli Street till you come to a fork which is sign-posted left to Thermai Kallithea, right to Lindos.
Bus Occasional buses during midsummer go direct to the Spa. Alternatively, inquire about a bus to Koskinou which should take you within walking distance.

Kallithea was built by the Italians in the late 'twenties as a watering-place for the treatment of rheumatism, arthritis, diabetic and kidney diseases. It is a curious pleasure-ground of green domes, pink and white buildings, arcaded walks and grottoes. It lies in an amphitheatre around a small bay; you can swim from the shore where the water is shallow (but rather hindered by flat rocks) or dive off the specially constructed quay into extremely pleasant deep water.

In my experience, the place is generally near to deserted. The spa no longer operates, though there is a restaurant in the season. Some coach tours and sea trips call in here and Rhodians come along at weekends. It is faded and somewhat seedy, yet it has a perverse charm. I once spent a hot, idyllic afternoon alone there, prone on a stone bench in one of the circular courtyards open to the sky. The sun dappled the pink wash of the walls, leaves fell gently from the tree that shaded me on to the cool, pebbled floor, there were bees at work in the dazed afternoon silence.

It costs nothing to go in, and presumably will stay that way until or unless the spa becomes a working proposition again.

ROUTES ON RHODES

Rhodes is the only town on the island and all major roads radiate from it. Similarly, all tours and excursions start from the town, unless otherwise stated, and return to it. In the following pages two main routes are suggested: Route 1 travels the length of the island down the east coast to Kattavia and Messanagros, and Route 2 follows the west coast road ending at Kattavia in the south. There are also three Link Routes (A, B and C). These are roads linking the two coast roads at various points down the island. Between them, the routes take in all the major sites and most of the secondary ones.

Please note that during 1974/75 major roads on the island are being remade and in some parts rerouted. In certain instances the newly made roads will by-pass villages or features of interest that appear along the following routes. The reader should also know that one or two entirely new roads will probably make their appearance by the end of this period.

However, because the final course of this new road system is not yet complete and possible access roads from the villages not even decided, the Routes recommended in this book and the distances between one place and another follow the original roads unless otherwise indicated. Sections of the new system will, of course, come into use when they are ready.

Route 1: Rhodes to Kattavia and Messanagros (East Coast)

The first 55 km. of this route (as far as Lindos) cover some of the most attractive coastal scenery of Rhodes. Beyond here, the countryside becomes sparer, but at the end of the route there is the exhilarating drive up to Messanagros, affording superb views of the Aegean on either coast.

Route Leave Rhodes by Archbishop Makarios Street. This becomes Athinon Street and runs round the west side of the walled town. Opposite St Francis' Catholic Church, the road bears right and becomes Stefan Kazouli Street (Route Exit B on Rhodes New Town map). From here you travel south along the coast road. This goes successively to Rodini Park, Asgourou, Afantou, Kolimbia, Archangelos, Malona, Massari (Lindos), Pilona, Lardos (Moni Ipseni), Gennadi, Lachania, Kattavia, Messanagros.

Bus K.T.E.L. line (near 'Son et Lumière' at end of the New Market, *Map* **17**). Apply to the bus offices for details about frequency of local services to Lindos and back and Kattavia and back. Tour buses also leave from concourse at *Map* **17**, departing three to four times daily in the season and returning the same day.

Taxi See p. 39.

Accommodation There are no listed hotels on this route. At Lindos there are rooms to let (see p. 101).

[3 km.] **Rodini Park.** (See p. 135 for details.)

[6·5 km.] Off the road and on the right is the minaret of the *mosque* of the village of **Asgourou** (pop. 285). This prettily situated mosque was originally the Byzantine Church of St John; it is now in poor condition. The village was Turkish and still has inhabitants of Turkish stock. Once the village was well secreted from the sight of passers-by or marauders and corsairs; today the minaret betrays its presence.

[7 km.] Left turn to **Koskinou**, a village sitting high on a hill in the near distance. (See Environs, p. 136, for details.) Near this turning is the settlement of huts, elaborate caravans and technical equipment of the 'Voice of America' radio stations.

[15 km.] Left turn to *Faliraki beach* (see p. 103 for details).

[18·5 km.] The new 18-hole golf course of Afantou lies to the left. (See p. 57 for further information.)

[20 km.] **Afantou** (pop. 2,555). This has the appearance of being

Rhodes
Diagram of Routes (1 and 2)
and Link Routes
(A, B and C)

one of the less prosperous villages of Rhodes: there is a somewhat Arab scruffiness of scratching hens and dishevelled streets that is not particularly characteristic of the island. Nevertheless, appearances can be misleading, for the village exports apricots and manufactures carpets; there is a handicraft industry and a fair amount of oil is produced.

Beyond Afantou there begins a stretch of fertile and well-ordered land.

[26 km.] Right turn to *Efta Pighes* (see Link Route A for further information about this beauty spot).

[27 km.] **Kolimbia** (pop. 222). This is an old and very pleasant little settlement. Hardly a village (it has no shops as such), the first feature you notice is the big square, made up of blocks of low dwellings for the aged and the refugee. The square has plenty of trees, there is a church and, on the right of the road, if you are passing at a time when the water is released, you will see a man-made waterfall with a splendidly steep and rushing torrent. This water comes tumbling down from Efta Pighes and is channelled into conduits which irrigate the whole of this rich and well-husbanded area.

Many of the farmers of Kolimbia live a few kilometres farther on, at Archangelos. The businesslike and prosperous air of the fields and orchards around Kolimbia is an inheritance from the time when Italian peasants settled here. New methods of fruit farming were introduced and the Rhodians were put on the right road to successful fruit husbandry. The land was divided up after the departure of the Italians, but the island farmers now in possession seem to have carried on the Italian techniques with success.

At the far end of the open square, a broad motorable path runs for about 3 km. through an avenue of eucalyptus trees straight down to the sea. (There is no bus: allow a good 45–50 minutes for the walk, depending on your pace and how often you halt for chats with passing children and housewives or stay to listen to the cool clatter of the water running down the conduits.) A short way down on the right you will see a modern bungalow with three white pillars. In a peach grove alongside this house there lies, hidden among grasses and with its walls no more than two or three feet high, the remains of a sixth-century A.D. *basilica* and some *mosaic flooring*. Though the ruin is so vestigial it presents a beautifully clear ground-plan – even though you have to peer at it through a wire fence. If you want to get a closer look, ask for permission from the Archaeological Service in Rhodes.

The avenue ends within a short distance of the sea and soon there is a fork. The path to the right takes you to a fine sandy beach below a rise. The left fork leads to a small cove with a jetty, a restaurant and a long sand-and-pebble beach (note more pylons of the 'Voice of America' station in the distance). To my mind, the best swimming here is from the jetty, as you can go straight into the very deep, clear water. Though the day-cruise boats from Rhodes often call at these beaches they are sufficiently far from the main road to be left in reasonable peace as a rule.

Returning to the main road, continue south.

[27 km.] A road to the left climbs to *Moni Tsambika*, the white monastery perched on top of the high, sharp peak of Mt Tsambika. One of the curious and apparently active religious observances of the island is centred on this Byzantine monastery. It seems that if a Rhodian woman fails to conceive she can make a pilgrimage to the monastery and there pray to become fruitful. This she must do on September 8th, when there is an annual festival. Her approach must be on foot (a long, hot haul up it is, too), and she must eat a small piece of the wick of one of the lamps in the chapel of the Virgin.

Should her prayers and pilgrimage prove successful, she names the child Tsambika if a girl, Tsambikos if a boy. Listen to Rhodian mothers calling to their children – and draw what deductions you like from the fact there are a startling number of children with these names.

[28·5 km.] Left turn to *Tsambikos beach* (5 km.). Sandy, relatively unfrequented.

[33 km.] **Archangelos** (pop. 3,000). They say nightingales sing at Archangelos and short of seeing a partridge in a pear tree it would be pleasant to hear those famous notes coming from among the glossy green leaves and bright fruit of the orange groves. Lemons and limes, mandarines and grapes also flourish in the fertile land of the valley; dark spears of cypresses surround the little white church, and in the scattered olive groves there grow also plane trees and fruiting walnut. The white cubes of the village houses lie among all this luxuriousness and if you can raise your eyes from the ground-level attractions there is a castle to be seen high above the village to your left, built by Grand Master Orsini in 1467.

Archangelos is famous for its boots. You will probably first notice these in Rhodes when the peasant women come to market. They stomp along looking very like Russian *babushkas* with their scarfed heads, plump shapes, full skirts and high, chunky boots. The boots seem to be made in two pieces, for the top half overlaps the instep and ankle and there is, apparently, a separate boot or shoe beneath. In fact, the boots are all one piece but the true leg length comes to well above the knee and is then pulled down in a fold over the ankle as far as the base of the heel. They are made of tough, hard-working hide or very soft goatskin. If you have time, you can arrange for an Archangelos shoemaker to run you up a pair; alternatively, there is at least one shoemaker in the old town of Rhodes (see p. 52 for address) who is expert at making them. They are wonderfully comfortable and look very dashing.

[39 km.] **Malona** (pop. 1,200). A left turn as you enter Malona and a walk of 4 km. (no bus) will take you to the *Castle of Feraclos* high above the village of **Charaki**. Feraclos saw both the first and the last of the Knights, for it was here that they landed on their arrival in the early fourteenth century and the *kastello* was one of the last strongholds to fall to the Turks, holding out well into 1523. In its day the castle housed prisoners-of-war and also Knights who infringed the rules of the Order. There is little to see now, but you can swim in the attractive bay and admire the view of Lindos far in the distance.

[42 km.] **Massari.**

[50 km.] **Kalathos.**

[52 km.] Fork left for Lindos.

Lindos

There are those, and I among them, who believe Delphi to be the most moving and beautiful site in Greece. Then one comes to Lindos and begins to wonder ...

Accommodation Rooms to let.

Restaurants There are two or three excellent beach restaurants on the Grand Harbour. On and near the bus square are the Lindos and Kleobule *tavérnas* and one or two small *kafeneíons*. W.C. on bus square.

Beaches The beautiful beach of the Grand Harbour is approximately ½ km. from the bus square. A smaller beach is at St Paul's Bay, about 1 km. from the square.

Lindos (pop. 650) still seems clad in the clouds of glory that attended the birth of civilization, radiant with discovery and clarity and hope. Unlike Delphi, where all is green and fertile, Lindos is bony and bare. Everything here is revealed and exposed to God and Athene Lindia. Though later civilizations and the works of the Knights of St John have set so massive a mark upon this place, there shines about these grand medieval walls the serene and golden genius of the gods and their creators.

Lindos village is barely a quarter of the size of the ancient city o the fourth and fifth centuries B.C. Nevertheless, it contrives to wind and interwind in complicated fashion and it is easy to lose one's bearings for a while. Fortunately there is a strongly marked spine which runs through the village from the bus square (the point of arrival) to the steps which ascend to the acropolis. This main street is clearly marked along its length with a series of sign-posts 'To the Acropolis'. The distance from the bus square to the point where the steps begin is approximately 300 yards.

HISTORY OF LINDOS

Lindos rapidly became and stayed the most important of the three great cities of antiquity. It is on the more sheltered east coast, it has a reasonable natural harbour and a magnificent headland crying out for a great temple.

The city begins to appear in history about the time of the Dorians (though there is evidence of Minoan settlement prior to this period).

About 700 B.C. Lindos became one of the parties to the Dorian Hexapolis, the others being her sister cities of Ialysos and Kamiros, together with Kos, Knidos and Halikarnassos.

The spareness of the land round Lindos was as grudging then as it is today. Livy points out that while the men of Ialysos and Kamiros – with their relatively more fertile and fruitful land – had no urgent need to adventure abroad, the unproductive land around Lindos forced the Lindians to turn to the sea and become traders and fishermen. Their ambitions reached far beyond mere coastal venturing and the Lindian sailors explored and colonized as far away as Italy, France and Spain.

Their seamanship was second to none: Torr quotes a tale of a Lindian captain whose ship was in danger of foundering in a storm. 'Well, Poseidon, you must own I'm sending her down in good trim.' Simultaneously, the land-based Lindians developed a shipbuilding industry which throve throughout the ancient world (it was said that at one point over five hundred vessels were being built or were in harbour at Lindos). This industry endured till very recent times and only dwindled and died at the outset of the nineteenth century.

As you look down on this little village and the bay and up at the acropolis, bear in mind that once this was a city famed for its commerce, its riches, its temples, its seamen. Picture the Grand Harbour in your mind's eye with the 'nine ships of lordly Rhodians' bound for Troy with Tlepolemos in the bow of one of them, bronze glittering, helmet plumes streaming. Look left across the bay and pick out with your eye the big circular stone building supposed to shelter the bones of Kleoboulus – and Kleoboulus was no less than one of the Seven Wise Men of the ancient world, along with Solon of Athens ('Call no man happy until he is dead') and others. Kleoboulus was tyrant of Lindos for close on forty years of the sixth century B.C., he built the first temple in stone to Athene Lindia and he, too, left a saying which you certainly know: 'Nothing in excess.' That was Kleoboulus, a composed and balanced man.

So flourishing and busy a city was bound to have a temple of some splendour; Lindos was fortunate in having such a headland to build it on, exposed and beautiful and proclaiming the calm and majesty and omnipotence of Athene Lindia for miles around.

Though Rhodes was founded in 408 B.C., Lindos remained a power for long after and though the propylaea was built very soon after the foundation, the great portico of the temple and the ranks of staircases which we see today were not added till some two hundred years later. Clearly, Lindos had stamina and did not easily relinquish her power to the new city.

Once into the Christian era, the inevitable happened: St Paul visited Lindos. He landed, it is said, at the little bay below the southern slopes of the acropolis. Then Byzantium came and left its mark: fortress walls around the acropolis, a church within the walls and, in the town, more churches. Some of the smaller Lindian churches, among them Agh. Georgios and Agh. Demetrios, are being studied now by the archaeologists of the island and are probably considerably older than the better-known Church of the Panaghia.

With the coming of the Knights, there was a new-look acropolis: massive medieval walls absorbed the Byzantine ones and the ancient propylaea and temple were virtually hidden behind the curtain of defensive stone. The Turks had their way with Lindos, too, though their coming and passing are less noticeable (but note the pretty Turkish carvings and stonework around the village spring in the square). Under Italian rule Lindos presumably went on much as always, for the Italians did little domestic building here and concentrated on excavations and the restoration and re-erection of some of the pillars of the portico and temple.

PRINCIPAL SIGHTS

Acropolis

Open Summer 07.00–sunset.
              Sundays and holidays 10.00–13.00.
                                           15.00–19.00.
          Winter 09.00–sunset.
              Sundays and holidays 10.00–13.00.
                                           14.30–17.00.
Entrance Drs 5.

The way to the acropolis leads from the bus square, past the *Church of the Panaghia*, and up the narrow streets (sign-posts 'To the Acropolis' all the way). You can either walk or take a donkey (plenty of donkey-men near the square). If you walk you may well be tempted to make side-sallies into churches or medieval houses. Once you are high enough to be clear of the village the path leads up the flank of the headland and there is a fine prospect of the bay to your left.

Your first encounter with the past comes when you step on to a stone-paved walled platform fringed with cypresses. Here are three large stone cisterns of Byzantine origin (*Map* 2), perhaps used for water or grain. As you turn right to start the steep ascent of the final flight of steps, you find in front of you an enormous carved relief of a *Hellenistic trireme* (*Map* 3), its graceful prow cut in deep sweeping arcs through the rock.

Jutting from the ship is a plinth designed to carry a statue. An

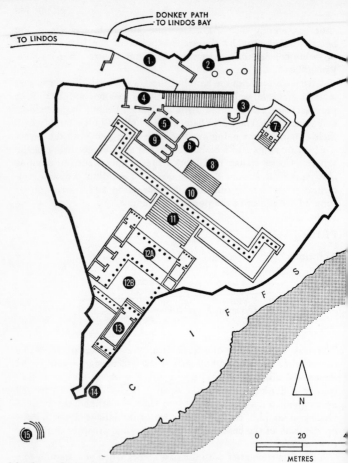

Lindos: Acropolis and Temple

1 Steps from village
2 Cisterns
3 Hellenistic ship carving and exedra
4 & 5 Castle of the Knights
6 Exedra
7 Site of Temple, possibly Roman
8 Stairway
9 Byzantine church of Agh. Ioannis
10 Doric portico
11 Broad stairway
12a Propylaea
12b Propylaea and forecourt of Temple
13 Temple of Athene Lindia
14 View of St Paul's Bay
15 Theatre

inscription tells that this was a gift from seamen to a seaman: from Lindos to Aghesandros of Mikionos. The statue was a likeness of Aghesandros himself and was the work of Pythocretos Timocharis of Rhodes. If you arrive at the right time of day when the shadows are driving deep into the sculptured lines of the ship it looks very beautiful; when the day is dull or the sun full upon it it is surprisingly easy to miss seeing it at all.

At all events, the ship makes a good excuse for a welcome pause, for the haul up the steps to the entrance of the fortress is the steepest part of the walk. At this point you are in the shadow of the walls built by the Knights (*Map* 4 and 5). The walls bear escutcheons of the Grand Masters, also some signs of later Turkish work. What makes these walls so attractive in spite of their severity and bulk is their inward slope, the harmony of the stonework and its colour, and the pleasing variants on the swallow-tail battlements which crown the whole.

You enter the fortress through a medieval doorway into a dark, tunnel-like hall, cluttered with Classical and Hellenistic pieces for which there is no better home. Until recently, a pen-and-ink notice warned (in English): 'DON'T APPROACH THE EDGE OF THE ACROPOLIS OVER THE SEA – DANGER – DEATH' (this last in red ink). You will see the wisdom of this very shortly. Immediately on the left is a spiral staircase leading to rooms which the knights on duty occupied.

Once you have groped in through this hall, you emerge into a grass yard with raw rock heaving up in the middle of it. Turn left through a medieval chamber with a barrel roof, and you come out into the lowest of the four terraces which, one above the other, mount to the temple proper. On this level the outer walls are on your left, some low, open storehouses (many containing cisterns) on your right, a high curved *exedra* (*Map* 6) with inscriptions almost facing you, and a considerable number of plinths, fallen and calcined capitals scattered about. There are also traces of a Doric and Corinthian temple at this level, probably Roman, and popularly called the *Temple of Psithyros*, the Whispering Temple (*Map* 7).

A short stairway takes you up to the ruined *Byzantine Church of Agh. Ioannis* (*Map* 9), built in the thirteenth century. This level is dominated by the *Doric portico* (*Map* 10) or arcade of the *Temple of Athene Lindia* (*Map* 13). This portico, built about 208 B.C., stretches some 90 metres on either side as you face it. Its shape is of an E without the middle stroke. The left-hand stroke of the E ends in a graceful assembly of pillars which look their best when you view them from the temple itself. On the right are more pillars and, ranked in front of a broad staircase, a further thirteen pillars, some with architraves and metopes replaced. Most of the re-erection is the work of Italian archaeologists.

The view up the flight of steps (*Map* 11), through the columns, is profoundly exciting. The steps are so pitched that you cannot see what is above, but you sense that some great mystery will be revealed and I always have a sneaking desire to find Callas appear at their head: imperious Athene, bearing shield and spear and commanding obedience with eye and voice. It is, you gather, an extremely theatrical composition.

What in fact is revealed when you have mounted the steps is the *Temple of Athene Lindia*. Standing in the wide *propylaea* (*Map* 12a) in front of the temple, you are somewhat surprised to find the house of Athene so small – only about 70 feet long and 28 feet wide. Yet so perfectly is it placed that it is an entirely satisfying climax. It forms the apex of the triangle upon which the whole acropolis is set. The base of this triangle is along the northern side, its two sides to your left and right as you mount towards the temple. The temple itself is at the point where these two sides meet. Beyond the medieval walls which enclose the area, the drop to the sea is nearly 400 feet, dramatic and deadly. Tragedies have happened here and the warning mentioned earlier is not a frivolous one. Immediately below the walls of the apex of the triangle is the little *St Paul's Bay*.

It is probable that there was some kind of religious centre here, if only a sacred grove, as early as 1700 B.C. Legend reports that the earliest temple was erected by Danaos who, after quarrelling with his brothers, departed from Egypt with his fifty daughters and found shelter at Lindos. Danaos felt so grateful to Athene for her help in conjuring the Lindians to accept him (and well he might, an uninvited guest arriving with fifty daughters) that he built a temple and presented the goddess with a wooden statue of herself.

It is possible that the temple of the Danaos legend is the one known to have existed on the site by about the tenth century B.C., a temple known to have contained a statue to Athene.

By the middle of the sixth century B.C. an elaborate stone-built temple was erected by the then tyrant, Kleoboulus, but this building was later destroyed and the statue with it. In 348 B.C. the Lindians themselves built a temple and put into it a new statue of Athene, fashioned of wood, gold, marble and ivory and wearing a wreath instead of a helmet.

This house of the goddess Athene became one of the most important religious centres in Greece and the Mediterranean. It is of Doric style and has four columns on each of its narrow sides (seven of these columns have been restored and re-erected). The temple was discovered in 1902 by the Danish archaeologist K. F. Kinch. He estimated that this version of the temple was built not earlier than the fourth century B.C.

A temple of such stature and fame was bound to attract many offerings (sacrifices, by the way, were bloodless here) and also the work of artists and writers. The artists – Apelles, Passaros, Protogenis – were some of them Rhodian, some of them from far beyond the island limits. One of the most treasured finds was the *Seventh Ode of Pindar* written in gold on a marble column. Other finds during the Danish excavation provided the archaeologists with a great part of their knowledge of the temple history. Look about you even now on the acropolis and you will find a rewarding number of inscriptions. On the exedra near the open vaulted storerooms on the lowest level is one naming Athene Lindia and bearing a reference to Halikarnassos.

The temple came to an end at the hands of the Emperor Theodosios of Byzantium, who removed to Constantinople many of its treasures, including the statue of the goddess. All these pieces were apparently destroyed in A.D. 404 but the statue was found unharmed in the following century. What Theodosios began, time and pillaging completed: many of the stones and marble decorations of the temple were built into other and later buildings.

Under the Knights, the temple and acropolis became a fortress. After the Knights departed from Rhodes the Turks took over and in the middle of the nineteenth century they built houses on the acropolis, lodged a garrison there, and generally acted in a highhanded fashion when any scholars or travellers arrived hoping to see the great site. Today, no one will act high-handedly, but if you chance to arrive just at one o'clock and the custodian decides he is going to stick to the letter of the law, you may earn a somewhat curt lift of the chin – that Greek way of saying 'no' which is more dismissive than any other I know. Otherwise, you can spend as long as you like seated on these steps and stones, high above the Aegean,

sunning yourself against a wall, while the sun beats down upon the
bare stones and goes braying back into the sky with a clamour like
armour. You are alone with Athene, with chivalry, and with the
birds that swoop and settle and are the only possessors now of this
site which was peopled probably for some 3,500 years.

After leaving the citadel and descending the outer stairway you
can either bear right down a donkey path which ultimately takes
you to the south shore of *Lindos Bay* (via the little *Church of Agh.
Georgios* and one or two Lindian fifteenth-century houses), or you
can return the way you came into the village square. On the way
down the steps, stop at the point where there is a small stall selling
pottery and look west across the village to *Mount Krana*. Here,
carved into the hillside, are rock-cut tombs of 200 B.C. The Doric
columns of the façade are still visible. From the same point, if you
look across the Grand Harbour to the north, you can see the pro-
montory on which is the large, circular tomb known as the *Tomb of
Kleoboulus* (though there is little evidence that it is). The tomb is
pre-Hellenic, with a passage leading to the burial chamber.

From the square, the beach is about $\frac{1}{2}$ km. down the road; there
is a restaurant halfway down and others on the beach.

Theatre
Map 15.

The theatre lies on the south-west slope of the Acropolis hill;
indeed, the apex of the triangle where the temple stands is almost
directly above it, though the curve of the hill makes it difficult to
see from here. The way to the theatre from the bus square takes you
a few yards past the *Church of the Panaghia* till you come to a corner
shop selling woven goods. Turn right into a narrow lane, which
takes you to the theatre: only a few minutes' walk. The amphitheatre is in fair condition: five of the gangways are clearly visible
and four climb up through the lower slopes of seats to the higher.
There is a decorated gangway dividing the two banks of seats. The
lower bank is of twenty rows and at ground level there is the cus-
tomary front row of stone chairs for the priests and other digni-
taries.

As you face the theatre, an excavated area with a good deal of not
very distinguished sculptural and foundation rubble lies on your
left. The rubble marks the site of an ancient temple, possibly dedi-

cated to Apollo. Later, a Byzantine chapel was built on the site; this was demolished by the Italians at the beginning of the last war.

Church of the Assumption of Our Lady (Church of the Panaghia)

Dominating the centre of the village is this beautifully composed late-Byzantine church in which all the features of the style – arch, circle, dome and cross – contrive to make marvellous exterior harmonies of deceptive simplicity. The subtlety of line and purity of materials – white-washed walls, domes and roof of red Byzantine tiles – make this a most inviting church. Indeed, I know of no church architecture of any period which is so inviting as village Byzantine or so restful. Maybe it is the curves that make it so? For here, with its soft lines, its domes, its breasts, is a mother church, comforting and absolutely rock-steady.

By contrast, the interior is remarkable for its richness. It is dark with frescoes and brilliant with gilt and silver and crystal. Raymond Matton dates the church somewhat prior to the period of the Knights (for the *escutcheon of Pierre d'Aubusson* on the outer wall of the church is believed to be a later addition). The frescoes are in excellent condition, date from 1779 and are by Gregory of Simi. Above the main door is a delightful sequence showing Man being weighed in the scales. Those found wanting descend to a series of explicit, hellish variations on a theme of how to fry a sinner; the victims demonstrate with expressions of unlikely sang-froid. To the right, the righteous are elevated on little clouds, three to a cloud.

Note the very handsome *Bishop's chair* and the excellent gilded *icon of the Virgin* on the iconostasis; she is unusually beautiful and has a jewelled tiara.

One of the nuns attendant on the church will probably take you through to see the burial chamber, which is in the form of an ante-room or enclosed courtyard at the far end of the church. It has a pebbled *chochláki* floor and was a burial-place of priests of the church and certain citizens of the town. In it are a number of icons well worth seeing, notably the three immediately above the door. The centre one is of a *Virgin and Child* enclosed in a lovely painted arc; on the left is a fine composition believed to be of an angel blessing a dying man in the presence of the Prophet David with his harp and a company of angels. All these are seventeenth-century. Below is an *Abraham and Isaac sacrifice* and on the adjoining wall are about a dozen smaller icons. All were the gifts of Lindians to the memory of relatives buried in the room.

Other churches

There are a number of small churches and chapels and if you have time to explore look for *Aghios Nikolaos* (in a small vineyard that is almost on the beach of the Grand Harbour); and *Aghios Demetrios* and *Aghios Minas* (both below the acropolis on the slope running down to the bay). You should be able to detect the roof of *Aghios Sotirou* fairly easily; it lies above and a little to the left of Aghios Nikolaos.

St Paul's Bay

From the acropolis you will have seen the small, seemingly enclosed cove of St Paul far below. You get to this bay by a path out of the village which leads over the hill and drops down near the little church. It is a very pleasant spot with a sandy shore and narrow entrance from the sea. When St Paul approached the island, they say, a great storm was raging; he was unable to reach Lindos harbour or to find landfall on the rocky coast. So the curtain of rocks at this point broke asunder in concert with a terrifying clap of thunder, the sea rushed in and the saint's boat was able to slip in to calm and safety.

Annually on June 28th and 29th (the saint's name-day) there is a festival of St Paul at Lindos; certainly worth joining if you are on the island at the time.

From the bay, you get one quite unexpected surprise: the near-400-foot headland on which the castle and temple stand is revealed as deeply undershot. It looks from here as though the whole acropolis has been quite undermined by some gigantic, rock-clawing scoop. The cavern goes deep under the site – how deep is hard to say – and in its vast gloom you can discern the dark arched entries of smaller caverns.

Lindian houses – inside and out

There is plenty of interesting domestic architecture to be found throughout the Aegean, but, to my mind, only on Skyros in the Northern Sporades and on Rhodes do you find interiors and exteriors developed to the extent of creating a distinctive and unmistakable local idiom.

The dominant features of the Rhodian village houses are best seen in Lindos (though there are examples and variants to be spotted in Archangelos, Koskinou and other villages). But Lindos has such a concentration of riches that it is easy to see a lot in a short time – several homes, incidentally, put a notice up outside saying that you will be welcome to come in (houses 125 and 143 for example).

First, there are the *medieval houses*, solidly built, four-square domestic fortresses, built with an eye to trouble but with a fondness for decoration, too. Byzantine doves and peacocks, flowers and graven inscriptions embellish the plain surfaces of grey stone blocks. Around the doors and windows run interlaced rope or chain patterns and the gently pointed arch of the doorway hints at Arab influence.

Perched above this there is a small upper room, like a ship's bridge. Known as '*the Captain's room*', this gave the head of the house a view of the harbour and his own ships and was probably a useful look-out in times of storm or trouble.

The first of these medieval Lindian houses I ever entered was occupied by a charming rattle of a black-clad old lady and a vari-coloured entourage of nine eager cats. Though the interior was more dilapidated than that of similar houses I saw later, there was the high, wooden ceiling painted with energetic floral designs, and the big, airy room had a distinct flavour of the medieval hall. Both the floor of this room and the courtyard outside were paved in black and white *chochláki*. The courtyard, in particular, was a cool, pebbled pleasure of lozenge patterns, chequered squares and an elaborate crystalline design with an affinity to the eight-pointed cross. (In other courtyards in the village you can see many more of these designs – cypress trees, anchors, running borders.)

The interior of the Lindian house of later date – sixteenth-century and after – has a number of features to look for. First, there is the big rectangular room known as 'the good house'. This will have a wide arch spanning nearly the full width of one wall. Within this arch is built a long, low platform, generally with a carved wooden balustrade along its length. There will be a low flight of three steps up to it. This platform was the family bed: it is generally laid with rugs or mats, and heaped in either corner are neat piles of square and rectangular pillows, boldly embroidered in green and red. The wall above the bed platform will almost certainly be hung with old and not-so-old Lindian plates and there will probably be a selection of embroidered cloths, runners and pillowcases hung on a rail or pinned to the wall.

In one house of the village, and one alone, there is a *spervéri*. (You can see others in the Benaki Museum in Athens and the Museum of Decorative Arts in Rhodes.) The *spervéri* is a tent-like, heavily embroidered linen curtain, suspended from the ceiling and fanning out to cover that end of the platform which was the bridal bed. There is an embroidered 'door' which falls to and quite encloses the area. This embroidered *spervéri* was not only heavy (often over 60 lb. in weight) but also expensive, so not all homes could afford the work and materials that went into making one. A *spervéri* would therefore sometimes be taken from one house to the home of a newly married pair and lent to them for the period of the honeymoon.

The designs which are worked into the *spervéri* and other cloths are some of them of Byzantine origin (the peacock is a common motif and the double-headed eagle has been found). But apparently there are so many sources of these designs that it is impossible to track each down to its source; sufficient that the results are delightful. Colours are mostly strong reds and greens; it is worth noting that most motifs are worked out in strictly geometric form with never a curved line.

The earthenware plates of Lindos have been collectors' pieces for some centuries and there are examples in most of the larger museums of Europe. On Rhodes you will find them in very many village homes and there are houses in Lindos which have extensive and valuable collections. You can see more of these plates in the Museum of Decorative Arts.

The best of the plates come from the sixteenth century: very Oriental in feeling, they exhibit a lovely freedom of design within the discipline of the shape. Flowers and leaves and buds sway about the plate as gently as in an evening breeze. Plates of the second period date from the seventeenth and eighteenth centuries and, while it is true that they show less delicacy of line and purity of colour, the subject-matter, which now includes Turkish-trousered women and high-legged, elegant horses, has a gaiety of decoration that is equally enjoyable in its way. Also in this latter period there appeared the ship motif, so popular in modern versions of the plates made at the Ikaros factory on the island today.

Expert opinion is apparently coming round to the belief that the plates of the first period may not have been made in Rhodes at all, so Persian are they in treatment. It is possible that they were discovered by Rhodian travellers to Asia Minor, brought back to the island as souvenirs and then introduced to the other islands of the Aegean in the course of Rhodian trade. The supporters of this theory point out that the plates were always regarded as decorative and valuable and were never used for everyday purposes. (Indeed, they were always pierced at the back so that they could be hung up.) They argue that, had the plates been made on the island and therefore easy to replace, they would not have received such special treatment. On the other hand, they might still have been made on Rhodes and yet treated with care simply because people thought them too pretty to spoil. Certainly, it is a combination of these same factors which colours my treatment of my own, modern Rhodian plates. I use them as decoration: because they came from far away and cannot be easily replaced, because they are relatively expensive, and because they look so pleasing and add grace to a room.

After visiting Lindos, return to the main road (Route 1). On meeting the main south-bound road, turn left to Pilona.

[53 km.] **Pilona** (pop. 22). There is little of note in this village and you pass through it en route for Lardos. Just before Lardos there is a right turn to Laerma (12 km.) and Moni Thari. (See p. 178, Link Route B.)

[56 km.] **Lardos** (pop. 700). Most of Lardos is well off the main road: not very attractive unless you need petrol. N.B. Some local maps show a loop road from Lardos via Pefki to Lindos. There *is* a road – very pretty – but it becomes unmotorable after 6 km.

On leaving Lardos the road becomes unmetalled though perfectly motorable; there is a badly sign-posted right turn to Moni Ipseni a few hundred yards beyond Lardos.

This detour takes you 5 km. along a pleasant, wooded road which dips steeply to where *Moni Ipseni* nestles between the hills. It is a pretty white monastery with blue gates, a lemon tree in a pebbled courtyard, and a church with an olive-wood screen adorned with angels and fierce, beast-like figures. Outside, a fountain with gushing water tempts you to drink or cool your feet; as it is generally alive with hundreds of wasps you may be able to resist temptation. But the oddest thing at Moni Ipseni is the rounded hill which rises in front of the monastery. A path winds up it in a series of almost militarily precise bends to a large cross which surmounts the hill. At every turn on this road to Calvary is a glittering white roadside shrine, each one a memorial and each one faced with a marble dedication.

[66 km.] Back on the main road, a minor road on the right leads to **Asklipios** (4 km.).

[70 km.] **Gennadi** (pop. 707). The village straggles as far as the roadside but the greater part is off the road. Gennadi possesses one of the few Rhodian industries, and the tall chimney of the brickworks can be seen from far away. To enter the village, take right turn at 70 km., sign-posted to Vati.

South of Gennadi the road runs close to the sea for a few kilometres and then edges inland. There are shallow dunes flanking the first part of the road and fine stretches of easily accessible beach.

[79 km.] **Lachania** (pop. 200).

[80 km.] Right turn to Messanagros, an alternative route to this village if you prefer to avoid the mountain road from Kattavia.

[83 km.] Left turn to the tiny seashore hamlet of **Plymiri**.

[88 km.] **Aghios Paulos,** now more or less deserted. Here there is a turn to the left. There is no great incentive to take this turning unless you wish to go to Vroulia. Just off the main road you drive past the empty shell of a barracks, turn right and in about 100 yards turn left again. The flat, wide path now stretches across the plain and over the hills to *Vroulia* and *Prassonisi*. Vroulia is some 10 km. from the main road and though you can do some of it by car, the rest you must walk.

In the early years of this century Danish archaeologists found traces of houses from the sixth and seventh centuries B.C., also the materials of a long wall. The site was tactically placed on top of a hill above the sea. Much later, in Byzantine days, a church was built on the site but there is very little to see now. Frankly, unless you are a dedicated collector of antique sites – however vestigial – or you fancy the walk for its own sake, Vroulia can be omitted from your sightseeing without any great pangs on your part. There is a lighthouse at *Akro Prassonisi*.

[90 km.] A right turn, which is the mountain road to Messanagros and Arnitha (opposite).

[91 km.] **Kattavia** (pop. 676). This is the most southerly village on the island, in an area with a reputation for weaving. I confess I find it characterless. Note: there is a Shell petrol pump at the entrance to the village.

The Rhodes–Kattavia bus stops here; the Rhodes–Kattavia–Messanagros bus continues up the mountain road to Messanagros. To reach Messanagros by car, leave Kattavia as if you were returning to Rhodes and take the left turn to Messanagros 1 km. out of the village.

[104 km.] **Messanagros** (pop. 300). There are 13 kilometres between Kattavia and Messanagros and they ride, high and winding, upon a thousand-foot ridge. Spectacular views of the sea spill out on either side of the ridge. The driving probably requires more care than anywhere else on the island but this should not deter you. It is an exhilarating road.

Messanagros is a small village of barely three hundred souls. From here you can descend a further splendid 11 km. to Arnitha (see pp. 180–81, Link Route C); or branch right at Messanagros to rejoin Route 1 at Lachania.

Route 2: Rhodes to Kattavia (West Coast)

A consistently interesting coast road taking in Ancient Kamiros as the high spot. Beyond Kamiros the villages are worth seeing and Monolithos Kastello is not to be missed. The road as far as Kamiros Skala is flat; thereafter it climbs and winds until, beyond Apolakia, it straightens out and runs along the flat coastal plain to Kattavia.

Route Leave Rhodes by Archbishop Makarios Street. Turn right just beyond Thermai Hotel into Venizelou Street and follow this road up the hill until it descends to join the west coast road near the Belvedere Hotel (Route Exit A on Rhodes New Town map). Continues via Kritika, Trianda (Filerimos), Kremasti, Paradissi (Petaloudes), Soroni (Agh. Soulas), Fanes, Kalavarda, Ancient Kamiros, Mandriko, Kamiros Skala, Kamiros Kastello, Kritinia, Embona, Agh. Issidoros, Siana, Monolithos Kastello, Apolakia (Skiadhi Monastery), Kattavia [117 km.].
Bus R.O.D.A. line from behind the New Market. Once weekly: usually returning the following day. Ask R.O.D.A. for details of this and other buses to villages on Route 2.

For visits to Ancient Kamiros only: several local buses and, from early June, R.O.D.A. usually run special round-trip buses to the site up to four times daily. There are also, of course, the tourist coaches (see p. 96 for addresses).

Accommodation Between Kritika and Trianda, you pass a series of new hotels: the *Blue Sky*, the *Posseidon*, the *Bel-Air*, the *Oceanis*, the *Miramare Beach Hotel*, the *Vellois*, the *Rodos Bay*, etc. There is an E Class hotel at Kremasti. (See pp. 97–100.) Simple accommodation possibly available at Skiadhi monastery.

[3 km.] **Kritika.** The name of this village, a straggling row of near-identical houses, contains a morsel of history, for it was settled by Turks fleeing from Crete in 1898.

[5 km.] **Ixia.**

[6 km.] Miramare Beach Hotel.

[8 km.] **Trianda.** A population of 3,150 makes this the largest village on the island. The bay of Trianda has been a holiday resort since pre-Christian days. The greater part of the modern village lies off the road (turn left at the petrol pumps: sign-post to Filerimos). The big yellow-washed church is worth a visit if only to see the intricately carved screen of olive-wood.

The road to the thickly wooded hill of Filerimos continues through the village of Trianda and climbs very steeply in a series of hairpin bends so acute that vehicles must adhere to a timetable that ensures that a bus or car going up never meets one coming down. (This timetable is set out on boards at Trianda and Filerimos.)

FILERIMOS (ANCIENT IALYSOS)

Open Summer Daily 07.30 till sunset.
Sundays and holidays 10.00–13.00.
15.00–19.00.
Winter Daily 09.00 till sunset.
Sundays and holidays 10.00–13.00.
15.00–17.00.
Entrance Drs 5.

Ialysos or Filerimos? Either name will be understood by the Rhodians. Ialysos is the ancient name, Filerimos the modern. Filerimos means 'one who loves solitude' and possibly came into use when a monastery was built on the site about A.D. 1000.

One snippet of learned gossip about Ialysos is both amusing and revealing. It seems that some two hundred years before Rhodes was founded in 408 B.C., Greek soldiers in Egypt took part in an expedition up the Nile. In the course of this expedition they came upon Abu Simbel. Like others since, they found these rock colossi irresistible and they carved into the person of Rameses II a message

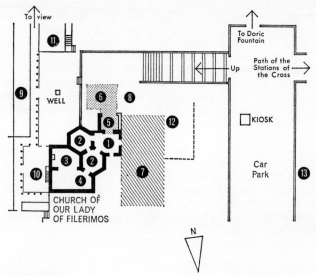

Filerimos

1 d'Aubusson chapel ⎤ Church
2 Two smaller chapels ⎬ our Lady
3 Larger chapel ⎦ of Filerimos
4 Early-Christian fish mosaic
5 Early-Christian church
6 Baptistry, early-Christian church
7 Temple of Athena and Zeus Polieus

8 Slates: probably Phoenician
9 Cloisters
10 Stairway to pulpit
11 Refectory
12 Subterranean chapel
13 Ruins of Byzantine church

recording their expedition. Individual soldiers added their names and at least one soldier gave 'Ialysos' as his home town. Professor Burn in his *The Penguin History of Greece* tells this story in greater detail.

Ialysos occupies a plateau at the top of the 875-foot-high Mt Filerimos. The plateau runs from west to east and is broadest at its western end. According to myth, the city was founded by Ialysos, the third of the three grandsons of the god Helios. The Dorians, under whom it grew from a settlement to a city named it after its mythical founder. The recorded history of Ialysos, however, goes back even farther than the Dorians. The Phoenicians were probably the first to settle here. When the Mycenaean Achaians arrived, about 1450 B.C., they called the place Achaia. That we remember today the mythical name and have quite forgotten the historical one simply proves once again that, whether we are tenth-century B.C. Dorians or twentieth-century A.D. realists, myth frequently exerts greater power than fact – or at least lasts longer.

The plateau was, in effect, the acropolis of the city. Some time during the Dorian period the city itself began to edge down the western slopes of the hill towards Kremasti and Trianda, and in this area an enormous necropolis has been found, containing tombs of every Archaic age since the Mycenaean. Museums throughout the world contain finds from this necropolis, which was first excavated by Salzman and Biliotti in 1876. In 1914 and again between 1929 and 1932 the Italians Majuri and Jacopi made still more discoveries.

After Rhodes was founded the inhabitants of Ialysos were probably not slow to see the personal and trading advantages of moving into the new city. By the first century B.C. it is reckoned that Ialysos had reverted to a village once more, but before this happened the city had thrown up its own crop of famous sons, among them the poet Timocreon and the Olympic victor Diagoras.

Church of Our Lady of Filerimos
Map **1, 2, 3**.

The bus deposits visitors on a large car park. On your left, behind wrought-iron gates, stands the almost wholly rebuilt Church and Monastery of Our Lady of Filerimos. You can estimate that upon or around this spot there have stood successively a Phoenician temple, a third-century B.C. temple to Athena and Zeus Polieus, an early Christian basilica, a Catholic church (converted from an Orthodox original), a stable (which is the use to which the Turks put the church), a restored twentieth-century version of the church, a war-damaged shell and, finally, the post-Second-World-War restoration of the Church of Our Lady of Filerimos.

The church was in five main parts. First, you enter the chapel built by d'Aubusson when he was Grand Master (*Map* **1**). Leading off this are two smaller chapels (*Map* **2**). From the left-hand chapel you enter the rear and largest part of the church (*Map* **3**). As you step in, look down at the floor just in front of you. Here, as it has lain for centuries, is a gay little red mosaic fish, part of the floor of the original early-Christian building (*Map* **4**).

You leave as you entered, through the doorway of the d'Aubusson chapel. Once outside, turn left and you come to a small, open

area abutting the church and, next to it, a sunken baptistry (*Map* 6).
Both are early-Christian.

Temple of Athena and Zeus Polieus
Map 7.

This third-century B.C. Doric temple runs north and south in front
of Our Lady of Filerimos. Foundations, bases, stumps of fluted
pillars are all there, but little else. The temple was similar in style to
the temple of Athene at Lindos but was much larger. It was built,
at least partly, over the site of the Phoenician temple. There is only
a relic of this latter temple to be seen – some stone slates (*Map* 8),
which lie in the right-angle formed by the southern wall of the
Doric temple and the western limits of the wall enclosing the sunken
baptistry.

Cloisters of the Monastery
Map 9.

Lying to the side and behind the present-day church are the restored
courtyards, galleries and cloisters. They are pleasant places to
wander in, with their silence and flowers and scents. Note the steps
that lead up to an open-air pulpit on the back wall of the church
that overlooks a small inner courtyard (*Map* 10).

On the southern side of the large courtyard is a refectory (*Map* 11)
and there is a stairway to a reception room. Beyond here, if you
walk through the trees, is a fine view.

Return now to the flight of steps which leads back to the
wrought-iron entrance gate. On your right and just in front of the
temple to Athena is a hump in the stony field. This is the subterranean Chapel of Aghios Georgios.

Chapel of Aghios Georgios
Map 12.

You step down into this tiny chapel and leave the sun above.
Almost every inch of wall is covered with frescoes. The chapel has
no apse: it is a simple, rectangular shape with a barrel vault. On the
right, a section of fresco has been removed to reveal part of a
Christian cross carved in stone beneath the plaster.

All the frescoes were executed in the fourteenth and fifteenth
centuries, though they have been repainted since. Among the most
interesting are a sequence of *Grand Masters kneeling before Christ,* a

St George, and also an exceedingly well-preserved and beautiful series of *incidents in the life of Christ* which compose the decoration of the barrel vault. In this chapel, too, we are given an excellent example of how the fresco painter liked to simulate a different form of decoration: all the frescoes of the side walls are 'looped' to a painted curtain rail to give the likeness of a tapestry or curtain.

Doric Fountain

As you leave the precinct of the church and emerge on to the bus park, turn left. A steep flight of ancient steps takes you to the Doric Fountain. The way is set with cypresses and flowers and the view down the valley is delightful. If you expect also to hear the cool splash of water you will probably be disappointed. On my visits no stream of life has issued from the lion's mouths that are set into the fountain and, even if it did, you wouldn't be able to cool yourself, for this lovely little building, with two of its fluted limestone columns and part of its architrave re-erected, is shut away behind iron bars. But don't miss it, not least because it was discovered quite by accident in 1926 when this part of the hillside happened to slip and revealed the fountain. This sets one's imagination to work on all the marvels probably still hidden beneath hillsides and villages throughout the island.

Byzantine church
Map 13.

This eleventh-century church lies on your left among the grasses and under the olive trees if you stand on the car park with the kiosk on your right. You can clearly see its three apses. Traces of the tiled floor and other details remain.

Stations of the Cross

The Italians set up fourteen copper reliefs of the Stations of the Cross along a path which leads to a small open place. There was a 25-foot cross here until it was taken down during the war. Until fairly recently you could see its replacement – a gun site.

Views from Filerimos

Filerimos is a wonderful strategic site and has been used as such many times. In 1248 the Byzantines directed operations against the invading Genoese from here, and Suleiman the Magnificent commanded the final siege of Rhodes from the hill in 1522. In the recent past both Italians and Germans held the hill and the two nations conducted a fierce battle for possession of it after the fall of Italy.

The views from Filerimos deserve recording. To the north is the wide *Bay of Trianda*. Looking south and west are the villages of *Paradissi* and *Kremasti*. *Mt Paradissi* rises from the fields, with that curious tilt towards the sea which is such a feature of nearly all the high ground along the west coast of the island. From the vantage-point at the end of the path of the Stations of the Cross you look down on the valley and the villages of *Pastidha* and *Maritsa* – and the near-by airport – and, farther south, the wooded peak of *Profitis Ilias*. More distant still, in contrast, is the treeless and much higher summit of *Mt Atavyros*.

From Filerimos return to Route 2 via Trianda. A few hundred yards after rejoining the main road and a little beyond the village look out for a good example of a *pírghos* house. This one sits on the right of the road near a pottery workshop. It is a rectangular stone tower with a small round turret high in the north wall. All the main windows are set high, too, because the *pírghos* was a domestic fortress, built at a time when it was necessary for every home to provide its own protection against corsairs. This example is now a well-tended home: doors and windows are painted blue and the garden is cared for. It is said that even today the people of the village call their houses *pírghoi* though they are often no higher or more defensive than a bungalow.

[11 km.] **Kremasti** (pop. 2,100). Just before the entrance to this village a road to the left goes to the airport and the villages of Maritsa and Pastidha.

Kremasti is an agreeable village; the main street is shady with trees and there seem to be more *kafeneíons* on either side than there are pubs in Rose Street, Edinburgh. There is an air of absorbed busy-ness: the little shops look fairly well-to-do, the stalls are piled with fruit and vegetables. Kremasti has a library, housed in a classic-ally pillared building which, according to the inscription above the door, was built in 1927. Almost opposite is the school, which has a flavour of American Colonial classicism, possibly because many ex-citizens of Kremasti now resident in America have made bequests to the village.

The gigantic, elaborate *Church of Our Lady of Kremasti* is at the entrance to the village on the right. Inside, the pillars are massive and are of marble and mock-marble; the floor is genuine marble; there is a pretty side-chapel, and some undistinguished modern wall paintings. The courtyard outside is glittering white; the black spears of tall cypresses and gilded wrought-iron gates look well against it. It is neat and well-tended. What it must have cost to build – it is entirely modern – beggars the imagination.

The village has a famous annual festival, beginning on August 15th, when the Panaghia of Kremasti is celebrated (her icon is to be seen inside the church). The festival lasts till August 23rd and is counted the greatest festival of the Dodecanese.

[13·5 km.] **Koufa.** Koufa is no more than a *tavérna* on one side of the road and a *kafeneíon* on the other, plus the little *Church of Aghios Ioannis* a few yards up the hill on the left. Ask the owners of the *kafeneíon* to show you the path and lend you the key.

Aghios Ioannis is worth a visit. The frescoes are in differing states of repair but those in the apse cover the whole area from roof to floor and include a *Raising of Lazarus, Christ on a donkey*, a *Last Supper* and the *Washing of Christ's feet*. There is a pebbled floor.

[15–16 km.] **Paradissi** (pop. 1,900). A sign-post announces 'Paradissi' as you enter the village and just beyond it are two small churches, *St Michael's* on the right and *St Mark's* on the left. St Mark's is the one to look at as it contains a spirited *fresco of St George* and also a painting of another saint who has the characteristic grave, dark-eyed Byzantine gaze.

The old name of Paradissi was Villanuova and the Italians chose to revive it. Now the village is named after *Mt Paradissi* which lies east of the village. The area is well-watered and almost everyone farms. The village is full of flowers before the sun of high summer burns them up; flowers in gardens, flowers in windows, flowers marching up flights of steps. If you arrive around Easter the houses will be bright with their coats of Easter paint. Paradissi has a canning factory which handles some of the fruit and vegetables grown in the area. (You will by now have become aware of the characteristic features of this part of the coastline: the small, metal windmills – made in Illinois, most of them – and the tomato fields, each plantation protected by a windbreak of tall bamboo.)

Two paths to the right in the centre of the village are each sign-posted to the beach.

[18 km.] From here you can make a left turn to Upper and Lower Kalamon and Petaloudes, the Valley of the Butterflies.

Petaloudes, the Valley of the Butterflies

Petaloudes is a total of 7 km. from the turn off the main road. At 1 km. there is a left turn to Damatria; at 5 km. you pass through Kalamon; at about 5·5 km. a right fork runs downhill to the Petaloudes Restaurant. You keep to the upper road and in a further 1·5 km. arrive at Petaloudes. Entrance is free and parking space is available.

The Valley of the Butterflies is a narrow and heavily wooded gorge. Flat shoes are recommended, for the authorities have indulged in some rustic bridges and handrails to add to the natural hazards of clambering up rocky paths. The going is easy enough, however, and should deter no one. Beyond the head of the valley is the Monastery of Kalopetra. (N.B. The butterflies appear only from June till September.)

Use your eyes on this walk, for you may otherwise be halfway up the valley and wondering where the butterflies have gone to – without realizing they are all about you, so skilful is their camouflage. They fold their wings so that the brown and cream colouring is upper-most and they cluster in the boles of trees and under leaves; they even blend perfectly with the rocks on which they rest. If you happen to be present when a guide is taking a party up the valley, he will blow a whistle. The shrill sound immediately sends thousands of butterflies – now red and gold – fluttering panic-stricken up-wards, fragile as leaves.

On returning to the parking place, note that the road continues to Psinthos (5 km.) (see Link Route A, p. 177). To rejoin Route 2, however, return to the main road the same way as you came. Turn left on to main road.

[21 km.] A left turn to **Tholos**: an abbreviation of the old name Theologos.

[24 km.] **Soroni** (pop. 888). Lawrence Durrell, in *Reflections on a Marine Venus*, has a tragi-comedy of a chapter about the events of the annual festival of Soroni which he attended just after the war.

This festival includes donkey races and horse races and celebrates the saint of Soroni, Agh. Soulas. July 30th is the date.

Do not, however, be misled: the large church on the rise to the left of the main street of the village is not Agh. Soulas but *Agh. Loukas*. It has high, narrow vaulting and a pale-blue ceiling sparkled with gold stars and set with oval medallions of the saints. The bishop's chair is painted gold and blue and the iconostasis (unsung in any guide-book I have read) is an extremely handsome one of carved olive-wood. It is a large, cool church, scented with incense and very likeable.

Agh. Soulas is 4 or 5 km. from Soroni village. To reach it, take the left turn to Eleoussa, Kolimbia and Dimylia just beyond Soroni. After 3 km. an open space opens to the left. Alongside it is a small race-track (for the donkey races). An avenue of trees passes the track and you come upon Agh. Soulas, a tiny, red-roofed chapel in the midst of cypresses and pines. There is little of note inside and this modest chapel of Agh. Soulas, it appears, is simply a focus for a very popular festival. The race-track, paved dancing floor and stone benches, the pretty clearing in the woods, are all evidence that the Rhodians have gone to unusual pains to set up permanent facilities for a favourite celebration.

[26 km.] **Fanes** (pop. 707).

[30 km.] **Kalavarda** (pop. 400). As you approach Kalavarda, the road forks. The left fork goes into the village and thence inland to Salakos (see p. 175); the right runs along the coast to Ancient Kamiros and beyond. Route 2 takes this coast road.

[34 km.] You arrive at the starting-point for a visit to ancient Kamiros. There is no village here, just a small restaurant at the foot of the hill where you swim and eat and can view a large tanker, beached and rusting and sinking lower every year, farther down the coast. The local buses stop near the restaurant; to get to the site you walk up a road to your left. Coaches and cars can drive up to the entrance.

The walk up to the site is pleasant, about 1 km. of gentle going on a road between pine trees. You breast a shoulder of the hill and, suddenly, the excavated city lies before you. (It is so well concealed that once, within half a dozen strides of the site, a man asked me: 'Tell me, will there be much to see at Kamiros?' Five seconds later he had his answer.)

ANCIENT KAMIROS

Open Summer Daily 07.30–sunset.
Sundays and holidays 10.00–13.00.
15.00–19.00.
Winter Daily 09.00–sunset.
Sundays and holidays 10.00–13.00.
14.30–17.00.

Entrance Drs 5.

This ancient city lies in a bowl in the hillside, a complete ground-plan of a city exposed to view. The roofless walls, the flights of steps, the fallen stones and tumbled pillars rest white and silent in the sun. Below and to your left is the sea, a large temple area spreads in front of you, the main street drives through the middle of the city and climbs to where the remains of the stoa and its portico look down upon all that remains of Homer's 'chalky Kamiros'.

It is a surprisingly large site; even if you come as one of a bus load it is easy for everyone to become dispersed and for you to feel quite alone. The owners of the city have gone, long gone – but they left Kamiros to you. Here is a gift of the past, quiet and still and stony: deserted by all but the bee-eaters who flit, chattering, among the pines as evening falls.

Principal sights

No evidence of an acropolis has ever been found, so it is assumed that Kamiros was an unfortified city. It has been extensively excavated (though there are sections still awaiting attention), first by Salzman and Biliotti when they discovered it in 1859, and then after 1929 the whole area was uncovered by Italian archaeologists. The funerary bas-relief of Krito and Tamarista now in the Museum of Rhodes was found here, and in the British Museum are a number of Kamiros finds: a small terracotta basket of fruit, a metal cup containing hen's eggs, and a delightful terracotta figure of a woman kneading dough.

Entrance is from the north-west. The area in front of you contains a vast, square temenos or *sanctuary* (*Map* 1). In the north-west corner of this sanctuary are the remains of a *Doric temple* (*Map* 2). A few pillars of the temple have been re-erected: it was designed *in antis* and the god to whom it was dedicated is unknown. Stumps of pillars are ranked along two sides of the temenos: on the east side they are backed by a high retaining wall (*Map* 3); on the uphill side the row of ruined pillars ends in a doorway (*Map* 4). Note that the

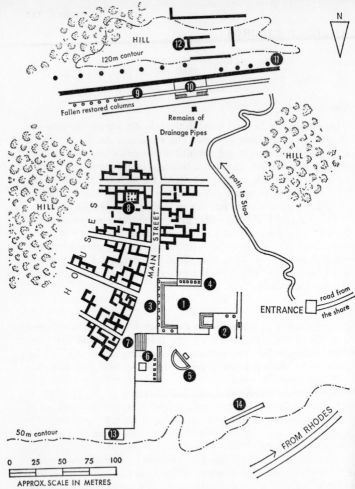

Ancient Kamiros

1 Sanctuary
2 Doric temple
3 Retaining wall
4 Doorway
5 Exedra
6 Sacrificial area
7 Steps

8 Hellenistic house
9 Stoa
10 Sixth-century B.C. cistern
11 Pits
12 Temple to Athena
13 Public baths
14 Ancient wall

N

HILL
120m contour
Fallen restored columns
Remains of
Drainage Pipes
HILL
path to Stoa
HILL
HOUSES
MAIN STREET
ENTRANCE
road from
the shore
FROM RHODES
50m contour
0 25 50 75 100
APPROX. SCALE IN METRES

four middle pillars of this group are curved on one face and flat on the other.

Below the sanctuary on the seaward side you can see the outline of a semicircular *exedra* (*Map* 5). Behind it, a low flight of steps leads to a *sacrificial area* (*Map* 6). Here are nine altars, six of them virtually undamaged, and also a large sacrificial altar. To the right of this a narrow, steeper flight of steps (*Map* 7) rises to the level of the main street.

From here you can wander uphill. Almost all the ruins to the left were houses and just after you start upwards you can see two standing pillars. These are part of the inner court of a small house. Within the house is a *calcined fireplace*. There are four clearly marked alleys running to the left off the main street. Flanking the highest of these is a *Hellenistic house*, easy to see because several of the pillars have been re-erected (*Map* 8).

Between here and the top of the hill you should be able to see signs of the extensive *drainage system* of the city where the pipes now appear on the surface of the road.

The *stoa* (*Map* 9) with its portico is very large, 640 feet long. It is Doric, of the third century B.C. and built in part over a large cistern of the sixth century B.C. (*Map* 10). The cistern is in two parts, one a narrow supply cistern with steps leading down at either end so that water could easily be obtained. The main section is the reservoir proper. It was coated with an impervious seal and has two drainage holes.

The stoa itself is a mess in its present state. During their work here the Italians (who did much of the admirable work of excavation) rebuilt six columns and their entablature but these have now fallen down, leaving only an unhappy stump or two to tell the tale. But the view of the town from here is magnificent and the great expanse of sea, islands and the coast of Asia Minor are peacemakers. Looking left – i.e., to the west – you face the island whence the original settlers came, Crete. At your back is the ridge of Mt Atavyros. On the slopes between here and Atavyros was the great necropolis where many of the greatest Archaic finds were made.

Behind the stoa and along most of its length there ran a narrow path and beyond here were shops and the agora. The demarcations of these shops can still be seen. Most noticeable, however, are a row of *pits* (*Map* 11) where treasures are believed to have been stored. Behind the pits are the remains of a *temple to Athena* (*Map* 12). The temple itself was built in the sixth or fifth century B.C., then restored and added to during the Hellenistic period.

When you return to the lower town you can detect some sketchy remains of *public baths* (*Map* 13), and part of the *ancient wall* (*Map* 14).

On rejoining the coast road, continue to Mandriko.

[44 km.] **Mandriko** (pop. 80). An undistinguished village. The road climbs out of the village and drops again. Soon you can see the small harbour of Kamiros Skala (the new sign-post simply calls it Kamiros, in contrast to Ancient Kamiros), lying a few hundred yards off the road to the right.

[47·5 km.] **Kamiros Skala.** There are two or three small *tavérnas* at this little harbourage; at one of them I have eaten excellent *souvlákia*, sprinkled with parsley and onion and stuffed into a roll. Fishermen from the offshore island of **Alimnia** come in here and you may even find a *caïque* departing on a trip to Chalki. But before you leap aboard, have a thought as to how you are to get back, as the boat will probably not return for a week and other boats calling at Chalki are infrequent.

There is a legend attached to the area around Kamiros Skala and the next village along the road, Kritinia. Kamiros Skala was probably the ancient port of Kritinia and Kritinia itself was named after settlers who came from Crete. These people came to Rhodes after an oracle warned Althaemenes, grandson of the then King Minos, that he would kill his father. Althaemenes fled from this fate and made landfall near Kamiros Skala. It is easy to guess how the story ended. Many years later, Althaemenes' father took it into his head to see his son again before he died. He set sail for Rhodes but, unfortunately, arrived after dark. The settlers were sensitive to invasion and they promptly killed the strangers in the night without stopping to inquire who they were. True to the rules of legend, the man who killed the Cretan king was Althaemenes.

It was these settlers who built the earliest city of Kamiros and so laid the foundations of the Rhodian Minoan period.

[49 km.] *Kamiros Kastello* (sometimes called *Kritinia Castle*). This is one of the fortresses used by the Knights to protect their west coast.

The Kastello was built – or rather, restored – by the Knights in the early sixteenth century. It has a masterful air and commands the approach up the narrow valley from the north. Its western aspect is perched on natural rock which stands sheer above the sea. It is extensively damaged, but you will find the arms of Grand Masters Aimerie d'Amboise and Fabrizio del Carretto on the outer walls. Inside, the grasses grow high over tumbled stones. The view is splendid: the nearest island is the little **Nisos Makri** and south of it is that even smaller **Nisos Strongili** (*strongíli* means round). This is a common name for circular but otherwise undistinguished islands and there is another Nisos Strongili farther down the coast near Monolithos. Beyond these two islets is the horseshoe shape of Alimnia.

[52 km.] **Kritinia** (pop. 760). Apart from the Althaemenes legend there is nothing of great interest in Kritinia, though a festival is held here on April 23rd.

The road to Embona runs out of the village then doubles back on itself, so that when you reach the far side of the valley you look back on the road you have just travelled.

[60 km.] **Embona** (pop. 1,450). The approach to Embona is across the western foothills of Mt Atavyros, well-wooded with pines and spruce. The village is not among the most attractive on the island. Indeed, a great part of it is set upon a grey, sandy escarpment which looks as though it has been dumped there by bulldozers and then given a going-over by tanks. But it is pleasant to sit in the square while the women come to the spring with their water jars (plastic and earthenware). They are sturdy women, famed throughout the Dodecanese for their costume and their skill as dancers. They are in great demand at festivals all over Rhodes. Their white blouses are embroidered from neck to breast; a petticoat, also embroidered, falls below the skirt. There is a draw-thread just below the breast, so the effect is high-waisted and full and the peasant boots set it off well.

The Atavyros range runs from north of the village to a point 15 km. to the south-west. *Mt Atavyros* itself is 3,986 feet high. From the village a path goes to the top but you would be wise not to attempt this without help. The village, like most villages, is confusing and I make no attempt to guide you through the lanes to the path – you must ask a local to lead you to it, and, if possible, up the mountain, too.

On the summit a Hellenistic temple of Zeus once stood; now

there is little or nothing to see – except, of course, the most extensive view the island offers.

2 km. out of Embona the road from Salakos and Profitis Ilias joins the route. (See Link Route A, p. 175.) You should bear right, however, and take the road to Agh. Issidoros. This road almost encircles Mt Atavyros and climbs fairly high. *Moni Artamiti* lies on the left of the road. Before you begin the run down into Agh. Issidoros there is a sight of the sea again; a little farther down you should also get a view across to Karpathos if the day is clear.

There is a left turn to Laerma (11 km.), Thari Monastery and Lardos (29 km.) before you enter Agh. Issidoros. Between Agh. Issidoros and Siana the scenery is rugged and bare. Watch out for a superb view across the *Gulf of Monolithos* to the small islets which dot it.

[76 km.] **Aghios Issidoros** (pop. 1,000).

[85 km.] **Siana.** A little before this village there is a track (motorable – just) which runs off to the right. You could make a little detour here and advance a kilometre or two towards the small peninsula of *Cape Armenistis*. It is a rough track but the views are delightful. You can't go far for two reasons: the going becomes too rough and you will soon be stopped by the resident beekeepers. (There are signs asking you to beware of the bees.) As the gentlemen behind black veils told me courteously, the car disturbs the bees.

Siana lies in the shelter of *Mt Akramitis* and is a pleasant enough village with a large late-nineteenth-century *church*. It is about here that you begin to become very aware that you are now in a part of the island that is much less well-to-do than the north. Here they live off the grudging land, reaping little or no benefit from tourism.

[89 km.] **Monolithos** (pop. 500). (The name of the village means 'one stone'.) The village is about 2 km. north-east of the *Kastello of Monolithos*, to my mind one of the 'musts' of Rhodes, not because of its interior but for its superb position. You first sight it – and this is the best view of all – from above. High as the castle is, the road is even higher. From the village it winds for 2 km. along the edge of a steep slope and there below, perched on its extraordinary Teutonic peak of rock, is the fortress, stark against the shining sea. At one moment it looks like some Wagnerian keep; the next, it seems to come straight from a nineteenth-century steel engraving of a corsair's fastness. Gradually, the road slips downwards and comes to an end in a neatly laid-out car park below the castle. Leave the car and walk up a sweet-smelling path between trees. On my first visit, the sun was low in the west and cast a brilliant path across the sea. *Cape Armenistis* thrusts out into the ocean a little north of the site. Within the castle is the tiny *Chapel of Agh. Panteleimon*. Until the middle of the last century it was still possible to detect traces of fifteenth-century frescoes in this chapel, but these have now succumbed to wind and weather. When you leave the chapel and walk towards the sea wall you notice the barrel vault of what appears to have been another chapel. Please take care when exploring these walls, for there is a sheer drop of about 500 feet beyond the walls and absolutely no safety measures. Return to Monolithos village and take the road to Apolakia.

[101 km.] **Apolakia** (pop. 550). There is not much to keep you at Apolakia, but the people are friendly and helpful. The road south of the village goes along the flat coastal strip. To your left the 1,500-foot range of Koukouriari rises steeply.

[108 km.] 7 km. out of Apolakia on the left is a sign-post ('Iera – Monastiri'). This is the way to the *Monastery of Skiadhi* (3·5 km. from the turn). If you aim to do a complete round trip of the island and want to spend a night on the way, this is your last chance before Kattavia. The monastery will probably be willing to give you shelter for the night, though it is *very* simple indeed. But the view and the sunset and the solitariness of resting here in the evening and awaking in the early dawn to step out into the courtyard of the white monastery make it worth any mild privation. The monastery is empty of monks and, on my last visit, was cared for by an elderly couple.

The road to Skiadhi from the coast road is through wheatfields and at intervals on the way up there are glimpses of the monastery. The track gets rougher and higher – first and second gear all the way. Abruptly, after one last grinding bout in bottom gear you emerge on the little grassy slope in front of the monastery. Facing you are white walls, white buildings, blue and white bell tower. Inside is a large courtyard with a plane tree in the middle and probably an amiable dog lolloping around. Turn to look back whence you have come. Taste the air, listen ... there are goat bells as flocks are led home for the night, men's voices, birdsong. These sounds drift upwards, linger briefly and then disperse into this shimmering aerial splendour in which the sea glitters. Monolithos is far distant, Karpathos lies ahead upon an insubstantial ocean and the tiny islets to the south look like a flotilla of boats. One, indeed, is shaped like a corsair galley and there is a tale to explain how it came to look like that. It seems that Skiadhi and district had been plagued with corsairs beyond their fair share and, when once again corsair vessels were seen on the horizon, the few remaining inhabitants – the others had all been killed or abducted – prayed to the Virgin to save them. And so she did, turning the pirate chief's boat into stone. Whereupon the others fled.

The charming church of the monastery was sadly damaged a few years ago by an earth tremor and the roof is reft by deep fissures. So the church can't be used till money is found and architects and builders arrive to repair it. Most of the contents of the church have been removed to a little room off the courtyard for safety. This room, or temporary church, is tenderly looked after by the old couple. There are icons, flowers are in vases, candles are lit, a lamp shines in the window all night.

The interior of the church proper is white and ochre. There are three pleasing motifs set among circles in the roof and the cupola is decorated with frescoes. The chapel in the east and the apse are Byzantine; the rest is eighteenth-century and later.

Your bed at Skiadhi will be a country one – a wooden base, a thin mattress – but the linen and the worn blankets will be immaculate. There is no standard price, but so slender are the commons upon which the two caretakers live and so kind are they that it is nice to pay over the odds rather than the other way about. I took food with me to eat but they would not hear of it and insisted that I share with them the dish of unsalted spaghetti with goat meat. This was the only true hardship of my visit but worth it to please them and for the talk we had over the meal and later when we sat over coffee in the lamplit sitting-room.

Return to the main road from Skiadhi and proceed to Kattavia, where, incidentally, you can get petrol from a Shell pump.

[117 km.] Kattavia. (See Route 1, p. 157.)

Link Route A: Kalavarda to Kolimbia

This route, beginning at Kalavarda on the west and crossing the island to Kolimbia on the east, can also be regarded as the southern leg of a round trip from Rhodes to Rhodes. (Whether you do it in half a day or a full day depends on how long you linger here and there.)

Route Leave Rhodes as for Route 2 (p. 157). From Kalavarda (Route 2) to Kolimbia (Route 1) via Salakos, Profitis Ilias, Eleoussa (Dimylia, Platania and Apollona), Archipolis (Psinthos), Efta Pighes, Kolimbia [45 km.].
Bus West coast buses (R.O.D.A. line) from Rhodes will take you to Kalavarda, Salakos or Apollona, but there is no bus which does the complete route. East coast buses (K.T.E.L. line) pass the turn to Efta Pighes. Tour buses will take you as far as Profitis Ilias but thereafter follow a different route.
Accommodation Two A class hotels at Profitis Ilias. See p. 100 for details.

Kalavarda (pop. 400); a sign-post directs you inland from this village towards Salakos.

[8 km.] **Salakos** (pop. 727). This village is in the foothills of Mt Profitis Ilias. Gardens and flowers abound. The *church* is one of the trio of four-apsed churches on the island; the others are St Nikolaos Fountoucli (see below) and the Chourmali Medresse in the old city of Rhodes.

[20 km.] *Mt Profitis Ilias*. The wooded mountain road from Salakos to the heights of Mt Ilias is clearly marked. When at last you reach the peak you are 2,620 feet high. Here are the hotels, the Elafina and Elafos: literally, the Deer Hotel and the Doe Hotel (see p. 100). The surrounding forests of sharp, pungent pines seem to have inspired the builders to a chalet architecture more suited to Grindelwald than Greece. The views from here across the west coast are very fine. There is a small *kafeneion* and also a little church (not notable though pretty). Grazing in disheartened fashion within a wire enclosure are a number of deer.

From Profitis Ilias take the road to Eleoussa.

[26 km.] The *Church of Agh. Nikolaos Fountoucli*. It is perched on a grassy shelf on the eastern and lower slopes of Mt Profitis Ilias. The view is delightful, the place both peaceful and exhilarating. The church is four-apsed. Imagine a blunt cross with four curved extremities and domes or half-domes placed above the centre and the extremities, and you obtain some idea of the shape and interior calm of Fountoucli.

Though some of the frescoes which cover the interior have been overpainted and touched up, these thirteenth- and fifteenth-century works retain plenty of power. Note the energetic treatment of the winged St Michael who bears a massive sword, also the simplicity of the standing figures of a man and wife who uphold, between them, the church of Christ. Look up, and you will see a Pantocrator in the dome of the north aisle.

Don't miss, either, the charming *St Francis and the Birds*, which is on the wall facing the husband-and-wife fresco. It is pleasing enough in itself, but what makes one leave the church smiling is the cheerful malice of the artist who painted a couple of decorative bosses at either end of the frame round the fresco. Look closely and you discover they are a pair of fat cats.

Outside the church, an old fig tree casts deep shade. Sit under it for a while and listen to the clatter of spring water that issues from a spout and spills into an old stone trough. There is a fine view, too, down the valley towards Dimylia and Eleoussa.

[29 km.] **Eleoussa** (pop. 300) is set around a large colonnaded square. At the far end is an imposing house so clustered with palms that I was not in the least surprised to see a group of people chatting over drinks at the top of the grand flight of stairs. It looked like a residency or governor's palace – and that is exactly what it was, during the Italian occupation.

It is worth taking your bearings as you enter the square from Fountoucli as there are three other roads leading from the square, one at each corner. To your right is the turn to Platania and Apollona and at the far end of the square the road to the left goes to Dimylia and the one to the right is the road to Archipolis.

You can make two brief excursions from Eleoussa if you wish. One is north and west about 2·5 km. to **Dimylia** (pop. 200). The village lies above the valley, which throws up odd humps and hills and is scattered with boxy houses. Here I once saw a travelling butcher doing business: the meat hung from a tree in a bloody sack, a table was set up below with scales and knives arrayed. The village population and the village flies clustered around.

The second detour from Eleoussa is 2 km. south of Platania (pop. 200) and from there a further 6 km. to Apollona. I find

Platania very likeable and it can be quite beautiful in the late after-noon when the lowering sun throws the eastern slopes of the hills beyond the village into dark, bruised shadows tipped with bright gold. The village residents have gay and nonconformist ideas on house-painting. One year every house was an immaculate variation of ochre and white; before my last visit they had all been freshly painted apple-green or viridian. One or two slowcoaches still adhered to the old ochre and white. Note the beehive shape of the bake-ovens.

Apollona (pop. 850) is a straggling, dusty village chiefly visited because the road goes through it and, in another 8 km., joins up with the road from Embona to Profitis Ilias. Now return to Eleoussa and Link Route A the way you came (note that 1 km. beyond Apollona on this return journey there is a right turn to Laerma).

[35 km.] **Archipolis** (pop. 363) is a small village perched on the side of a hill. From here you can continue along Link Route A to Efta Pighes or make a detour to **Psinthos** (10 km.). This village was the scene of the Battle of Psinthos in 1912. When the Italians landed on Rhodes the Turkish garrison withdrew to Psinthos, where the Italians engaged and finally overcame them and occupied the island. From Psinthos you can either return to Rhodes via Kalithies or rejoin Link Route A just beyond Archipolis, whence the route takes you to Efta Pighes.

[40 km.] Right turn to *Efta Pighes* ('Seven Springs'). To get to this meeting of many waters, you bear right off Link Route A for 1·5 km. up a steep, unmade road which descends into a dell. This is Efta Pighes.

There is a busy restaurant with tables set under the trees – some are even perched on flat boulders in the middle of a stream. On the return journey along the unmade road, halt near a sign marked LIMIN. This directs you to the little lake where the seven streams meet, though you have to scramble down a steep path to get there. At the bottom a rushing cascade topples into the pool where the streams converge and the water is carried by conduit to irrigate the orchards and fields around Kolimbia. On returning to Link Route A turn right.

[45 km.] Here Link Route A joins Route 1 just north of Kolimbia. From here you can return to Rhodes or turn right to Lindos.

Link Route B: Aghios Issidoros to Lardos

This is an attractive country road that runs first down the eastern flank of Mt Atavyros and continues through the Laerma–Lardos forests and valleys. Though Thari is recommended only as an optional detour, any traveller passing up the opportunity to see this retiring but remarkable survival of Byzantine and post-Byzantine frescoes is missing one of the newly discovered treasures of Rhodes.

Route From 1·5 km. before Aghios Issidoros (Route 2) to Lardos (Route 1) via Laerma (Thari), Lardos [23 km.].
Bus None is particularly convenient. Bus tours don't yet include Thari in their schedules. A car or taxi is the best solution.

Having taken Route 2 from Rhodes to Embona, proceed from there towards Aghios Issidoros. Approximately 1·5 km. before Aghios Issidoros there is a sharp turn to the left sign-posted to Laerma. Take this turn.

[11 km.] **Laerma** (pop. 676). As you enter the village, take the right turn marked Moni Thari, Profilia and Istrios. The *Church of Aghios Georgios* on the right as you pass through the village has a pretty blue gallery where women worshippers sit. The windows have the same stylized cross as a framework between the panes as at the monastery of Skiadhi and the use of ochre to pick out the oval medallions of paintings of the apostles is also similar to Skiadhi. Outside, note the attractive fenestration of the light sources high in the walls.

From Laerma, you can make a 4-km. excursion to *Thari Monastery*. 2 km. along the Thari–Profilia–Istrios road out of Laerma, turn left until you come in a further 2 km. (along a bumpy but motorable road) to Thari.

It is a small, domed church set in a clearing between low hills. The period of its greatest development was between the ninth and thirteenth centuries and as these were times when the island was plagued by pirates and other raiders, the church is carefully hidden away off the public highway.

The north and south walls contain the oldest, twelfth-century parts of the existing building but there are some ninth-century remains in the ground surrounding the church. It is even possible that an early Christian basilica preceded the ninth-century masonry, but for confirmation of this we have to wait until the extensive study of the church now being done by the Dodecanese archaeologists is complete.

But the great glories of Thari are its wall paintings. The walls of the nave, the dome over the truncated crossing and the apse all carry frescoes and some are of such quality that the experts are convinced that a great artist in the medium once worked in the church – and had his school of followers, too.

Some areas of the church carry as many as four layers of paintings and these are dated *circa* A.D. 1000, 1200, 1500 and 1700. The apse bears three layers: two are of the thirteenth and sixteenth centuries and the still hidden earliest layer may be contemporary with the older frescoes above.

Other points of interest include the following:

(a) There are two periods represented on the dome. Work has been going on to attempt to remove the newer, sixteenth-century frescoes and place them in the museum, thus revealing the older ones which are probably of the late twelfth and early thirteenth centuries.

(b) The frescoes of the nave and part of the crossing are seventeenth century.

(c) On the curve of the roof is some work of the thirteenth century.

The frescoes in the apse are the easiest to see. They depict the hierarchy of apostles in tones of burnt red, ochre, black and cream. Above them is a group of prophets. On the right wall of the apse is a splendid head of a horse, dappled and caparisoned – probably part of a painting of St George or St Demetrius.

From Thari, you can either return to Link Route B at Laerma and then continue for a further 12 km. to Lardos (Route 1) or after completing the 2 km. of track back to the Laerma road you can turn left and join Link Route C taking in Profilia and Istrios on the way (see p. 181).

Link Route C: Apolakia to Gennadi

This short link route between the west and east coasts offers the choice of climbing high into the hills or keeping to pleasant foothills and valleys.

Link Route C(i): From Apolakia (Route 2) to Gennadi (Route 1) via Vati [17 km.].
Link Route C(ii): Via Istrios and Profilia. [26 km.].
Link Route C(iii): Via Arnitha. [21 km.].

Link Route C (i)

This route takes you through pleasant, cultivated countryside to the sea. From Apolakia the road strikes inland, due east.

[2 km.] Here the road forks left and right. Take the left fork which immediately passes over a flat bridge. On the far side of the bridge is another fork. Link Route C (i) takes the right fork to Vati.

[10 km.] **Vati** (pop. 242). This is a pretty village, huddled in a narrow green valley. The population farms (the main crops are vegetables). There is an attractively situated ruined mill with a peaked roof just outside the village.

[17 km.] Link Route C joins Route 1 at **Gennadi.**

Link Route C (ii)

Follow Link Route C (i) to the bridge at 2 km. This variant of Link Route C climbs through fir and spruce to the heights of Mt Skiadhi and then rejoins C (i) before Vati. Starting from the far side of the bridge (see above) take the left fork to Istrios and Profilia.

On the way to these two high villages with their spectacular views you should step aside for twenty minutes to see the – admittedly vestigial – remains of the early-Christian *Church of Aghia Irene.* The font and fountain in Argyrokastrou Square in Rhodes Old Town were found here, also the pillars now standing in the courtyard of the Palace of the Grand Masters.

The site of the ruins lies about 150 yards off the road to the left. The easiest aid to pinpointing the location is to suggest that, between 1·5 km. and 2 km. from the bridge, you look to the right where you will see a wide track sign-posted 'Moni Ioanni'. Approximately 200 yards along the road beyond here there is a line of low pines on the left. Follow a path parallel to the trees, bear left ound a ruined house and then right round a large fig tree. The walls of Aghia Irene are virtually razed to the ground and the interior crackles with stubble and wild thistles. Among all this lie marble columns and the baptistry near which the font was found. A respectable patch of mosaic Byzantine pavement remains in the baptistry: arcs and squares and lozenges and peacocks. Now return to the Istrios road.

7 km.] **Istrios** (pop. 280). Sprawling among hills, its cobbled streets climb towards Profilia.

10 km.] **Profilia** (pop. 180). Sits very high on the mountain ridge; splendid views. From here the road descends 8 km. to join Link Route C (i) just before Vati, passing a left fork to Laerma on the way.

Link Route C (iii)

Another gentle way to the east coast with some good views from Arnitha. Follow Link Route C (i), forking right 2 km. from Apolakia instead of passing over the bridge.

4 km.] **Arnitha** (pop. 222), a picturesque village on the side of a hill, has a number of small churches and a ruined *mosque*. The road connects with that from Messanagros (see p. 157, Route 1). Alternatively you can retrace your steps to rejoin Link Route C (i).

KOS

Kos lies about four hours' sailing time by inter-island steamer to th
north-west of Rhodes. It is the second-largest island in the Dodeca
nese (49 km. long and between 8 and 10 km. wide). It is a lon
narrow tadpole of an island with a flick of its tail at the western en
The northern coast is low-lying and very fertile: this garden islan
produces oranges, lemons, pomegranates, grapes, melons, walnut
almonds, artichokes, tobacco, honey and tomatoes. From the plai
there rises a ridge of mountains which runs the length of the islan
from east to west, and then turns sharply south down the 'tail' o
the tadpole. The south coast, with the exception of a flat plai
around Kardamena and a smaller area below Kefalos, is mour
tainous.

The island has a population of just over 18,000; half the ir
habitants are Greek Orthodox, half Muslim. There are five mai
villages other than Kos: Asfendiou, Pili, Antimachia, Kardamen
and Kefalos. The farthest – Kefalos – is 43 km. from Kos.

There is only one harbour to speak of and this is the delightfu
waterfront of the town of Kos. It looks across some three miles o
water to Turkey. Bodrum (the ancient city of Halikarnassos) :
twelve miles away.

INFORMATION FOR VISITORS

All map references are to Kos Town map (p. 191).

Getting to Kos For information about sea connections see pp. 33, 37.
Air Kos Airport is 27 km. south-west of Kos town (see Route 1, p. 204), close to th
village of Antimachia. Airport buses wait to collect incoming passengers. *Olymp.
Airways* terminal is in Vass. Paulou Avenue (*Map* **12**).
Shipping agents These are to be found for the most part on the waterfront and u
Vass. Paulou Avenue.
Boat trips From Kos you can take day-excursions to Patmos, Kalymnos, Lero
Nisyros, Simi and Rhodes. There are also day-trips to Bodrum on the mainland ♦
Turkey. Book through your hotel or any travel agency.
Public transport Local K.T.E.L. buses call at all five main villages. Note that it ma
not be possible to get to and from the farther villages in a single day. Inquire at th
bus station in Pissandrou Street, off Vass. Paulou Avenue (*Map* **11**). To date, n
local bus goes to the Asklepieion, though tour coaches do.
Taxis The taxi station is on the waterfront, below Platanou Square (*Map* **4**
Drs 6·50 per km. one way only: Drs 4·0 per km. return. (Inflation may have increase
these prices since the time of writing.)

There is a set fare to and from the Asklepieion but for this trip, as for longer journeys, arrange the fare before setting out.

Tourist coaches There are half-day and full-day tours round the island. These can be booked through your hotel or direct with any of the travel agencies below.

Travel agencies A selection of tour agencies includes Viking Tours, Stamadiadis, Olympia, Oskar, Tirinipoulos, Loukopoulos, V Tours, Andriotakis. Many of these are also the shipping agents (see above) for inter-island scheduled boats, day-excursion boats and the vessels such as the *Panormitis II* and *Radiosa* (see Rhodes, Information for Visitors, p. 95).

Car and bicycle hire Car-hire agencies are Safari, Pampris, Smaragdakis and Viking. Scooters for hire at Drs 140 per day from Antonios Pis in Hippokratous Street. But the bicycle is the most common form of Koan transport. Almost everyone cycles. The reason – the town and the northern coast are flat and the roads are metalled. So you can simply walk into one of the many cycle shops or parks scattered about the town and hire a machine as you need one. Rates : approximately Drs 5 per hour for one of the new, small wheelers and a little less for a rattle-trap. N.B. If you leave your cycle while you look at a site or go for a walk, *remember your licence number* so that you will recognize which is your cycle when you return. All bicycles in Greece are licensed.

Information The Tourist Police office is on the waterfront: Viking Tours at Akti Miaouli 2 (on corner of entrance to Port Quarter), Stamadiadis and other tourist agencies – all of them helpful – are on the waterfront or near by.

Mr George Soultanos is an officially appointed, English-speaking guide. Ask for him at the Kos Hotel or through the Tourist Police.

Bank National Bank of Greece, Perikleous Ioanniki Street; Ionian and Popular, on the waterfront.

Post office In Eleftheria Venizelou Street: walk up Vass. Paulou Avenue and turn left (*Map* **10**).

Hospital Hippokratous Street.

Shopping and souvenirs The island has little to offer in the way of local arts. You might like to buy a tin of one of the island jams and chutney-type spreads : *nerantzáki* (made from a fruit like an orange but not so sweet), *tomatáki* (from tomatoes) and *melitzanáki* (from aubergines).

The Kos Gift Shop in Platanou Square contains souvenirs well worth the giving. Though not native Koan work, the jewellery, bowls and ashtrays of vivid or sultry enamel on copper, the silk batik ties and scarves are each of them designed and hand-made by Mrs Cocconi who is usually on duty at the shop when she is not busy in her workshop. Almost everything here is far removed from the run-of-the-mill tourist souvenir.

Spirits, petrol, etc., are at the special Dodecanese rate (see p. 50). English and American cigarettes are less easy to get than on Rhodes and are just as expensive.

There is an attractive fruit and vegetable market (*Map* **9**) at the far side of Liberty Square. Buy your picnic fruit here.

Early closing Thursday.

Festivals See pp. 55–57.

HOTELS

Kos Town

As on Rhodes, most of the hotels are in the main town.

A Class   *Atlantis*. Opened 1973. Situated north-west of Kos town at Lampi, approximately 1·5 km. out of Kos. All 200 rooms have private bathroom, telephone and sea views.

Public rooms, modern but restful and cool, patios with sea views to Turkey and north to Kalymnos. Private beach, swimming pool due to open 1974, swings, etc., for children. Free buses hourly to and from Kos throughout day.

B Class   *Theo-Xenia.* On the beach, looking towards Turkey; built 1961. Probably the most attractively situated hotel in the town: covered with bougainvillaea and climbing shrubs. Only two or three minutes' walk from the centre of Kos. Restaurant, bar, private beach, chairs, umbrellas.

Kos. Opened 1967. All 80 rooms have bathrooms. Lift, bar, restaurant. About 10–15 minutes' walk from centre of town by road parallel with sea and flanked with shady trees.

Alexandra. Built 1969. Just behind the waterfront with views out to sea and inland to the hills. All rooms with private bath, telephone. Restaurant. Roof garden.

C Class   *Zephyros.* From the Theo-Xenia about 1-km. walk from centre of Kos along the tree-lined shore road. A large rambling house turned into a cool and simple hotel. If you ask nicely, they'll let you do your own ironing here. No private baths or showers, but you can have your breakfast under the trees in the garden and wonder whether you might take a trip to Turkey – just across the water.

Milva. Konitsis Place. Built 1971.

Doris. Venizelou Street. Built 1970.

Elli. Themistokleous Street. Built 1971.

Christina. Near the *Kos* and *Zephyros.*

Acropole. P. Tsaldari Street. Just off the waterfront in the centre of Kos. A biggish Greek house turned hotel. Delightful garden.

Veroniki. P. Tsaldari Street.

Koulias. 11 Riga Ferou Street.

Elizabeth. Venizelou Street.

There are several pensions – one of the best known is the *Villa Vassilliades*, on the same shore road as the Theo-Xenia. Rooms on Kos are excellent. Ask the Tourist Police for addresses of pensions and rooms.

os environs

imitra Beach Hotel. This modern B Class hotel was opened in 1973
1d is 7 km. south-east of Kos town on the road to Thermai. You
1n choose to stay in the main hotel (all rooms have private bath or
1ower, telephone, radio and balconies facing the sea) or to occupy
1e of the bungalows. The dining-room is pleasant as are all the
1blic rooms and patios (the chairs, tables, etc., have a sense of
yle unusual in most new Greek hotels). Canoes, pedalloes, chairs
1d umbrellas are available, there are bikes for hire and buses run
1 and from Kos town.

The hotel has a very large expanse of beach (some of it sandy,
1me of it shale) and if you want comfort, a certain isolation and
1lendid sea views it should cater admirably to your needs.

N.B. Some 3 km. out of Kos on the Dimitra Beach road another
1tel, the *Ramira Beach*, is being built. Ask the N.T.O.G. for up-to-
1te information.

utside Kos Town

1t *Kardamena* there is a small D Class hotel, the *Paralia*, also some
1oms to let. A large new hotel is being built approximately 3 km.
1ong the beach to the east of the village. Ask the N.T.O.G. for
1test information about the opening date.

Kefalos village is a mile inland from the wide sweep of Aghios
1tefanos beach and up a steep hill. There is no hotel but a few rooms
1 let here and near the beach. (See p. 186 for mention of a very
1rge beach hotel, halted before completion.)

ESTAURANTS AND ENTERTAINMENT

estaurants and cafés

1n the harbour are the *Limnos*, *Romantica*, *Archontissa* among
1veral others. The *Limnos* is regarded as the smartest and it is
1mong these harbour restaurants that you may find *donér kebáb* and
1atzíki as well as the more usual dishes. A favourite lunchtime
1staurant is the *Drosia* near Platanou Square, with its tables spread
1ut along the roadside under pink and white oleander trees.

Beyond the avenue of palm trees on the way to the *Theo-Xenia* are
1 group of attractive restaurants and cafés under trees and among
1owering shrubs. Of these, try *I Prasini Akti* for a meal (look for its
1d-checked tablecloths and red chairs) and the *Oasis* for evening

coffee and cakes. Farther along still, the *Miramare* restaurant is o the right of the road – unpromising to look at and to date even fai ing to announce its name. But in the modern kitchen meat sizzles o hot plates, the ingredients of salads are chopped crisp and fresh an as in the old *tavérnas*, you are positively welcomed inside to choos what you fancy.

An attractive *kafeneíon* on the waterfront is the *Syndrivani*, oppo site the Town Hall. A little beyond the busiest part of the wate front is a quiet *zacharoplasteíon*, *O Foikos*, where you sit under a enormous tropical tree. There is an arcade of small cafés in Libert Square. Kos also has a *patsás* shop near this square. *Patsás*, the dic tionary says, is tripe soup: it can also be more freely interpreted a offal soup and is eaten with relish by Greek workmen as a mornin staple, much as Scots eat porridge.

Nightlife

Cinemas: *Orfeus* (past Theo-Xenia Hotel and Miramare); *Astro* (waterfront); *Splendid* and *Kentrikon*, both in the town behind th waterfront.

Night-clubs: There is usually a night-club and a discotheque but th names and locations tend to change from year to year. The Touris Police or your hotel will give you up-to-date news.

BEACHES

Stretching from the castle, past the Theo-Xenia Hotel along to th Kos Hotel there is the *Meropis* beach, a long, narrow stretch of sand Beyond here is a wider, better beach, the *Psalithi*. To the north o the harbour is the *Pharos* town beach.

At Kardamena the village is so close to the sea it is practically i it – indeed, the shore is so narrow that you have to walk round th bay a bit before it widens out into a beach proper.

Below Kefalos is a mile to a mile and a half of sandy beach that i the first edition of this book I called magnificent. However, sinc then an immense complex of hotel and bungalows covering at leas a quarter of a mile of the beach has been built. The offence i greatest when you look down on the bay from the Kos road – vandal's hand has destroyed a heart-stirring view of pure sea, san and a tiny islet with a white chapel on it. For lack of money, thi vast hotel has not been completed, so hotel and bungalows stan derelict and I am in two minds whether or not this is nastier than the completed project would be. It is a dreadful example of 'how not to do it'.

Nevertheless, Aghios Stefanos beach is still extensive, the sea still glitters and if you keep severely to the far end of the bay you can avert your eyes from the sprawl. But the Byzantine pillars of the basilica of Aghios Stefanos lie near to the hotel.

There are numerous other beaches around the island; those along the north coast at Tigaki, Marmari and Mastichari are easily accessible. Beaches with the best facilities are those of the Atlantis and Dimitra Beach hotels (see pp. 183 and 185), and the Ramira Beach Hotel (see p. 185) when completed should also be well equipped.

HISTORY OF KOS

The history of Kos is broadly similar to that of Rhodes (see p. 63), and after the arrival of the Knights follows an almost identical pattern.

The ascertainable ancient history of the island begins near Kefalos, in the far west of the island, where a cave has yielded up Neolithic remains. The Achaians colonized the island in the latter part of the fourteenth century B.C., and in about 1100 B.C. there began the same process of Dorian invasion and development as on Rhodes. Later, as a member of the Dorian Hexapolis, the island capital was at Astypalaia, not far from Kefalos. Only when the capital moved to the side of modern Kos in 366 B.C. did Koans begin to wield true power and for some time it was one of the most famous and powerful of Aegean islands. During the fifth century B.C. it became a tributary of Athens, but tried to escape from Athenian rule towards the end of the century. This uprising brought Alcibiades to the island and you can still see part of the wall he built to strengthen the garrison. In 336 B.C. the island was occupied by Alexander the Great.

However, Kos did eventually gain independence and used it to make alliances with Egypt. As one of the consequences, the island became a favourite holiday resort of the Ptolemies of the day and the third Cleopatra even left her jewels on Kos for safe keeping.

Several Roman emperors left their mark. Claudius I, in particular
not only ruled Kos but was its most constructive and generous
benefactor.

Kos was later absorbed into the Byzantine empire until Constantinople fell to the Crusaders in 1204. It then had Genoese rulers for
about a hundred years until the arrival of the Knights of St John
(who, however, did not manage to seize Kos till 1315 – six years
after they took possession of Rhodes). 1523 saw the Knights ousted
by the Turks and thereafter the controlling powers were as on
Rhodes, with the Italians taking over in 1912 and the British holding the island for a brief period at the end of the war until the island
was united with Greece in 1947.

Kos has produced its quota of famous men and many others have
lived and worked here. Both Theocritus, author of the *Bucolics*, and
the painter Apelles – a contemporary of Praxiteles – worked on
Kos, and Herodotus was a Koan on his mother's side. But the
greatest figure of Koan history is Hippocrates. Born in the ancient
city of Astypalaia about 460 B.C., he was one of the figures of antiquity who lives today. What Shakespeare is to Stratford, Hippocrates is to Kos. His sons and grandsons were physicians, the Koans
put his head upon their coins and made a statue of him, and today
land has been bought near the Asklepieion on which to build an
International Hippocratic Institute.

KOS TOWN

Kos – the town, at least – is Greece tamed, domesticated. It has a
population of approximately 8,000. The streets are lined with trees
and every garden blossoms; the houses are painted and well cared
for. It has none of the harshness and bareness of Cycladic islands.
Its houses do not glitter and glimmer under layers and layers and
years and years of whitewash. It is unfair to describe the pleasances
of Kos as suburban, but by comparison with almost every other
Greek island here indeed is something approximating to the comfort and neatness and assurance of a middle class. Kos has had
much effort applied to it to make it good to live in. Many of its
houses and public buildings are less than forty years old, for in

1933 a severe earthquake virtually destroyed the town. It was re-built by the Italians and the result is highly successful of its kind; a planned town yet full of felicities and grace-notes.

The modern Koans describe their town as *ísichos*: 'quiet, calm', they say. They use the word to cast a disparaging stone at Rhodes and one sees what they mean. Here the chaffering and the trading are muted. There are more fishing-boats than international liners; even the pop is Greek pop and not Bob Dylan. It is often so quiet you can actually hear the birds sing. It is no backwater, for Kos is busy and prosperous, but its bustle is that of a small fishing town rather than an international port. But 'times they are a-changing' and Kos town is already somewhat more sophisticated than once it was, with new hotels and flights of new arrivals rather than small clusters stepping from *caïques* on to the waterfront. There are gains among the losses, of course – notably, the number of Dodecanese islands you can visit on day-trips from Kos.

It might be helpful if you think of the town as divided into four areas: the first is the waterfront lying between the Astron cinema and the castle; the second lies immediately behind or parallel to the waterfront: here are Platanou Square, the Mosque of the Loggia, the excavated agora and port quarter, the Museum and Defterdar Mosque, Liberty Square, the shops, the post office, etc. The third area contains all the major excavations other than the agora and port quarter and runs inland from the Theo-Xenia hotel, along Korai Street to the Casa Romana, the theatre, the western excavations and other sites. Finally there is the long stretch of beach and hotels which extends from the castle along the coast to the Kos Hotel and Psalithi beach.

The Asklepieion of Kos lies some 3–4 km. out of town to the south-west.

Your first sight of Kos if you arrive by sea is of the very fine medieval castle which forms one arm of the harbour. Its walls and battlements proclaim it a minor Rhodes (though in some ways it is even more interesting than the military works of Rhodes, for the castle of Kos has not been restored in any way).

A new mole allows all but the very big cruise-boats to land passengers immediately below the castle walls. From here you can walk inland or take a taxi the short distance into the town centre.

PRINCIPAL SIGHTS

Waterfront

If you stand with your back to the water, halfway round the curve of the waterfront, you face the *Town Hall*, or Demarch's office, a low building with a squat tower at one end. On the ground floor of this building are the *Tourist Police office* and the *Customs*.

To your left are the *Castle of the Knights* and an avenue of large palm trees; to the right, the northern arm of the harbour curves round past the Astron cinema. Between the Town Hall and the Astron are most of the waterfront restaurants. Beyond the castle, the road passes under a footbridge and emerges on to the shore road along which are several hotels.

Side streets lead from the waterfront into the town which is centred around *Liberty Square* (*Map* **7**).

Castle of the Knights
Map **1**.

Open March 16th–October 15th 08.00–18.00.
           Sundays and holidays   08.00–13.00.
                                     15.00–18.00.
           October 16th–March 15th 09.00–13.00.
                                     14.30–17.00.
           Sundays and holidays   10.00–13.00.
                                     14.30–17.00.
Entrance Drs 10.

Here the wind blows through the crumbling battlements, and wild flowers toss about the stones in the overgrown keep and bougainvillaea clambers over the escutcheons of Grand Masters. This part-destroyed, unrestored fortress is for wandering in and noting the signatures of time – the grace of a Hellenistic stone vase, the block of marble on which some happy sculptor carved a school of gay, inquisitive and vividly alive fish.

The original fortress was begun in 1450 and was the work of the then governor of Kos, a member of the Venetian Quirini family. It was completed in 1478 by a Genoese governor, de Carmadino. The outer enceinte, part of which runs from the road into the sea where it forms an arm of the harbour, was added after the Turks had attacked the city in 1480. Grand Master Pierre d'Aubusson – that indefatigable military architect – started building in 1495 and the structure was completed by another Grand Master del Carretto in 1514. Both men are remembered within the stones of the castle; the

KOS TOWN

1 Castle of the Knights
2 Platanou Square
3 Mosque of the Loggia
4 Taxi Rank
5 Museum
6 Defterdar Mosque
7 Liberty Square
8 Metropolis Church
9 Market
10 Post Office
11 Bus Station
12 Olympic Airways Terminal
13 Acropolis
14 Hellenistic Temple
15 Altar of Dionysos
16 Baths
17 Casa Romana
18 Theatre

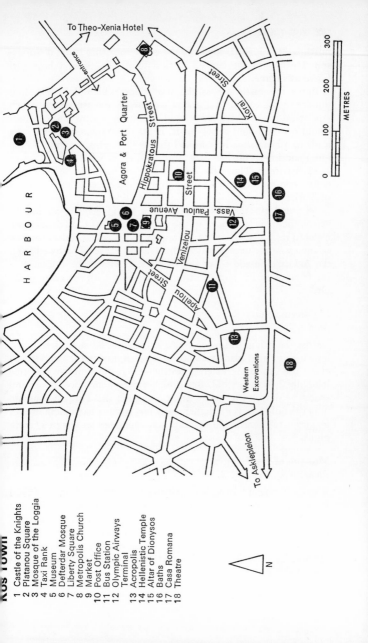

north-west polygonal tower of the outer enclosure is the d'Aubusson Tower and the curved bastion to the south-west bears del Carretto's name.

Enter the castle across the footbridge which links Platanou Square to the castle. In a grassy well below the terrace on which you stand is the *Antiquarium*, with numerous herms and carvings found on the island set about it. From the terrace a sloping way leads to a horseshoe ravelin and thence through a doorway to the inner enceinte. This is a very large open space with a round tower at each corner. The walls are embellished with blazons and you obtain commanding views through the embrasures to the mainland of Turkey.

As you leave the castle, look up at the Hellenistic carving set across the main doorway on the outer side. This is a frieze of the classical masks of comedy and tragedy and much of the stonework of the castle includes pieces of this era and earlier, borrowed from the Asklepieion and other ancient sites. The escutcheon alongside the frieze is of Pierre d'Aubusson, quartered with the arms of the Order.

Platanou Square
Map **2.**

Across the bridge from the castle is Platanou Square. Here is the hunched, twisted plane tree beneath which, says tradition, Hippocrates used to teach. Patently untrue – even this world-weary tree is hardly 2,400 years old. But it makes the square cool, green and shady by day and to sit by night alongside the Turkish fountain under the old tree is a delight; many lovers must have memories of magic shared here amid the scents and aching tenderness of a Greek night.

Mosque of the Loggia
Platanou Square; Map **3.**

Also in Platanou Square is the eighteenth-century Mosque of Gazi Hassan Pasha, or Mosque of the Loggia. It is three storeys high and has a minaret at one end. Arched and fretted windows look down on the square and an elegant exterior staircase of marble climbs to the entrance. The interior is rotting away and you are not allowed in; but, happily, there is news that money may be found to part-restore this graceful mosque.

Agora and Port Quarter (excavations)

Behind the Mosque of the Loggia is the excavated area of the agora and port quarter. Part of the medieval city of the Knights was built over this section of the old city. It is a very confusing excavation and you are recommended to enter it at the point indicated on the map.

This entrance is through two arches joined by an antique pillar and supporting a pediment. On the far side is a small avenue of eucalyptus trees; to the left of the avenue is the *Church of the Panaghia* standing among cypresses and to the right is *Aghios Ioannis*, a restored basilica-shaped Byzantine church with a barrel roof.

At the end of the avenue, look left and you see the medieval *Schlegelholz Bastion* which bears, on the far side, the arms of Grand Master d'Hérédia. Together with a bastion-cum-gateway which stands just off Liberty Square, it marks part of the medieval city boundary. The earthquake of 1933, in destroying many remains of these medieval buildings, revealed a great part of the antique city. Excavation proper began a few years later and the area now exposed is the result.

Standing at the end of the avenue you face a broad path dividing the site. A few yards down it, a track turns right towards the *Mosque of the Loggia* (*Map* 3) and at the end of this path you can see the six pillars of a stoa of the fourth and third centuries B.C.

As you walk down the broad path, you will see a few low walls to the right surrounding some mosaics. These are overlaid with gravel for protection but you may be allowed to sweep away some of this with your hand to look at the mosaic below. Near by this is a ruined basilica from the fifth or sixth century A.D. built upon a Hellenistic site. The remaining excavations include the stylobate and stumps of pillars of what is believed to have been a temple of Aphrodite and, at the far end, two standing pillars of a Roman temple of the second century A.D.

Museum

Map 5.

Open March 16th–October 15th 08.00–18.00 including Sundays and holidays.
October 16th–March 15th 09.00–13.00.
14.30–17.00.
Sundays and holidays 10.00–13.00.
14.30–17.00.

Entrance Drs 5.

Most Italian public buildings of the 'thirties are less attractive than domestic ones, and this is no exception. However, once inside you will find a charming reconstruction of a courtyard which displays a fine mosaic pavement. Statues excavated from various sites stand round all four sides. Look for a *Greek Artemis* and her dog; for an unusual, small statue of a boxer, his arms bound with protectors and wearing bulky gloves; for *Hygieia*, goddess of health and daughter of Asklepios, and for a figure of the god himself. Finally, don't miss a *Dionysos* of such doubtful sex that the guide said to me joyfully: 'See – hermaphrodite, kyria!'

The pride of the museum is the figure of *Hippocrates*, found when the theatre was discovered. I also liked an *Athena*, calcined by fire but emerging pure and unharmed. Look, too, for a headless *Artemis of Ephesus* (about 200 B.C.). She is 'many-breasted Artemis', an Asian fertility goddess far removed from the Greek huntress. She is, in fact, that Diana of the Ephesians whom the silversmiths of Ephesus defended when St Paul preached against the making of false idols. 'Great is Diana of the Ephesians!' cried the Ephesians. (See Acts xix 24 ff., *New English Bible*.)

Liberty Square and Defterdar Mosque
Map **7** and **6**.

Liberty Square is entirely modern and unremarkable except for the eighteenth-century Defterdar Mosque in one corner and for one of the gateways of the medieval period which, overgrown with bougainvillaea, provides a picturesque note. A covered fruit and vegetable market is within the arcaded building behind the mosque: busy and cheerful, this is where to shop for grapes (Koan grapes are delicious), peaches, pears, melons in season.

Hellenistic Temple and Altar of Dionysos
Map **14** and **15**.

On the corner of Vass. Paulou Avenue and Korai Street the remains of a Hellenistic Temple and Altar of Dionysos are sunk below the level of the road. You pass this site en route to the Casa Romana.

Casa Romana
Map **17.**

Open   March 16th–October 15th 08.00–18.00.
           Sundays and holidays   15.00–18.00.
           October 16th–March 15th 09.00–13.00.
                                    14.30–17.00.
           Sundays and holidays   10.00–13.00.
                                    14.30–17.00.

This Roman villa is built on the foundations of a Hellenistic one. It lies on the left of the road leading to the theatre; easy to spot, as it has been reconstructed with blank walls and red tiles edging the flat roof. It has some handsome mosaics, notably a carefully protected seascape with fishes. (Bear in mind that many Koan mosaics of similar or even better quality are now to be seen paving the salons of the Grand Masters' Palace in Rhodes, transported there by Mussolini. A pity in many ways – but at least they are preserved.)

Before you enter the Casa Romana step aside to look at the large *Roman baths* (*Map* **16**) – you won't often see the baked discs of the hypocaust in such good condition as they are here. A few of the marble slabs of the floors are in place, too; some so thin and cracked that they have the texture and appearance of water icing.

Theatre
Map **18.**

From the Casa Romana a short walk along the same road brings you to an avenue of cypresses. Framed between them at the far end is the theatre (Hellenistic) with fourteen rows of seats (the top seven being original). The theatre is in working condition and is sometimes used for performances of classical drama. In the *cavea* at the back was found the statue of Hippocrates now in the museum.

Western Excavations (Roman houses, House of Europa, Baths, Baptistry, etc.)

Cross the road when you leave the theatre and you come to an L-shaped excavated area that is much more rewarding, to my mind, than the remains of the agora and port quarter. In order to start exploring this area at the right point, walk back a few yards towards the Casa Romana (*Map* **17**) until you come to the beginning of the site, parallel with the roofed Roman houses mentioned below. Here, a short flight of steps descends to the site. A low hill rises above the site, crowned with a minaret. This is the old acropolis of Kos (*Map* 13).

At the foot of the steps is about 160 yards of paved Roman way in splendid condition, running parallel with the modern road. The ruins of Roman houses lie between the paving and the slope of the acropolis, many of them roofed over with corrugated iron for protection. You may get the same kind of pleasure from exploring these houses as I do. It is rather like wandering around unfinished houses of an evening when the workmen have gone home. Here it is the tenants who have gone, but their choice of paint and wall decoration are still there to see and it is touching and exciting to stand in a tiny bathroom of the third century A.D. which still displays its owner's choice of terracotta designs and figures on its walls. The Pompeian style of these paintings is echoed in the mosaics of the House of Europa, a little farther west. Some of the mosaics found in this house are now in the museum, but the *Europa and the Bull* still decorates the floor of what was probably the showroom of the house – for the walls also bear some particularly attractive paintings.

Beyond the *House of Europa*, the site takes a dog-leg turn towards the harbour. Here, you come to another length of Roman paving and to the left of this there stretch an assortment of ruins: a large *Roman thermal establishment*, a *gymnasium* with groups of pillars of the re-erected Hellenistic *colonnade* and an early-Christian *basilica*. In the bath is a mosaic of the *Judgment of Paris*, concealed by the usual layer of fine sand. The basilica was built over part of the baths and the most interesting features are the restored marble doorway and, near by, a small marble immersion font sunk into a mosaic floor. Both the doorway and the font belong to the baptistry that formed part of the basilica.

Return now to the paved way and you pass the remains of a row of taverns on the right. Beyond here is a restoration of the latrines of the baths which were set around a peristyle court. At the far end of the site is a large open shed; here, again under sand, is a very large mosaic area. Some argument exists whether the figures are gladiators or duellists. *At the time of writing, this mosaic has been lifted and a new, firmer base has been laid. The mosaic should be back in place within a few months.*

ENVIRONS

Asklepieion

Route There are no local buses to the Asklepieion though coach tours include it.
A taxi will do the journey for a set fare (see p. 182) or you can hire a bicycle or walk.
Avoid the heat of the day: in early morning or late afternoon it is a pleasant and easy
excursion. Leave Kos as for Route 1 (see p. 203). You pass through the village of
Kermetes (note the stone and brushwood huts) and thence up a fine cypress avenue
to the site (4 km.). At Kermetes there are two or three *kafeneíons* and restaurants:
friends report that the first on the right coming away from the Asklepieion provides
an excellent meal.

Open Summer Daily 08.00–13.00 and 14.00–18.00.
Winter Daily 09.00–13.00 and 14.30–17.00.
Entrance Drs 10.

Asklepios – who was he? There are several legends describing the
birth of the god of healing. One says that Apollo saved him from
the pyre on which his mother met her death and took him to Mt
Pelion. There he was cared for by the Centaur, Chiron, and was
taught the rudiments of medicine. Asklepios revealed astonishing
powers of healing, even to the point of restoring the dead to life.
Unwisely, he demonstrated his ability to do this particular feat and
Hades complained bitterly to Zeus. Asklepios, he said, was assum-
ing powers of life and death. Zeus agreed and struck the offender
dead with a thunderbolt.

However, by now Asklepios was firmly entrenched as a divinity
and his fame and cult grew. (It is interesting that his association
with Apollo also invested him with powers of light and fire, probably a metaphoric 'warming back to life'.)

The god is sometimes represented as a serpent (and the serpent
remains the signature of the doctor), but statues of him as a man
translate him into a somewhat conventional, benign, middle-aged
gentleman.

Asklepios had a number of daughters, Iaso, Panacea, Aegle and
Hygieia. The latter was herself the goddess of health.

The two great Greek sanctuaries of Asklepios are at Epidauros
and Kos. Almost to a man, visitors come away from Epidauros
feeling that the very place heals: that a few days spent there would
mend and renew. The Asklepieion of Kos creates much the same
impression though perhaps less powerfully. The ancients had
genius in their choice of sites (the grandeur and Olympian terror of
Delphi, for instance). Believers in the power of environment as an
ingredient of healing, they chose their medical sanctuaries with
equal skill. At Kos, where the temples were dedicated to religion,

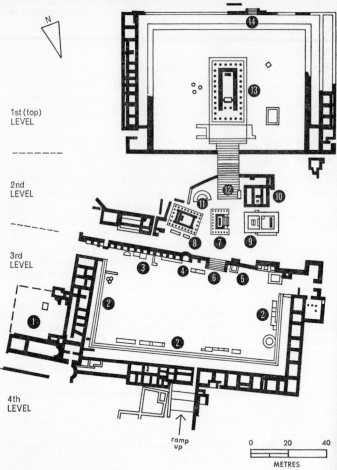

1st (top)
LEVEL

2nd
LEVEL

3rd
LEVEL

4th
LEVEL

ramp
up

0   20   40
METRES

Asklepieion of Kos

1 Roman baths
2 Location of Doric portico
3 Retaining walls with niches
4 Fountain
5 Small Temple of Xenophon
6 Central stairway
7 Altar of Asklepios
8 Ionic Temple of Apollo
9 Ionic Temple of Asklepios
10 Remains of priest dwelling
11 Exedra
12 Grand staircase
13 Doric Temple of Asklepios
14 Steps to woods

health and the arts, you are made free of the view across the sea to the purple mountains of Turkey, and the architectural cunning of the four terraces upon which the sanctuary is built. There is a clatter of cicadas in the woods at your back (even as there was in the third century B.C. when Theocritus wrote of them); a rustle among the long grass turns out to be not Asklepios' snake but a determined wild tortoise.

The Asklepieion was built about the middle of the fourth century B.C. (after the death of Hippocrates in 357). It stands upon the site of an earlier sacred grove. Whereas at Epidauros healing was largely a matter of suggestion, the Asklepieion of Kos was administered very much according to the teaching of Hippocrates. The physician-priests of the sanctuary were so-called descendants of the god and jealous of his rites, but they also knew that the ways of Hippocrates could produce results. Thus a patient was studied as a whole man, his ailment diagnosed and medically treated – but he was also made to observe the various practices of the cult of the god. Purification, fasting, sleeping in the temple on the skins of sacrificial animals, willing a vision of the god to appear in the night and to make a pronouncement which the priests could interpret – these were part of the regimen. On the whole, little was left to chance and patients got the benefit of the cult and of Hippocrates.

A number of famous doctors practised at the Asklepieion; the most renowned was Xenophon, court doctor to the Emperor Claudius. According to Lemprière: 'He enjoyed the emperor's favours ... He had the meanness to poison his benefactor at the instigation of Agrippina ... first with mushrooms and, when they failed, a poisoned feather was thrust down Claudius' throat as an "emetic".'

During the sixth century A.D. the sanctuary was destroyed, possibly by earthquake, possibly by invasion. In the fourteenth and fifteenth centuries the Knights used the ruin as a source of building materials and in 1902 a German archaeological team started to excavate the place; their work was continued by the Italians who are also responsible for the fairly extensive restoration, most of it modelled on the pattern of the Hellenistic sanctuary as it was enlarged and developed over the centuries.

The sanctuary occupies four levels. The fourth, and lowest, is the starting point. To the left rise the remains of the *walls* of first-century A.D. *Roman baths* (*Map* 1). Within the walls are rooms telling of the function of the building, notably, two with the hypocausts of the hot rooms. The next level, the third, has relatively little to show in the matter of ruins as it was probably the working hospital area of the sanctuary and was therefore devoid of temples. Doric porticoes (now vanished) bordered three sides of this terrace (*Map* 2) and the fourth side is faced with a massive retaining wall with blank niches set in it (*Map* 3). This reconstructed wall is broken in the centre by a flight of steps. To the left of the steps is a spring that was running when the sanctuary was built; today it emerges from a tiny Roman *sculpture of Pan* (*Map* 4) and spills over wet green foliage into a deep stone basin. To the right of the steps were a number of mineral springs used by patients seeking a cure. There are also traces of a small *temple* dedicated to Xenophon (*Map* 5).

The central stairway (*Map* 6) leads to the second terrace. This was the province of the priests and their temples. Almost facing you as you step on to the terrace, but a little to the left, are the ruins of the *altar of Asklepios* (*Map* 7). In here were statues to the god and his daughter, Hygieia. (The statue of Asklepios was in the person of Nero, impersonating the god.) To the left of the altar stand seven white marble pillars of a large *Ionic temple of Apollo* (*Map* 8). This is partially restored. It is oriented at an angle to the altar and is peripteral (i.e., the central core of the temple was surrounded by a colonnade of pillars on all four sides). Some of the elaborate and particularly handsome entablature lies upon the ground.

To the right of the altar is the oldest building in the sanctuary: the *Ionic temple of Asklepios* (*Map* 9), built in the third century B.C. It was this temple which housed Apelles' famous painting of Aphrodite Anadyomene. This temple was of a simpler form than the temple of Apollo, having only two columns at either end set between the side walls (*in antis*). Behind this are remains of what is believed to have been a priest's dwelling (*Map* 10).

There remains one more ascent to make; before you start, look to the left of the stairs where you can see a curved *exedra* (*Map* 11), or platform, with niches for statues.

This final staircase (*Map* 12) is grand and monumental. It is divided into two flights and an altar and a third, small flight once rose on what is now a flat landing separating the flights. You emerge upon the level of the immense *Temple of Asklepios* (*Map* 13). In the early second century B.C. it became necessary to enlarge the sanctuary and it was at this time that the Doric temple was built.

One can easily envisage, from the size of the stone and marble stylobate, how it must have dominated the entire sanctuary. The form is peripteral, with six columns front and back and eleven along each side. A porch or *pronaos* had two columns *in antis*. You will undoubtedly note a fine Byzantine capital set upon a Doric drum; this is a reminder that a Christian chapel once stood upon the foundations of the older temple.

Behind the temple are the pine woods; just on the right are a few worn and overgrown steps (*Map* **14**). If you walk up these you are doing what patients over two thousand years ago did – setting off for a quiet, convalescent stroll among the healing air of the pines. The view from here is superb: across Kos and the harbour to Bodrum, and farther across the sea to the peninsula of Knidos to the south (where there was another Asklepieion). Kalymnos lies to the north and west, with the small island of Pserimos between it and Kos.

About 3 km. south of the Asklepieion is the *Vourinna fountain*, the ancient spring which supplies water to Kos even today. It is contained within a 23-foot-high tholos with a dome, the oldest building on Kos. (Though it is not unlike the Mycenaean beehive tombs, it cannot claim to be as old as they are.) You approach the tholos through a passage some 115 feet long.

ROUTES ON KOS

Kos is a very easy island to drive around. Roads are adequate and some are being repaired or slightly rerouted. (See p. 94.) The northern part is flat and the hilly or mountainous areas are not difficult. You can do a round trip in a day quite easily. The following two routes are based on the use of a car or taxi. For details of coach tours see p. 183.

Route 1 extends the length of the island from Kos to Kefalos and Route 2 branches south to Pili and Kardamena. This pair of routes plus detours enable you to visit the five main villages on the island. Distances are from Kos unless otherwise stated.

You can also take a short trip to Thermai, approximately 13·5 km. south-east of Kos. There is a tiny thermal establishment here, open only in the high season.

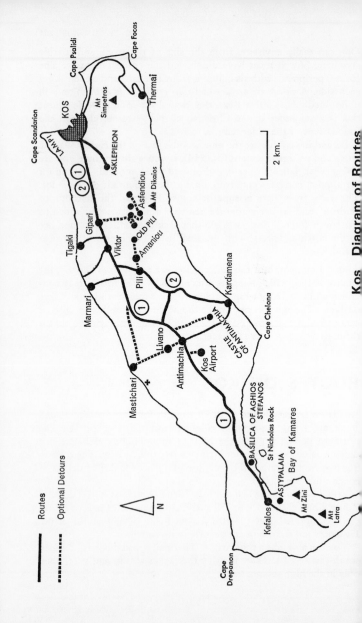

Kos   Diagram of Routes

Routes

Optional Detours

N

2 km.

Cape Scandarion

Cape Psalidi

Cape Focas

KOS

LAMPI

Mt Simpetros

Thermai

① ②

ASKLEPIEION

Asfendiou

Tigaki

Gipari

Viktor

OLD PILI

Mt Dikaios

Marmari

Pili

Amaniou

Kardamena

①

②

Mastichari

Livano

Antimachia

O CASTLE OF ANTIMACHIA

Cape Chelona

Kos Airport

BASILICA OF AGHIOS STEFANOS

St Nicholas Rock

①

ASTYPALAIA

Bay of Kamares

Mt Zini

Mt Latra

Cape Drepanon

Kefalos

Route 1 : Kos to Kefalos

This is the master route, travelling nearly the whole length of the island, taking in many of the major sights on the way and presenting the leisure and pleasure of Aghios Stefanos beach at the end of the journey.

Route Leave Kos by Korai Street in a westerly direction. This road passes the Casa Romana and the theatre. Just beyond the outskirts of the town is a fork. The left-hand road goes to the Asklepieion (p. 197). Take the right fork marked 'Chora'. Drive via Gipari, (Asfendiou), Viktor, (Mastichari), (Castle of Antimachia), Antimachia, Kefalos [43 km.].
Taxi or bicycle hire See pp. 182–83.
Accommodation Rooms to let at Kefalos. (See also p. 185.)

[9 km.] **Gipari.** A left fork here goes 7 km. up the mountainous hillside through tall forests to the five hamlets comprising the village of **Asfendiou**. This village clusters in little groups on the side of *Mt Dikaios* (at 2,780 feet the highest peak on the island). Mt Dikaios, and the Oromedon range to which it belongs, are noted for a profusion of springs, and the area is consequently green and refreshing. From Asfendiou return to Route 1.

[10 km.] A right turn goes to **Tigaki** (swimming: approximately 3 km.).

[11 km.] **Viktor.** Another right turn to the sea past a large salt-lick. The islet visible from this part of the coast is **Pserimos**.

[13 km.] The road forks left here to Pili (see p. 205) but Route 1 continues towards Kefalos. A few hundred yards farther on is a right turn to *Marmari* (beach).

[16 km.] A dust track to the right goes to **Mastichari** in 7 km. Mastichari is a popular seaside hamlet. There is a fine beach of silver sand, a *tavérna* and not much else. (Along the coast to the west are the remains of the fifth-century A.D. Byzantine *Church of Aghios Ioannis*.) The sea at Mastichari, as along all this coast, can be boisterous when the wind is blowing from north or east. To rejoin Route 1 from Mastichari, either return the way you came or drive 4·5 km. inland through **Livano**; one more kilometre brings you to Route 1 at **Antimachia**. The Castle of Antimachia lies on the Kos side of Antimachia, so if you visit Mastichari and then take the Livano road to Antimachia you will have to return along the Kos road for about 1 km. in order to visit the castle.

[24 km.] At this point, approximately 1 km. before Antimachia, you will see a windmill. A little beyond this a path leads off the main road to the left. It is unmarked, with only a cave and a large rock near by to help to identify it. This path takes you in 3 km. to the *Castle of Antimachia* (marked in some local tourist maps as 'Soroko'). The path is perfectly motorable though bumpy – so you should take reasonable care. This very handsome castle was built by the Knights as an aid to fortifying Antimachia and you can judge for yourself how well-positioned it is, commanding both the approaches from the sea at Kardamena and the inland routes. It is a very fine castle indeed, marvellously isolated and correspondingly exciting. It is triangular in shape; the massive walls and battlements remain in good condition. Don't expect, when you arrive at the end of the path and halt below these imposing walls, to see an equally imposing doorway ahead of you. This lies to the left behind a curved bastion – there was a drawbridge at one time. A second portal leads you into the inner keep and over this doorway is the escutcheon of Pierre d'Aubusson as a cardinal. The interior is wild and tumbled yet there remain some beautiful arched doorways and keystones, also some marble lintels. The views are exhilarating and so is the wind. From the castle return to Route 1 and proceed towards Antimachia.

[25 km.] **Antimachia** (pop. 1,540), notable for its production of melons.

[26·5 km.] Left fork to *Kos Airport*. The main road continues over a series of rocky ridges which run diagonally across this narrow neck of land.

[38·5 km.] Soon after this point the road begins to run nearer the sea and soon descends in a number of hairpin bends towards the *Bay of Kamares*. From the summit you can see the chapel on the tiny offshore islet of **St Nicholas Rock** and, near the islet, the ruins of the *basilica of Aghios Stefanos*. Beyond, there rise the mountains that run down the tail of the island, *Mt Zini* in the foreground and the higher *Mt Latra* farther south. On the horizon is the island of **Nisyros** and its satellite rocks, *Giali* and *Strongili*.

[43 km.] **Kefalos** (pop. 1,400). To reach Kefalos you have to go down to sea level and then climb high again, for the village is perched, like hard white sugar, on the heights overlooking the bay.

The way up is pitted with innumerable caves; near by, in a cave similar to these – Aspropetra, or White Rock – were found some Neolithic remains. Kefalos itself is not a very engaging village, and the land around is so harsh and arid that its people reap none of the lusher benefits of luckier settlements on the island. For the most part, therefore, the men of Kefalos are fishermen rather than farmers; some minerals – perlite, for example – are mined and exported.

From the village a track (not good, and it gets worse) runs due south along the ridge of mountains towards the tail. It would be foolish to attempt to take a car too far along, but it is worth going a short way as the air is so dazzling and the views so splendid. It was on the slopes of Mt Zini, far below, that Astypalaia, birthplace of Hippocrates, was situated. The ancient capital was sacked by the Spartans during the Peloponnesian War and in 366 B.C. the capital moved to Kos. Return to Kefalos and descend the hill to sea level where a path forks to the beach and a pleasant *tavérna*. The swimming and sand are superb. A walk along the beach brings you to the ruined basilica of Aghios Stefanos with its pillars. The water between the shore and St Nicholas Rock is very shallow at this point and you can wade a good part of the way across.

Other sites (somewhat vestigial) in the vicinity of Kefalos include the remains of a *medieval castle*, a *Hellenistic temple* and a *theatre*.

Route 2: Kos to Kardamena

This route crosses the hilly spine of the island; the views to the south and east are very rewarding.

Route Follow Route 1 (see p. 203) to just beyond Viktor and continue via Pili (Old Pili), Kardamena [27 km.].
Bus, taxi, bicycle hire For details see pp. 182–83.
Accommodation D Class hotel and rooms to let at Kardamena. Large new hotel being built. (See p. 185.)

[12 km.] Fork left to Pili.

[14·5 km.] On entering **Pili** look for left turn to **Amaniou** (1 km.). This path is marked only by a small and battered sign-post and is easy to miss. To get to Old Pili take this track, which is motorable as far as Amaniou but becomes a mule-track thereafter. At Amaniou stop in front of a blue and white church; the path continues ahead to Old Pili (approximately 3 km. of winding track from this point). Before setting out – or instead of setting out – you can obtain a view of the *Kastró of Old Pili* if you stand on the courtyard at the back of the church and look across to the high ridge of mountain beyond. Below is a spur of rock. On top is perched the Byzantine *kastró* of Old Pili. The ruined village is on the far side of the spur, also a church with fourteenth-century frescoes. Return from here to Pili.

[15 km.] **Pili** (pop. 2,000). Modern Pili has little of interest except an unusual fourth-century B.C. subterranean chamber, the *Charmyleion*, possibly named after a King Charmylos. It lies on the Kardamena side of Pili, so, as you leave the village, look for a group of houses on the left. Here is a sign-post marked 'Charmeli' (the tomb has given its name to the settlement) and a track runs past the houses. A few hundred yards down the track you come to a small *Byzantine church*, built above the tomb. The barrel-vaulted chamber lies below this. On either side are six rectangular, built-in 'coffins' – each occupied by one of the twelve apostles, according to well-endowed local imagination.

From Pili, Route 2 continues south and west to Kardamena. The views along this road are continuously splendid and from the highest point you look down upon the *plain of Kardamena* and across to Asia Minor and Nisyros.

[27 km.] **Kardamena** (pop. 1,230). This attractive fishing village-cum-*caïque*-port (there are very occasional *caïque* connections with Nisyros, for instance) is a popular holiday spot with Greek holiday-makers. The narrow waterfront is packed with *tavérnas* and how many there are becomes very apparent if you happen to arrive on a feast day when the whole village is dancing, feasting, singing and music-making. All this gaiety is of a reasonably unspoilt and local nature, though buses and transistors are not unknown. On other than high days and holidays the village reverts to being quiet and sleepy. The shore line is so narrow here that the beach proper only begins some way out of the village. Kardamena is well off for water and is noted for its tomatoes and tomato juice. To the west are ruins from a *temple of Apollo* and a *Hellenistic theatre*.

From Kardamena you can either return to Kos via the same road or take the climbing inland road to Antimachia and Route 1. At many points on this route you will get tantalizing glimpses of the Castle of Antimachia to the east of the road (see p. 204 for details).

KALYMNOS

Kalymnos lies south of Leros and the northern tip of the island is separated from its close neighbour by a channel under 1½ miles wide. The island is 13 km. long by about 8 km. wide and covers 42 square km. in all. The Admiralty charts spell out its geographical features with meticulous clarity: three mountain ranges running diagonally from west to east across the island, separated by two valleys. Another range of mountains stretches along the full length of the finger of land in the north that points to Leros. The capital is Kalymnos (or Pothia) on the south coast and there are two smaller centres, Myrties, a holiday village at the far end of the Kalymnos valley, and Vathy, a fishing port at the head of the second valley. The population is just under 14,000 and over 10,000 of these live in Kalymnos town. Industries include fishing, sponge-diving and sponge-exporting. There is a fair amount of fruit growing.

Distances on the island are small – just over 8 km. from Kalymnos to Myrties on the far side of the island, for instance. For this reason no routes are given, but four excursions from Kalymnos town are suggested: to Vathy, to Myrties, to the islet of Telendos and to the cave of Kefalos.

INFORMATION FOR VISITORS

Getting to Kalymnos For information about sea connections with other islands, see pp. 33, 37.

Shipping agents All are on or near the waterfront.

Boat trips You can engage a boat from a willing fisherman. Popular boat trips are to the cave of Kefalos and to Vathy and from Myrties to Telendos Islet. Ask police or boatmen on waterfront.

Public transport Daily bus to Vathy and return from stop behind clock tower square. No bus to Myrties.

Taxis Taxi station in the square at far end of shopping street (see p. 213). Taxis are the common transport of the island and five or six housewives, at the end of a shopping trip to Kalymnos, will pile into a taxi to return to Chorio or Myrties. The shared price is rarely more than Drs 7 each.

Information In Town Hall, on clock tower square.

Banks The National Bank and the Ionian and Popular Bank are both just off the waterfront.

Post office Clock tower square.

Shopping and souvenirs Sponges, of course. These are magnificent but, because men risk their lives to obtain them, expensive. Look for the 'confection' of sponges sold by some dealers, a veritable bouquet of sponges and, like a bouquet, wrapped in cellophane. The dark Kalymnos honey has been famous ever since Ovid spoke well of it, but it is heavy and liable to spread itself over your belongings unless carefully wrapped. The Astoria café on the waterfront generally has some in stock.

There are also several tourist souvenir shops. The 'Greek Corner' is staffed by a Kalymniot who speaks good English and is very helpful and informative.

Early closing Thursday.

Festivals As national festivals (see pp. 55–57). On Kalymnos there is also a spring gathering (April 10th–20th) to bless the men and boats before they set off for the sponge-fishing season and a late summer celebration to welcome them back. Most Kalymniot sponge-divers of today work off the North African coast.

Museum The small museum is closed pending removal to a new home, now being built.

Public W.C.s On far side of clock tower square.

HOTELS

Kalymnos town and environs

C Class *Thermai.* On the waterfront. Typical Greek hotel of its kind; unpretentious.

D Class *Chrystal.* Also on the waterfront; adequate hotel of its type.

Alma. Inexpensive. No private bathrooms. Hot and cold running water in rooms.

Iamatika Thermonika. This is a tiny spa hotel about 20 minutes' walk south of Kalymnos along the coast. It offers sulphur baths and hot springs, and has a small restaurant and eight bedrooms. It is on the sea and there is a small pebbled beach.

N.B. A large, new, A or B Class hotel is being built on the waterfront. Ask the N.T.O.G. for up-to-date information.

Panormos (which includes the districts of Linaria and Kandouni)

C Class *Drossos.* Opened 1973. Cool, spacious, splendidly placed about Kandouni Bay. All rooms have private bathrooms, some look out to sea, some inland. Large patio, dining-room door from hotel down path to beach. Garden at back with fruit trees, seats, mini-golf. Swimming pool should be ready by 1974. Endearingly eccentric furnishing of public rooms. Reliable report regards this as a delightful hotel run by delightful people.

Plaza. Stands in own garden off beach. Restaurant.

D Class   *Katina Beach*. Near the Drossos. A largish house, 26 beds. Pleasant balcony off salon. No restaurant but breakfast provided.

Myrties

C Class   *Delfini*. Painted blue and white, inside and out, clean, attractive. All rooms with private bathrooms. No restaurant but breakfast provided. Situated just above beach, fine views across to Telendos.

D Class   *Myrties*.

Pensions

At Panormos
Kypreos. New. Inexpensive. No restaurant.
At Myrties
Marilena. (Bungalows.)
At Masouri
Marias.

Rooms (Kalymnos town and elsewhere)

Apply to the police. There are a fair number of rooms to let in Kalymnos town; those belonging to George Psarramotis are excellent.

RESTAURANTS AND ENTERTAINMENT

Restaurants and cafés

O Paradissos is a restaurant in a cool white courtyard just off the waterfront. Also recommended is *Kappa's*. Tables under the trees and across the road alongside the water. Good food, good value for money.

The various cafés and bars around the harbour include the older, more traditional cafés, and a number of modern ones. Recommended for an excellent, old-style Greek breakfast (rolls crisp and early morning fresh, honey and butter on the same plate, good tea, Nescafé or *métrio*) is the little establishment next door but one to the Thermai hotel. It has no name but the owner's name is above the door – Magkli.

There are a few beach restaurants on either side of the island at Linaria, Myrties, etc.

Nightlife

Two cinemas, both in the square housing *O Paradissos* restaurant.

BEACHES

The most accessible are on the west coast at Linaria, Kandouni, Myrties and Masouri.

HISTORY OF KALYMNOS

Together, Kalymnos and Leros are believed to be the Kalydnian Isles of Homer's Catalogue of Ships. Michael Volonakis, in *The Island of Roses and her eleven sisters*, quotes an ancient theory that the name 'Kalydnai' was possibly an amalgam of two Greek words '*kalai udnai*' or 'good comrades', certainly a fair description of the nearness of the islands to each other.

The first people to settle here were probably Karians from south-west Asia Minor. In the eleventh century B.C. the Dorians arrived and, as elsewhere in the Dodecanese, they were the most important of pre-Classical influences. Little is known about the island history during the three or four centuries immediately preceding the birth of Christ except that Kos held some kind of authority over it. In time, Kalymnos was absorbed into the Roman Empire and later entered the sphere of Byzantium. From the Middle Ages onwards, the island history was very similar to that of Kos, and the Venetians, the Knights of St John and the Turks have all placed their signatures on the island.

An earlier chapter has noted Kalymnian hostility to Italian rule. A cheerful outward sign of this is the many houses painted alternately blue and white, the Greek national colours. Surely a Greek manifestation of 'they only do it to annoy, because they know it teases'? A more serious outbreak of antagonism occurred in 1935 when the islanders rebelled against Mussolini's attempt to ban Greek in the schools and to introduce an independent Church of the Dodecanese.

Visitors are sometimes puzzled to hear Kalymniots remark that they are going to 'Brosta' because 'Brosta' isn't on the map. The solution is that the word is simply the local, idiomatic term for the 'front' or Myrties side of the island (*embrós* = 'in front of'). 'Back' is Kalymnos town itself.

KALYMNOS TOWN

Some years ago Charmian Clift wrote an admirable book about Kalymnos and called it *Mermaid Singing*. The picture she painted was harsh and true. A rocky island and bare. An island of crippled sponge-divers and crippling poverty. An island hard on men and women alike; riddled with superstition, crying out for work. Somehow, it did not seem that Kalymnos had much to offer the holiday-maker.

PRINCIPAL SIGHTS

The truth is that Kalymnos has a great deal to offer, but you must accept it for what it is. It is poor and it is rocky, but the hills are austerely beautiful in the late afternoon when their bones are cast into deep violet shadow. It is arid and eroded, but lying between the mountain ranges are two valleys and both are abundantly blessed with fruit and flowers. The houses of the waterfront are tall and Victorian and wear a good deal of wrought iron (you will find decorative iron lunettes above the doors here as on Patmos). The architectural appearance of the town as you view it from the sea is extraordinarily appealing. Blocks and rectangles mount one upon the other, a child's town, neatly painted in blue and green and white and ochre.

The town lies in an amphitheatre and climbs up either side of the valley, curving round the harbour like a pincer. A mountain crag above the northern slopes acts as sentinel, dizzyingly pure and inviolable in sunlight, a brooding mass when night falls.

Though the island is not yet ready for any large influx of foreign tourists, it is very popular with Greek families, so there are a fair number of excellent rooms to let. The harbour is large and the waterfront long; here are shops, *tavérnas* and an open square – the 'clock tower square' of this chapter – in which stands the delightful eighteenth-century *church of Aghios Christos* (of which more later), a free-standing *clock tower*, the *Town Hall*, the *Post Office* and

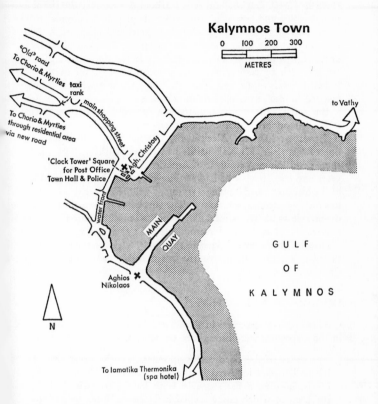

the *Police Station*. Running inland at the far end of this square is Venizelou Street, the main shopping street, and at the top of it you come to another square. This is the town taxi station where a considerable number of taxis wait for custom. From the square a right fork takes the 'old' road to Chorio and Myrties, while a left fork passes through the residential part of the town and you can then bear right and rejoin the 'old' road or continue straight ahead to take the 'new' road to Myrties.

The town is well supplied with neo-Byzantine churches. Among them is *Aghios Christos* and it is a treasure. Outside, the dome is powder-blue and sits on a drum which is pierced by circular discs of stained glass. Inside, the church is gold and blue and brown; colours that give it an oddly Carolingian air. There are four large arches on pendentives, twelve windows in the dome and, painted on the arch of ceiling over the iconostasis, two Greek crosses linked to each other by a lozenge. The gallery has elegant, bow-fronted 'boxes', each with painted panels.

But what adds to the unusualness of Aghios Christos is that it is also an art gallery. The artists represented are nearly all Kalymniots: Manglis, Alachouzos, Oikonomou, Kalafilaikis. On one of my visits, Mr Kalafilaikis was there, working high up on some scaffolding. A resident of America, he comes home every few years and on this visit he had set himself to touch up the gold leaf of the interior. 'And I am also trying to get the priests to use a little less *liváni* – incense, you know. The smoke soils the paintings and the marble so badly. I would like them to use just enough for people to *smell* the idea, you understand.' He did not sound very hopeful.

None of the other churches in the town, not even the vast *Aghios Nikolaos* on the hill above the main quay, can touch Aghios Christos.

DIVERS OF KALYMNOS

Charles Newton describes in *Travels and discoveries in the Levant* how, in 1854, sponges were brought to the surface:

> The cause of the dearness of sponges ... is the great risk of life and capital incurred in the first instance. The diver decends, holding a flat stone in both hands, to assist him in sinking, on which stone a cord is fastened. When he gets to the bottom he puts this flat stone under his arm, and walks about in search of the sponges, putting them in a net hung about his neck ... he then pulls the cord as a signal, and is drawn up again.

Until relatively recently this was still the method; now the islanders buy such modern diving equipment as they can afford, though even this, according to Ernle Bradford, is often old and in poor condition. The net – a long bag fixed to a circular frame and slung round the neck – is still used.

EXCURSIONS ON KALYMNOS

Excursion 1 : Myrties

This 7·5-km. excursion takes you to the best and most accessible beaches on the island.

Route See map of Kalymnos town for exit routes to Chorio and Myrties. N.B. This excursion route follows the perfectly good, motorable 'old' road, as the new one by-passes Chorio and other features of interest.
Accommodation See list of hotels and pensions on p. 210.

As you leave Kalymnos town look to the left and in a very short while you see three old, but now restored, windmills on a hillside. Above those are the remains of a *Castle of the Knights*, also a small *church*. This acropolis, with its stout walls and commanding height, was one of those sanctuaries to which Greek villagers fled when pirates attacked their island. Throughout the Aegean you will find, time and again, these inland *kastros* which sheltered the villagers in time of danger. The population lived and worked on the land or in the ports when things were quiet, but retreated behind walls until the invaders went on their way.

[2·5 km.] **Chorio**, the old village (pop. 2,600 approximately), lies in the flattest part of the valley, overlooked by high hills. *Mt Parasiva* (sometimes called Profitis Ilias) to the north is nearly 2,230 feet high. In the village is a *church* with a very old iconostasis. Here also is another *castle* which acted as bolt-hole during the Middle Ages and later.

[4 km.] To the right of the road is the site of ancient *Damos*. This site was partially excavated by Charles Newton in the middle of the nineteenth century. The site is extensive and lies on either side of a dried-up stream and has little to show today for some rather hot and tiring scrambling. However, the assiduous should be able to find remains of a theatre, rock-cut tombs (Mycenaean) and the site of a *temple of Apollo*. With less endeavour, you can see a third-century B.C. *burial chamber* on the roadside between Damos and the Plaza Hotel. It is in a small green patch, is overgrown with morning glory and a plaque marks it as an ancient site.

[5·5 km.] **Linaria** (pop. 480). With Kandouni, Linaria is part of the district known as Panormos. The road descends into the *Bay of*

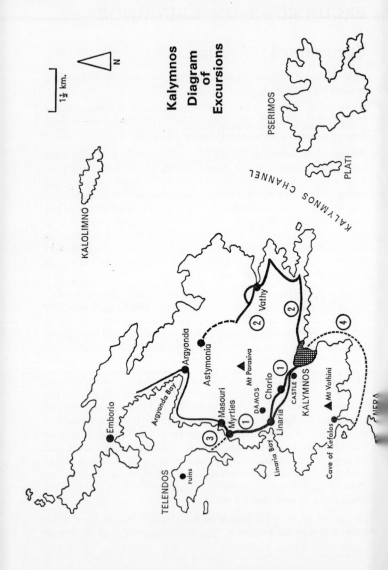

Kalymnos
Diagram
of
Excursions

N

1½ km.

KALOLIMNO

PSERIMOS

PLATI

KALYMNOS CHANNEL

Emborio

Argyonda Bay

Argyonda

Astymonia

Mt Parasiva

DAMOS

Chorio

Masouri

Myrties

Linaria

Linaria Bay

CASTLE

KALYMNOS

Cave of Kefalos

Mt Vothini

Vathy

TELENDOS

ruins

NERA

Linaria which is divided into two by an outcrop of rock known as *Kandouni*. *Kandouni beach* is the sandier, has some beach restaurants and offers the better bathing.

The road continues to Myrties and Masouri through vineyards and groves of cypress, lemon, pine, olive, orange, fig, tangerine, oleander and eucalyptus. It is all so varied and so plenteous that one wonders if one has not, somehow, strayed into Marvell's sensuous land:

> What wondrous life in this I lead!
> Ripe apples drop about my head;
> The luscious clusters of the vine
> Upon my mouth do crush their wine;
> The nectarine and curious peach
> Into my hands themselves do reach;
> Stumbling on melons, as I pass
> Ensnared with flowers, I fall on grass.

7·5 km.] Myrties (pop. under 60). This residential and holiday village has two hotels (see p. 210). Its beaches are rockier than those of Masouri and swimmers will find the short walk to Masouri worth while. At Myrties is the jetty whence you can get a boat across to the islet of Telendos (see below).

8·5 km.] Masouri. There is little here except the sandy beach and a few houses.

From Masouri the road ceases to be metalled and continues as a somewhat rough-going track to **Argyonda.**

Excursion 2: Vathy

Although there is less of historical interest to see on the way than in Excursion 1, the views from the coast road to Vathy are superb. This part of the coast is deeply indented and far below the road lie bays of jade and aquamarine, water glittering, pure and barely stirring.

Route You can get to Vathy by road [12·5 km.] (see map of Kalymnos town for exit route) or you can hire a boat. If you approach by sea you should ask the boatman if he is prepared to take you to the entrance of the Grotto of Daskaleios, a cave where numerous Neolithic and Bronze Age artifacts were discovered and where stalactites and stalagmites probe towards each other from ceiling and floor.

Vathy village (pop. 700) embraces three smaller villages: **Rina** on the coast, **Platanos**, inland, and **Metochi**, beyond Platanos (The entrance to the cave of Daskaleios is in the little bay of Rina. Some antiquities are to be found. There is a '*throne*' carved from the rock and, on the far side of Platanos, some *cyclopean walls* which are clearly visible from the road. However, the charm of Vathy is in its beauty rather than its history, and groves of tangerines do the immediate hinterland.

Higher up the valley beyond Metochi, the fertile soil bears figs. The metalled road ends at Metochi to become a mule track to Stimenia. Beyond this point there is no road and to reach the tiny settlement of **Argyonda** you must take the track from Masour (see Excursion 1).

From Argyonda the mountains that make up the northern extremity of the island fall away steeply into the sea and though there is a track of sorts to the hamlet of **Emborio** a boat from Myrties is far more practical. Near Emborio is a Mycenaean *tomb*.

Excursion 3: Telendos Islet

It may seem a paradox to write that possibly the most exhilarating feature of Kalymnos is its satellite isle, Telendos. You first sight Telendos (pop. 75) from the summit of the high hill above Myrties, on your way from Linaria. Below you lie the little village and its sunny shore, a boat or two bobbing at the wooden jetty and the narrow channel of sea between island and islet blue and glittering. Beyond is the 1,300-foot peak that is Telendos, virtually a mountain in the sea. On its shore is a fishing village, near enough to be seen, distant enough to be desired. It is irresistibly tempting.

Route By small motor-boat from Myrties, probably the *Michal*: on a windy, sunny morning this is an exultant trip, the boat tricked out in blue-and-white stripes over its engine cover (Greek national colours again). Time: about 10 minutes on a calm day; on the blustery day of my visit about 20 minutes.

In the channel between Kalymnos and Telendos there lies a sunken city, believed to have been uprooted in some long-past disaster. An American diving expedition recently explored the area and is reasonably certain from the relative positions of roofs and founda-

ions that an earthquake was the cause. You can't see anything
rom the surface, alas. I spent some time craning over the side of
he *Michal*, but the evidence lies deep.

There is a tiny fishing community on Telendos and a *tavérna*
where you can get a drink and a very simple meal. The scene from
ere across to Kalymnos on a fine morning is marvellous: in front
f you on Telendos hang vivid orange, red and yellow nets, and
cross the water the deeply overhung and undershot mountains
f Kalymnos are plunged in velvety, black-grape shadows. The
illagers can direct you to the local ruins: those of the *Monastery
f Aghios Vassileos* and also of a medieval *castle*.

Back at Myrties, people will urge you to stay till evening because
t sunset the islet takes on the features of a woman. The story you
re told is that 'many years ago' a king and his queen lived on
Telendos and the king deserted her. Ever since, she has remained
n the islet, grieving and looking out to sea for his return. I like to
hink that, perhaps, unknown to her, the king remained on the
hore of Myrties, spellbound and for ever gazing at her profile. It
s certain that those who today set their eyes upon her will ever
fter carry in their minds the image of Telendos, the mountain isle.

Excursion 4: Cave of Kefalos

The cave lies to the south and west of Kalymnos town and below
Mt Vothini. Kalymniots may look blank if you ask to go to
Kefalos; ask for Vothini, however, and they will understand. The
boat trip from Kalymnos town takes about 40 minutes. Thence
by mule. Kefalos is a stalactite cave (entrance: Drs 5), and once
served as a sanctuary of Zeus.

LEROS

Leros has barely 7,000 inhabitants. It is gently mountainous (the highest peak, Mt Kalavati, is only 1,073 feet high) and the coastal lowlands are fertile, allowing vineyards and orchards to flourish. The island is 9 miles long by 4 miles wide. The sea cuts deeply into the land as it does at Patmos, and two necks of land are only 1 km wide. There are four large bays, Partheni in the north, Gourna and Porto Lakki on the west and Alinda on the east. Two smaller bays are Panteli and Xirokampos.

INFORMATION FOR VISITORS

Getting to Leros For information about sea connections with other islands, see pp. 33, 37.

Shipping agents The main agent is at Platanos but you can book at Porto Lakki too. The agent usually sits at a desk in a *kafeneion* near the jetty but, as this location is likely to change from time to time, inquire from local inhabitants.

Boat trips Negotiate with fishermen on waterfront at Porto Lakki or Platanos. During the summer months, inquire about local cruises to Kos, Kalymnos, Bodrum (Turkey).

Taxis A fair number. Most assemble near the quay at Porto Lakki; they are also available at Platanos and Aghia Marina.

Information The main police office is at Platanos but there is a squad of local police in the town.

Early closing Thursday.

Festivals Carnival reaches its height on the Sunday before Orthodox Shrove Monday; the latter, incidentally, is known as *'Káthará Deftéra'* or 'Clean Monday'.

HOTELS

Porto Lakki

C Class   *Leros.* Large, echoing, Italian-built. Restaurant. Views across bay.

Pension *Angelou's Guesthouse.* (Agent: Greek Tourist Agency, Morley House, 320 Regent Street, London, w1.)

Platanos and Aghia Marina

Flisvos. 'Restaurant with rooms'. Simple, Greek. (Aghia Marina) Hotel under construction (*Platanos*).

Alinda

B Class *Xenon Alindon*. New, modern, but only about five rooms
as yet. Restaurant.

RESTAURANTS

Porto Lakki

A beach restaurant about 1 km. from the town provides a typical
beach lunch. Otherwise, Porto Lakki has almost nothing to offer
except one or two disheartened cafés, and you will do well to eat at
the *Leros Hotel* restaurant.

Platanos

A few *tavérnas* and cafés.

Alinda

Two beach restaurants and the restaurant of the *Xenon Alindon*
Hotel.

BEACHES

The island is not very well off for sandy beaches. Porto Lakki,
Xirokampos, Alinda Bay and Gourna Bay provide the best and
most convenient swimming.

HISTORY OF LEROS

Leros shares its earliest history with Kalymnos; it was one of the
two Homeric Kalydnian isles and it also received the Karians as its
first settlers. Probably on account of its deep and sheltered bays and
many coves, it later became a favourite haunt of corsairs. In this as
in the rest of its medieval history, the island story is very similar to
that of the Dodecanese as a whole.

Leros has one very individual oddity, however. Property is
inherited through the female line and thus the real estate of the
island is almost all in the hands of women. How this came about is
not fully determined, but Ernle Bradford suggests that it may in
some way be an outcome of the Lerian cult of Artemis (see below).

The recent past of the island is of vivid interest. During the last war, Rhodes, Kos and Leros featured largely in British plans to control the Aegean and the Anatolian coast. After the fall of Italy, several Dodecanese islands were occupied by British units, the Italians acquiescing. Of these Kos and Leros were the most important. We failed to occupy Rhodes and this failure rendered our hold on the other islands very uncertain. Thus, on November 16th, 1943, Leros fell. In *The Second World War* (Vol. 5) Churchill writes:

> The garrison was alert, but too few. The island of Leros is divided by two narrow necks of land into three hilly sectors, to each of which one of our battalions was allotted. Early on November 12 German troops came ashore at the extreme north-east of the island, and also in the bay south-east of Leros town. The attack on the town was at first repulsed, but that afternoon six hundred parachutists dropped on the neck between Alinda and Gourna Bays and cut the defence in two. Previous reports had stated that the island was unsuited for paratroop landings and the descent was a surprise. Very strong efforts were made to recapture the neck. In the last stages the garrisons of Samos, the 2nd Royal West Kents, had been dispatched to Leros but all was over. They fell themselves a prey. With little air support of their own and heavily attacked by enemy aircraft, the battalions fought on till the evening of November 16, when, exhausted, they could fight no more.

Churchill's feelings are expressed in a telegram to Anthony Eden dated November 21st: 'Leros is a bitter blow to me ...' And elsewhere he commented: 'Leros fell on Nov. 16, the British losses in the whole business being about 5,000 and the enemy scoring his first success since Alamein.'

PORTO LAKKI

Though the capital, Platanos, with its small port of Aghia Marina, is on the east coast, passenger boats are much more likely to disembark you at Porto Lakki on the west. Porto Lakki (pop. 1,700) is a weird survival. The great depth of the bay has had understandable attractions for modern navies, and first the British and then the Italians set up a naval base on its shores. Under the Italians, the base grew into a vast establishment and was, indeed, the only reason for the existence of the town. Now the place has lost any purpose in life. Gigantic Mussolini-inspired public buildings echo emptily along the shore, all of them peeling and dreary. The town and its people are expiring of ennui in this pointless desolation. (Fortunately Platanos is considerably livelier and if you have the misfortune to arrive at Porto Lakki don't judge the island too quickly or too harshly.)

The still, lake-like bay is undoubtedly the most attractive feature of the appropriately named Porto Lakki. The Customs House, the Harbour Master's office and the main hotel of the island, the *Leros*, are all on the waterfront. On the opposite side of the bay is another series of buildings, once hotels and naval schools.

As you enter Porto Lakki harbour you can see how effectively the Frankish *kastró* high above Platanos commands the approaches to the island.

A number of smaller islands which are administered by Leros include Peganisi, off the south-east coast, Farmakonisi to the north-east, and, far to the west, the lonely and unpopulated islands of Levitha and Kinaros. These two are stepping-stones to the most easterly of the Cycladic islands, Amorgos.

EXCURSIONS ON LEROS

Excursion 1: Platanos, Alinda and Gourna Bay

Route Turn left off Porto Lakki waterfront and leave the town via a wide, tree-lined avenue. After about 1 km. the bay of Panteli appears to the right and there is a splendid view of the castle at Platanos. Continue through Platanos to Alinda and then cross the island to Gourna Bay [6 km.]. Total distance from Porto Lakki: approximately 6 km. excluding detours.
Accommodation Modern hotel at Alinda. Small restaurant. (See p. 221.)

From the road above Panteli, there are views down into the bay and left towards Platanos with its houses climbing up either side of a narrow valley. From here you can also see that there is a row of ruined mills and watch-towers in line with the castle.

[3·5 km.] You reach Platanos.

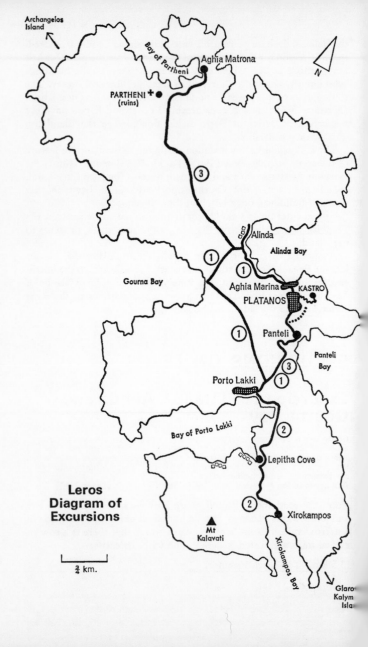

**Leros
Diagram of
Excursions**

¾ km.

PLATANOS (LEROS TOWN)

Platanos is a busy, fairly thriving town (pop. 2,690 with Aghia Marina) and has a vitality sadly missing at Porto Lakki. The approach to the castle is up a steep and narrow cobbled lane which challenges the taxi-driver with the twin hazards of extreme narrowness and multiple hairpin bends. Near the top you can look down on the rooftops and see that there is also a long, long series of steps from the town to the castle.

Principal sights

The *Church of the Panaghia* is at the castle entrance. It has been badly damaged and though old is not particularly interesting.

The *castle* was built by the Byzantines and was restored and strengthened by the Knights of St John. The best reason for visiting it today is that from the look-out (in use during the last war) it offers some magnificent views. You can look back to Porto Lakki, across the island to the Bay of Gourna and beyond Platanos to Aghia Marina and Alinda. Far to the east is the coast of Turkey.

Back in Platanos, continue down another cobbled street past a school and so enter **Aghia Marina**. (In effect, Platanos is the inland and larger part of the town and Aghia Marina the port.) The small square on the waterfront is pleasant and there is a restaurant with rooms, the *Flisvos*.

From Aghia Marina continue round the bay towards Alinda. On the way is the British War Cemetery in which rest the Allied dead of the battle for Leros in 1943.

[4·5 km.] **Alinda** is no more than a narrow beach with a small restaurant, a few houses and the *Xenon Alindon* hotel.

From Alinda to Gourna Bay, retrace your steps past the Xenon Alindon for a few hundred yards and then turn right. Here an unmade road runs past the German War Cemetery under some pine trees. The road soon forks left (the right fork goes to Partheni, see Excursion 3) and crosses the narrow neck of land between east and west coast, passing through a wide fruit-growing valley.

[6 km.] *Gourna Bay* is large and wide, though the beach is not outstanding and is marred by scrubby grasses and shale. The water, however, is shallow and clear.

Return to Porto Lakki by the same route or by another unmetalled road which cuts across the hills and rejoins the Platanos–Porto Lakki road about 1 km. from the port.

Excursion 2: Xirokampos

Route From Porto Lakki follow the road round the head of the bay. At Lepitha cove bear left inland to Xirokampos [4 km.].

The road soon turns gently downhill through a shallow valley in which are several villas. At the far end of the valley is the hamlet of Xirokampos. It is a fishing settlement and the *tavérna* and *kafeneíon* make a hospitable viewing-base. The northern finger of Kalymnos lies directly ahead, with the satellite isle of **Glaros** in front of it. Together they so block the mouth of Xirokampos bay as to make it appear landlocked. The channel between Kalymnos and Xirokampos is the narrow Leros Strait.

Excursion 3: Partheni Bay

Route From Porto Lakki proceed as for Excursion 1. Just before entering Alinda turn left and in a short distance you come to the fork to Gourna Bay already mentioned. Take the right fork and follow the road north and west [12 km.].

Partheni Bay is another deep and isolated bay which drives deeply into the body of the island. There are some ruins near by and from the shore you look out towards the small island of **Archangelos** which shelters **Partheni** from the worst of the winds.

The ruins are of a *temple to the Virgin* (hence Partheni), but Bradford asserts that it is almost certainly wrong to assume that this virgin was Christian. She is much more likely to be the Artemis of Leros, a virgin goddess of fable to whom the islanders built a temple. The fable tells how the daughters of Oeneus, grieving incessantly over the death of their brother Meleager, were taken pity on by Artemis. She transformed them into Meleagrides (guinea-fowl) and took them to Leros where they sat upon a mountain top and continued their lament. The guinea-fowl thereupon became sacred (that is, Artemis was worshipped in the form of a guinea-fowl) and were bred in the area around the temple.

On the site of the temple ruins you will also find the remains of a *Byzantine church*. A little before the road peters out there is a tiny settlement which the Italians called **Porto di Rina** and the Greeks **Aghia Matrona,** probably yet another echo of the influence of the virgin goddess of Leros.

PATMOS

Patmos is an island of extremes. It is the northernmost of the islands of the Dodecanese, one of the smallest, one of the most arid, one of the most famous, certainly the most holy. It has a mere 25 miles of coastline and there are two main centres – the port of Skala (pop. 1,117) and, 750 feet above it, the monastery and fortified town of old Patmos, commonly called Chora (pop. 975). The population of the whole island is 2,500. There are only four roads. One goes north to Kambos, one south to Grikou (beaches and *tavérnas* at both places) and one mounts the hill to Chora, 2 km. from Skala. The fourth is a branch of the Chora road and winds round the base of the monastery and thence down the hill to join the coast road to Grikou.

INFORMATION FOR VISITORS

Getting to Patmos For information about sea connection with other islands see pp. 33, 37.

Shipping agents On and around waterfront and main square.

Boat trips To Kambos and Grikou and round the island.

Public transport Bus to Chora and Monastery from Skala, also to Kambos and Grikou beaches in season.

Taxis A few only. Assemble on waterfront. Arrange fare before setting out.

Information Police Station near jetty.

Guides Monks of the Monastery of St John.

Estate agent Mr Capranis, Skala, Patmos.

Banks Agents of the Bank of Greece and the Ionian and Popular Bank carry on business in shops in the main square.

Post office In the main square, Skala.

Early closing Thursday.

Festivals The monastery observes not only its own saint's day (May 21st) and national festivals, but goes to some pains to observe many others, too, including a unique representation of the Washing of the Feet on Holy Thursday. Two festivals are peculiar to Patmos and commemorate the founder of the monastery, the Blessed Christodoulos. On March 16th there is a festival in memory of his death and on October 21st the monastery celebrates the return of his bones to Patmos from Euboea where he died.

    The tourist should note that some of these observances are often preceded by a week or two of serious fasting and that during this time the island may exist on genuine short commons (though no one could accuse it of living sumptuously even in ordinary circumstances).

HOTELS

Skala

B Class   *Patmion*. Long, low, pink-washed. 21 bedrooms, some with private bathrooms. Overlooking the bay.

C Class   *Chris*. Next door to *Patmion*. 26 bedrooms, all with private bath or shower.

            Astoria. Convenient, unassuming.

D Class   *Ethnikon*. Pleasant, some rooms with private bath or shower.

            Rex. Modern, simple.

E Class   *To Neon*. On corner of waterfront and main square. Simple, good value.

            Nireus. Has its own small beach.

Grikou Bay

B Class   *Xenia*. 36 bedrooms, all with shower or bath. Open early April till end of October. Meals available to non-residents. Transport to Skala by taxi or boat. Pleasant, 3·5-km. walk. Attractive situation on beach.

E Class   *Flisvos*. Small, perched on bluff above the sea. Very simple. No running cold water; it comes in painted cans hitched to the wall of your bedroom. Common shower. Restaurant. (See also Pensions and Rooms below.)

Pensions

Pension prices are similar to those in other small islands. A double room (with private shower) in an A Class pension will cost approximately twice that in a D Class pension.

In Skala, the Pension *Gryllis* is an excellent A Class example of its type. It lies in Pteri Street, immediately off the main square to the right as you face inland. A matter of 100 yards brings you to a general store and the pension is above it.

Rooms

There are rooms to be had in Skala plus a few in Chora and at Kambos, a few km. north of Skala. Prices per bed vary between Drs 30–50.

N.B. The owner of the *Flisvos* on Grikou Bay has four flats to let in a house on the bay, all with mod. cons.

RESTAURANTS

Skala

Restaurants – mostly cheap – include the *Avra, Arion, Drosia, Patmos*. The *Doris* is good, clean and open for breakfast. There are a number of cafés in and around the small main square.

Chora

Small *kafeneíons* and *tavérnas*.

Grikou Bay

Lunch and dinner are available at the *Xenia Hotel*. The *Flisvos* provides simple meals.

Local dishes

There are no outstanding island specialities, though there is some white and dryish Patmos wine. A sweetmeat called 'Patmos pudding' is sometimes on sale: wine, flour and nuts are compounded into a kind of paste, then cut into portions.

BEACHES

The town beach is the narrow *Aghios Theologos* beach, near the Patmion Hotel. At Grikou there is a good beach divided by a spur of rock on which is the small Flisvos Hotel.

There are a number of delightful small beaches off the road to Kambos beach, though not all are easy to get to and some are bristling with sea urchins. Round the small island there are numerous inlets but you need a boat to reach most of them. *Livadhi ton Kalogiron* ('Monks' Meadow') is popular, and the very beautiful *Lambis Bay* is renowned for its coloured pebbles.

HISTORY OF PATMOS

Among the pieces in the Treasury of the Monastery of St John you will be shown some enchanting gold, silver and enamel pendants in the form of sailing-ships. These rich and elaborate fancies were presented by the masters of sailing vessels to their wives in the seventeenth and eighteenth centuries. Encrusted with jewels, generally with five sub-pendants dangling from their keels, these pendants must have bounced bravely on the bosoms of the captains' ladies. Yet these are more than lovely jewels, they are also indications of a curious turn of history. Where else among the Dodecanese islands can one imagine captains rich enough (and rich in the time of Turkish occupation, too) to bestow this kind of bauble? The fact is that, almost alone among the Dodecanese, Patmos prospered under Turkish rule. The enormous prestige of the monastery, good relations with the Pope (who protected the island, threatening to excommunicate any who were tempted to pillage it) and, until the mid seventeenth century, good relations with Venice, provided the island with conditions under which it was able to flourish. For centuries the monastery had built up its own trading fleet and when the Knights left Rhodes for Malta, the Patmian fleet made alliance with them and actually sailed with the flag of the Knights of Malta flying from its masts.

The beginnings of Patmian history are slenderly supported. On the summit of the hill called Kastelli at the back of Skala are the remains of some sixth- to fourth-century B.C. walls, and enough pottery and other domestic relics have been found in the area between the harbours of Skala, Mericha and Chochlachas, or built into later buildings, to indicate that a fair-sized city once stood here.

However, it was the Roman decision to exile St John the Theologian that marks the start of Patmian fame. Some time between A.D. 81 and A.D. 95 (he was released from exile in A.D. 96) St John was granted, in the grotto cave of the Apocalypse, the great Revelation which went forth from Patmos as a message of hope and terror to the seven great churches of the world.

Prochoros, a 'disciple' of St John writing some centuries later, is the source of most of the stories we possess about the saint and how he came to write the Revelation. Both he and his work are among the living legends of Patmos. Among Prochoros' tales is an account of how St John overcame Kynops, a heathen magician. Islanders will point out the spot where Kynops lies, a petrified rock beneath the waters of Skala harbour. There is a portrayal of this event on one of the frescoes in the outer narthex of the Monastery of St John.

Between the fourth and seventh centuries Patmos became a place of pilgrimage, but thereafter the island was abandoned to the invasions of Islam, Arabs, Byzantium and eastern-Mediterranean pirates. But its great days were yet to come and they began in 1088 when Christodoulos – monk, doctor, a Superior, soldier and scholar, and one of the significant men of his time – founded the monastery. He obtained from Constantinople the gift of Patmos in order that he might build a monastery dedicated to the saint. In the monastery library today are three Chrysobulls of 1088, the first signed by Alexis Comnenos I, the Byzantine Emperor, bestowing the island upon Christodoulos, the second giving him free use of a ship for monastery purposes and the third exempting the island from taxes.

Over the succeeding centuries the monastery laid the foundations of its riches and reputation as a seat of learning. Notably, it acquired large monastic estates as far afield as Asia Minor and also a fleet to keep them supplied. It was this fleet and this power that enabled the monastery if not the island to ride above Turkish occupation, which began in 1453. With a break in 1659 when the Venetians captured the island, Patmian prosperity continued and the original Theological Seminary, the Patmias, was built in the eighteenth century. From the Patmias priests went forth to build Patmian colonies in central Europe, Russia and Egypt.

Patmos enjoyed eleven years of freedom after the War of Independence in 1821 but again fell to the Turks in 1832. They held it until the Italian annexation of the Dodecanese in 1912. The island was reunited with Greece in 1947.

SKALA AND CHORA

Skala, though it has neither the atmosphere nor the history of Chora, is the most *useful* place to stay in. Roads to the beaches start here, most of the hotels and eating-places are here, and you don't have to climb the formidable hill to the high town every time you forget your dark glasses. Skala has its own charm, anyway, for the small, neat houses are scrupulously whitewashed and the sills are painted a sober indigo or ochre. In truth, one needs to do little more, for the purity of Patmos needs no decoration.

**Patmos
Diagram of
Excursions**

CHORA (THE HIGH TOWN)

As you sail into Patmos, the vertical ramparts, battlements, square
towers, steep ramps and glacis of the Monastery of St John (see
p. 236) deceive most newcomers into thinking that here is a fortress
and to seek the monastery elsewhere. First impressions are, however, correct for the Monastery of St John the Divine is one of the
great fortified religious houses. Pirates and Mediterranean powers
of the Middle Ages found Patmos attractive prey and in order to
protect the spiritual stronghold it was necessary to give it teeth. It
rides superbly above Chora, a medieval village that was acolyte
to the holy place.

Some think Chora entirely delightful and certainly it has fascina-
tion. It is, to me, an oddly dead village. Perhaps this is because the
first time I went there it was a Sunday and a very monastic Sunday
at that. Shutters remained closed and there was a disturbing silence
as of a deserted, unpeopled place. Was it only Sunday silence?
When I have been there since I have found little more animation;
even shops are few, so there is not a great deal of daily come and go.
Architecturally, the village has some charm. Houses are tall and
Turkish influence is clear. You can find plenty of windows that
once were rounded, later changed to a pointed arch and, still later,
have had a semicircular lunette inserted, similar to those of Kalymnos. There are some charming slatted 'country' doors and fitted
into these doors are second doors, rather low – head and shoulder
height and prettily arched. The lanes of the village are narrow
and winding with bends that blunt the strength of the tremendous
winds that can blow up here, winds that sweep the stone paving
clean and send the leaves rattling down the dry runnels. There are
a few *tavérnas* and three finely situated windmills; from just below
the approach to the Monastery a partly metalled road runs down
the far side of the hill to join the coast road to Grikou.

The monastery itself is the jewel of Chora – or, perhaps, one
should say the jewel in the crown that is Patmos. For it is from here
that one looks down on the unparalleled beauty of this island and its
position. I cannot name, in my experience, any other Aegean island
which has so magnificent a prospect of islands. In 1743 Dr Charles
Perry called this view 'perhaps one of the most beautiful views in
the whole world', and it is every bit as tenable an opinion now as it
was then.

The island itself, fantastically indented, is formed of three land masses, each linked by a narrow isthmus of land. The southern mass is the smallest, the middle one is larger and the most northerly the biggest of all. So thin is the soil that the bare hills have the grey abrasive look of pumice overlaid by a fine brown veil. On the heights and along the coast the maggots of time have eaten into the pumice. Encircling these pockmarked and forbidding rocks is the sea, and so elaborate is the pattern of bays and coves and inlets that here and there it seems that the Aegean is glittering in the midst of a field like a blue lake. And all about you are the islands. From the monastery you can see as far as *Mykonos*, *Naxos* and *Paros*. The peak of *Mt Kerketeos* on Samos rises, strong and unmistakable, to the north. West of it is the ridge of high cliff that runs down *Ikaria*. *Amorgos*, *Leros*, *Kalymnos* lie on the blinding horizon and the long, flat tail of *Kos* is visible beyond these. The nearer islands – *Hiliomodi* (which, at last count, had a population of four), *Grilussa*, *Lipsos*, *Arki* and *Agathonisi* – are a foreground to the great land mass of Asia Minor and that prospect of *Cape Mycale* so familiar to those who know Samos. Friedrich Hölderlin, who never visited Patmos, yet wrote a great, mad poem about it, spoke with the truth of instinct as this extract indicates:

> But around Asia's gates there murmur,
> Extending this way and that
> In the uncertain plain of the sea,
> Shadowless road enough;
> Yet the boatman knows the islands.
> And when I heard
> That of the near islands one
> Was Patmos,
> I greatly desired
> There to be lodged, and there
> To approach the dark grotto.
> For not like Cyprus,
> The rich in wellsprings,
> Nor any of the others
> Magnificently does Patmos dwell, ...

MONASTERY OF ST JOHN THE DIVINE

Open   Summer Daily 08.30–12.00 and 15.00–18.00.
          Winter   Daily 09.00–13.00 and 14.30–17.00.
          Sundays and holidays 08.00–12.00.
Entrance Drs 10.

The *Central Courtyard* (*Map* 1), which you enter after passing through the covered way from the main entrance, is pebbled, and pots of flowers stand about it. Its clean, spacious air is accentuated by the double arcade and the four arches of the outer narthex of the main church. ('Narthex,' says the *Concise Oxford Dictionary*, is a 'portico or ante-nave in early Christian churches for women, penitents and catechumens'. Catechumen? A convert under instruction before baptism.)

Generally there will be one or two monks sitting in the benches in the *Outer Narthex* (*Map* 2); another may lean from one of the first-storey arches to talk to one below, a third may strike a simantron before the monastery bells themselves are rung. (A simantron is a large wooden or metal beam that is struck with a hammer.)

The Outer Narthex contains stones and carvings taken from the earlier church that was on this site when Christodoulos began to build.

The *paintings* on the walls and vaults of the Outer Narthex are exceedingly decorative, though it is true that they are not of very high quality. But you will enjoy the group which depicts Prochoros' version of the Life of St John. Some of these frescoes are of the seventeenth century; the latest is as recent as 1891. From the Outer Narthex wooden doors (seventeenth-century) lead into the Inner Narthex and to the right the *Founder's Chapel* (*Map* 4) – the chapel where the bones of the Blessed Christodoulos lie in a marble sarcophagus surmounted by a silver shrine (late-eighteenth-century).

The *Inner Narthex* (*Map* 3) is vaulted, blackened with smoke from incense, and has some damaged frescoes of the early nineteenth century. The treasure to see here is the very fine *icon of St John the Theologian*; the gaunt, massive head of the divine is inclined over a Gospel of his own writing. The icon is of the eleventh century, though it has been repainted since.

Passing through the main body of the *Church* (*Map* 5) which lies beyond the Inner Narthex, you come to the *Chapel of the Virgin*

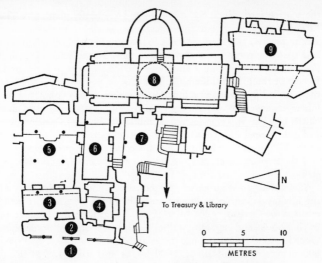

Monastery of St John the Divine, Patmos

1 Central courtyard
2 Outer Narthex
3 Inner Narthex
4 Founder's Chapel
5 Church

6 Chapel of the Virgin
7 Inner Courtyard
8 Refectory
9 Kitchen

(*Map* **6**) (late-twelfth-century). This chapel is full of interest: an *iconostasis* of the very early seventeenth century and carved and inscribed pieces from the early church. But it is the *frescoes* that make the Chapel of the Virgin memorable. The noblest of these, and the best-preserved, are on the east wall. Among them is a *Virgin with Child, attended by the Archangels Michael and Gabriel*. Above this fresco is a splendid *Abraham and the Holy Trinity*: note the guileless yet modern treatment of the table and the bowl of fruit.

Leaving the Chapel of the Virgin and turning left, you come to the *Inner Courtyard* (*Map* **7**), thence to the *Refectory* (*Map* **8**).

The major features of this eleventh-century hall with twelfth- to thirteenth-century ceiling and dome are the two long marble-faced *stone tables*. At each place there is a 'place setting', a recess carved in the marble into which the monk placed his knife, plate, etc. The *Kitchen* (*Map* 9) is close to the Refectory.

The *Treasury* and the *Library* have recently been rehoused, in cool and spacious rooms, one above the other. Nevertheless, it is still possible to display only a small part of the monastery's treasures. In one of the glass cabinets of the Treasury you will find some of the jewelled pendant ships mentioned earlier in this chapter. Elsewhere are seventeenth- and eighteenth-century vestments and altar cloths bearing, in some instances, miniature works of art in silver and gold thread and coloured silks – scenes of the life of Christ and of the Virgin and the Saints. Note the collection of handsome gold and silver pectoral crosses, chalices, jewelled mitres and bishops' staffs.

The *Library*, the pride of the monastery and the university of the medieval Aegean, is immediately above the Treasury. It is the creation of Christodoulos himself, who instituted the practice of buying books and engaging scribes to copy or write additional ones. Once it contained even more material than it does today. Just over 900 manuscripts and about 2,000 books and some 13,000 documents lie in the archives of the monastery. Much of this material is of interest only to the historian, but on display is an early-sixth-century A.D. parchment of the *Gospel of St Mark*. Only thirty-three pages are here in Patmos; others are scattered far and wide – in the libraries of Leningrad, Vienna, the Byzantine Museum in Athens and the Vatican. There are four in the British Museum. This famous book, on tissue-thin, purplish parchment, is inscribed in letters of silver (note that 'Jesus' and other sacred names appear in gold). The text reads continuously, with no spacing between words or paragraphs.

The monks have framed the original *Chrysobull* signed by Alexis Comnenos when he gifted Patmos to Christodoulos and there is a selection of brilliantly illuminated *codices*, some of them tenth- and eleventh-century portrayals of the Evangelists.

One of the features of the library is the contribution it has made to knowledge through the series of catalogues carefully prepared through the centuries. The earliest one extant (1201) is in the archives today: a rare Byzantine index of volumes which records possessions and also records that the monastery was not jealous of its learning and that books were lent to other religious houses as near as Kalymnos and Samos and as far away as Asia Minor.

The Library also contains a number of *icons*. Of these, the greatest treasure is the small silver-framed mosaic *icon of St Nicholas*, representing the moment when the saint dreamed he was to be raised to the episcopate. The pieces of mosaic are minute: the largest measures only one twenty-fifth of an inch across. The saint, eye directed slightly to his right, stands in the centre of the work. The robes draped on his narrow body are depicted in severely linear style. He stands against a golden background and on a dull greenish-blue ground. On one side of his head Christ offers him the Gospel and on the other the Virgin presents him with the vestments of a bishop. The whole is framed in silver. As this was a portable icon it is small – just over 8 in. by 7 in.

Of the others, there is a fine, soldierly figure of *St Theodore Tyre* (thirteenth-century) and a number by icon painters well known in their day. As the icons on show are likely to be changed from time to time, the best advice this book can give is to suggest that you look for works by Andreas Ritzos (sixteenth-century), Theodore Poulakis and Emmanuel Tzanes (both seventeenth-century).

You may also find a sixteenth-century *polyptych* of unusual interest and charm, a central panel flanked by rows of small paintings, each row telling its own religious story.

Don't miss the *roof terraces* from which emerge the domed roofs of Byzantine chapels. On a very bright day up here the dazzle is so great that photography is extremely difficult, so if you take a camera beware of over-exposing.

Back in the main courtyard there is a very efficient little tourist shop. The monks of Patmos have set themselves to produce really high-quality postcards, transparencies and a guide-book which is among the best produced in the Aegean, if not in Greece.

MONASTERY AND GROTTO OF THE APOCALYPSE

Halfway up the road to Chora is the Monastery of the Apocalypse. This contains the modern buildings of the *Patmias*, a college of theology founded in the seventeenth century which still schools young men for the priesthood.

A little above here is the *Grotto of the Apocalypse* (clearly signposted). The *Chapel of Aghia Anna* has been built around this dark, bleak grotto where tradition says that St John slept and woke and received his Revelation. You are shown, set in silver, the place where the saint's head rested and the ledge on which he wrote. (Some versions have it that this desk of natural rock is where the 'disciple' of St John, Prochoros, set down the Revelation at the saint's dictation.) This symbolic bringing together of the saint and his follower of many centuries later is illustrated in a miniature in Gospel Book No. 81 in the *monastery library*. The cave is heavy with symbolism. The guide will point to the three fissures that appeared in the rock as it was rent by the mighty coming of the Son of Man: these, say the guide, are symbols of the Trinity.

EXCURSIONS ON PATMOS

Excursion 1: Grikou Beach

Route Take a taxi or a boat (see p. 228 for details of taxi and boat hire). Otherwise walk from Skala or Chora (see Excursion diagram). [From Skala 3·5 km.]
Accommodation Two hotels (see p. 229). *Tavérna* on beach.

On arrival at Grikou beach you come first to the strip upon which the new Xenia hotel stands. Beyond here is the Flisvos hotel and beyond the Flisvos yet another beach backed with trees. You can walk from here along a narrow strip of land to a rock in the middle of the bay. This is *Kallikratsou* (some ancient remains). Still farther on you come to the narrow isthmus of *Stavros*. You can pause and swim at pretty well any point along these beaches. (But don't be misled into believing that all the lovely, lonely, unpeopled bays on the road to Grikou are going to be wonderful to swim in. There is generally a good reason why they are left alone and the reason is usually sea urchins. One gruelling hot afternoon I scrambled down to cool off and found a veritable barrier of urchins lying under the blue water.)

Excursion 2: Kambos and Lambis Bay

Route Follow the road north from Skala to Kambos Bay [8 km.]. From Kambos the road continues to the hill above Lambis. (You can go by boat to either bay.)
Accommodation A few rooms to let in Kambos.

There are two small restaurants on the wide Kambos Bay. The sand is coarse, becoming stony here and there but the beach is shallow and very sheltered. The islets of **St George** and **Kentronisi** lie south of the spur that thrusts out north of the bay.

Lambis Bay is approximately 4 km. from Kambos. The road becomes bumpy beyond **Christos** village but is perfectly motorable. It stops altogether at the summit above Lambis but a track goes down to the bay where there is a small restaurant. It is a very attractive place and famous for its coloured pebbles.

Excursion 3: Round the Island

Route Start off early in the morning by boat, take some food, return in the late afternoon.

You can pass or call in at any of the following bays or beauty-spots: *Kambos, the Hermitage of Apollos, Lambis Bay, Livadhi ton Kalogiron* (*'Monks' Meadow'*) in the north where you can swim and enjoy the pretty church and orchards; *Lefkis Bay* on the west, *Mericha* – the narrow bay just behind Skala – and *Chochlachas* just south of Mericha.

Farther south is the beautiful *Kipos tou Ossiou* ('the garden of the Blessed Christodoulos') and, in one of the deeply indented inlets of the island, a magically still and peaceful place called *Kouvari*. It seems right that the little church here is called a hermitage.

THE MINOR ISLANDS

The minor islands include Simi, Tilos, Nisyros; Chalki, Karpathos, Kasos; Astypalaia and Kastellorizzo. The first three of these islands are grouped between Rhodes and Kos. Chalki, Karpathos and Kasos lie between Rhodes and Crete, with Chalki nearest to the west coast of Rhodes. The final pair are geographical extremes. Astypalaia is the farthest west of all the Dodecanese and Kastellorizzo the farthest east. Of all these islands, the best-equipped for visitors is Karpathos, and the next best Simi.

These minor islands share the common history of the Dodecanese, though they are supporting players rather than the stars. To the Knights, directing operations from Rhodes, they represented vital outposts against the Turks, and Simi, Tilos, Nisyros, Chalki and Kastellorizzo were all fortified to this end. Karpathos and Kasos were of lesser strategic importance and though the Knights occupied both islands in 1313 they left again in 1315, allowing the previous ruler, Andrea Cornaro, to resume stewardship on behalf of Venice. Of the entire Dodecanese only Patmos and Astypalaia remained wholly untouched by the Knights, Astypalaia, because it was too far west to be useful (and was also in the care of Venice), Patmos because it was what it was.

The Turks acquired these islands in the early 1520s and held most of them till the coming of the Italians in 1912. Reunion with Greece took place in 1947–48.

Simi

Getting to Simi The inter-island steamers call at Simi town on the east coast. (See p. 37.)
Accommodation *Nireus* pension. Also some rooms available.
Festivals Two festivals at Panormitis (Whitsun and November). (See pp. 56, 57.)

The island (pop. 3,100) is about 9·5 km. by 9·5 km. It is flanked by the Gulf of Doris to the north and the Gulf of Simi to the east and is poised within the open jaws of two Anatolian peninsulas.

The coast is much indented, deeply bitten into here, nibbled away there. There are many bays, offshore rocks and islets. Inland, the island is almost wholly mountainous and so notoriously short of water that it installed a solar still, the first on any Aegean island. The still is out of action, so that water continues to be in short supply.

HISTORY OF SIMI

The *Iliad* states that Simi took part in the Trojan War on the Greek side and that King Nireus of Simi contributed three triremes which he led himself. Homer implies, a trifle acidly, that the king, though beautiful, was ineffectual: he was virtually the handsomest man to come to Ilium 'yet he was a weakling and his following was small'.

At some point the Karians crossed from neighbouring Anatolia and settled on the island. During the Peloponnesian War a naval battle between Athens and Sparta took place in nearby waters. Simi was occupied by the Knights and the Turks and was the first Dodecanese island to rise (unsuccessfully) against the Turks in the War of Independence. Its reputation as a boat-building island began in antiquity and continued until the nineteenth century. Today the great days of Simiot boat-building are past. And they were really great days. Volonakis records that the Knights greatly favoured the light, manoeuvrable craft which the Simiots manufactured. They called the boats '*skaphés*', and the Turks, who had reason to have considerable respect for Simiot boat-building, singled them out as '*Simibequir*', the boats of Simi.

An earlier chapter has referred to one of the legends about the naming of Simi. Another tells how Simi, the daughter of King Ialysos, was raped by the sea-god Glaucos who then took her to the isolated island off Karia and gave it her name.

Today almost the entire population lives in the capital. Industries are traditional: farming, fishing and diving. The earth is persuaded to produce small quantities of cereal, honey, olives, tobacco and wine. Sponge-fishing, though declining fast, remains the basic industry and Simiot divers are reputed to be the best in the Aegean.

SIMI TOWN

The old name for the town was Aigialos and a form of the name persists, for the lower town is still called Gialos by the islanders. Chora, the upper town, is partly on the site of the ancient acropolis and on its slopes are the remains of a necropolis.

There is a *Byzantine kastró* above the town and within it is the

Church of the Panaghia with some worthwhile frescoes. East of the *kastró* is a *ruined mill*; near by are the *towers of Simi*, pillars dating from the time when Simi played a part in the Dorian Hexapolis.

EXCURSIONS ON SIMI

Offshore islands

Of the offshore islands, *Nimos* protects Simi Bay from the north and only the narrowest of channels separates it from the main island. It can be visited by *caïque* from the harbour. To the south of the island are *Seskli* and *Trompeto* and among many other rocky islets are *Diavates*, *Oxa*, *Plati* and *Khondros*.

Emborio and Pedhi Bay

Emborio (called Nimborio by some islanders) is 2 km. west of Simi. It is a small summer beach resort; there are some Byzantine mosaics in the yard of a ruined *Byzantine church*. Pedhi Bay is 2 km. east of the capital.

Panormitis Monastery

Route You can get to Panormitis on foot or on muleback (4 hours approximately). You will need help to find the track; if you hire a mule, hire a muleman, too. Alternatively, a boat from Simi approaches the bay down the attractive eastern coastline; allow about two hours for this sea trip.
Accommodation Rooms to be had at the monastery but don't count on getting one during festival time.

Probably the best-known bay on the island, certainly to day-excursion visitors from Rhodes or Kos, is Panormitis on the south-west coast. The eighteenth-century *Monastery of St Michael Panormitis* spreads along the shore of this large bay; the interior is attractive and the *iconostasis* handsome. A few houses, about twenty inhabitants, and one or two restaurants complete the life of the bay. Two festivals are held here, one at Whitsun (Orthodox Whitsun) and the other from November 7th to the 9th. Both centre upon the monastery, both are lively, and the Whitsun celebration can be extremely exhausting because Panormitis tends to become very, very hot. Temperatures of 100° upwards are not unusual.

Roukounioti Monastery

Another monastery, Roukounioti, lies approximately 2–3 km. inland between Simi and Emborio.

Tilos

Getting to Tilos Inter-island ships put into Levadhia Bay once a week. (See p. 37.)
Accommodation Rooms only. Very few and very simple.

The island was noticed by Pliny and others and was known for the quality of its unguents. From the fourteenth century until the present day, the island history has been the familiar one of foreign domination by Knights, Turks and Italians until union with Greece at the end of the Second World War.

The medieval name for Tilos (pop. 790) was Piskopi; the Italians revived the name and many maps today still use it. It is a combination of the Greek words *epi* = over and *skopós* = lookout, and refers to the watch-towers on the island. Tilos was the name of a settler who colonized the island in earlier times.

EXCURSIONS ON TILOS

Tilos lies 22 miles north-west of Rhodes and is shaped something like a sea-horse. Two of the three villages bear the severely matter-of-fact names Greeks often fall back on: **Megalochorio** (literally, big village) has a population of 362 and **Mikrochorio** (small village) has 38 inhabitants. **Levadhia** is the island capital and inter-island ships put into Levadhia Bay. Megalochorio is the old capital and is on the site of ancient Tilos. The ruined *castle* is Venetian (note a Classical doorway) and is perched high on a hill beyond the village. The *church* has an unusual number of Byzantine icons.

Distances are small: from Levadhia by a dirt road to Mikrochorio is about 1·5 km. This track continues uphill to Megalochorio for another 9 km.

North of the island is a little offshore island called **Gaidaros** while to the south-east is **Antitilos**.

Nisyros

Getting to Nisyros Inter-island ships call at Mandraki once a week. (See p. 37.)
Accommodation Rooms only. Very few and very simple.
Festivals See p. 55.

Approximately 8 km. by 7 km., with a population of 1,790, Nisyros
is as nearly circular as an island can be, for both coast and interior
repeat a unique circular shape rather like a giant egg-cup. From
the shore the land rises steeply until it halts on the rim of a huge
depression, 4 km. across, which fills the centre of the island and is
pitted with smaller craters. The island was probably detached from
Kos as a result of volcanic action and within the giant crater there
is still a warm volcanic cone rising to 2,290 feet.

Strabo produced an endearingly ingenious myth to explain the
volcano, reporting that the island was a fragment which Neptune
severed from Kos with a blow of his trident. As Neptune at the
time was pursuing the giant Polybotes the fragment came in useful
to hurl at his enemy. It struck Polybotes, settled into the sea and
pinned the giant beneath it who ever after has been shaking the
island as he struggles to get free. Strabo also noted that the island
had an abundance of millstone for grinding stones. Pliny says the
island was once called Porphyris on account of the profusion of
shells which yielded a purple dye greatly prized by the Phoenicians.

EXCURSIONS ON NISYROS

There are four small villages on the island, linked by a dust road.
Mandraki (pop. 1,100) is on the north coast and is the island capital.
It is close to the site of ancient *Nisyros* and there are some traces of
the ancient *harbour walls* still to be seen. The *Church of the Panaghia ton
Spiliani* (literally, Virgin of the Cave) is partly hewn into the rock.
The Knights built one of their fortresses here (ruins). Behind the
village are woods and one of the charms of Nisyros are the almond
trees that cover many slopes; lovely to look at in spring, the fruit
extremely good to eat in summer.

Along the coast are some of the medicinal watering-places that
have been celebrated since antiquity. **Loutra** (approximately 1·5 km.
east of Mandraki) was one such thriving spa; present population
numbers four. **Pali** (pop. 152) is about the same distance farther
east from Loutra and also has spa waters near by. The other two
villages are **Emborio** (pop. 265) and **Nikia** (pop. unknown). Both
are high up on the rim of the central crater and both afford fine
views, although Nikia is thought to be the better vantagepoint of
the two.

Outside these villages, transport is by foot or mule. Although neither of the following excursions is particularly lengthy bear in mind that they are fairly time-consuming, climbing as high as 1,400 feet on dust tracks.

Mandraki to Nikia

In the centre of Mandraki the road forks left and right. Take the right fork and follow the dust road upwards until it reaches the edge of the central depression. From here the road follows the curve of the rim south and east. Approximately half a kilometre before Nikia there is a left turn to Emborio and Pali (see below). From Nikia a path strikes due south down the steep slope to the sea, but you can also either return to Mandraki or, possibly, strike north to join the Mandraki–Emborio–Pali path. Total distance to Nikia approximately 8 km.

Mandraki to Emborio and Pali

From Mandraki take the left fork which climbs to the rim, crosses the crater and meets the northbound path from Nikia. At this point, turn left to Emborio and Pali. Total distance approximately 9 km.

Chalki

Getting to Chalki Inter-island steamer once a week.
Accommodation Extremely limited; rooms.

Chalki (pop. 500) is the largest of a small group of islands which can be seen from Ancient Kamiros on the west coast of Rhodes. It is mountainous and very short of water. The highest point is Mt Merovigli (1,954 feet) to the south-east of the mountain range that crosses the island diagonally from north-east to south-west.

EXCURSIONS ON CHALKI

The island capital is variously called, even today, **Nimborio** or **Emborio** or **Skala** and is situated on *Emborio Bay* in the south-east. Old Chalki or **Chora** is on a height above the harbour. In this it conforms to medieval custom but differs from similar examples in the Dodecanese in that it is unusually far from the waterfront and nearly 1,000 feet above sea level. Many empty, shuttered houses are evidence of the depopulation of the island. Inland from Chora is the site of the ancient capital which was overbuilt with a *medieval castle*.

North-east of Chalki is the horseshoe-shaped **Alimnia**; the waters between and round about are scattered with tiny rocks and islets. There is no way to get to Alimnia save by the good graces of a willing boatman. If you do manage to set foot on it, there is a *Castle of the Knights* as a reward.

Karpathos

Getting to Karpathos Inter-island steamers or local steamers on the Rhodes–Crete run call at Pighadia once weekly, sometimes putting in at Diafani also. (See p. 37.) By air from Rhodes, daily in season, weather permitting. (See p. 36.) The airport, on the flat, bare, south-west tip of the island, is approximately 20 minutes' bus ride from Pighadia.
Transport *Buses* connect with all the main villages except Olimpos. Inquire locally for timetables and routes. Several *taxis* ply from Pighadia. (These are in great demand by the islanders and are not always available on call.) *Caïque* from Pighadia to Diafani once or twice weekly, returning next day, weather permitting.
Accommodation *Pighadia*: the *Pension Porphyris*, delightfully situated above a large, sandy beach; also the smaller *Anesis, Flisvos, Zephyros* and others. Some rooms in private houses.
Diafani: three *pensions*.
Festivals See p. 55.

Karpathos is 48 km. long and nearly 9 km. across at its widest. In all but population (6,700), therefore, it is nearly as large as Kos. It lies in the Karpathian Sea, 40 miles from the eastern tip of Crete and 30 miles from Prassonisi on the southern limits of Rhodes. From Pighadia, the largest village (pop. 1,280), a boat trip of 75 miles will circumnavigate the island.

From north to south, down the very centre of this long, narrow island, there runs an unbroken range of high mountains. For most of the way they slope steeply towards the sea. In the southern part of the island there is a fine tracery of streams and a number of springs.

Visible far out to sea is the 4,000-foot peak of *Mt Kalolimno*, virtually the navel of the island. It effectively divides the island in two. The land north of it is harsh and thinly populated, albeit the more interesting half in some ways, for the north clings to old customs and the village of **Olimpos** offers several unusual survivals.

South of Mt Kalolimno the island is well watered, and there are the high Lastos Plain and the fertile land around Pighadia, where gardens and orchards and olive groves flourish behind the sandy Vronti beach. The islanders farm and fish and in the past have also mined silver and iron and quarried gypsum.

The prevailing wind is from the west and evidence of its strength can be seen on the way from the airport or on any bus ride round the island. Seldom have I seen trees so hunched and cowering against the ferocity of the wind as the trees of Karpathos.

The sea round the coast is booby-trapped with sunken reefs, some of them of coral which was much in demand among the ancients. However, **Pighadia** is a good harbour. The old harbour of **Tristoma** on the extreme north-west of the island is dangerous and little-used. It is well known for the two rocks which lie across the harbour entrance and challenge the new arrival to guess which is the correct way in. The Admiralty chart provides a charming engraving of a 'captain's eye' view of the problem. One channel is marked 'Boat Passage', another 'False Entrance' and the third 'True Entrance'.

Saria is the little satellite island sitting like a helmet upon the head of Karpathos. Only 30 yards of water separate island from islet, which is deserted except in summer when shepherds visit it. The site of old *Palatia* is on the east coast of Saria.

HISTORY OF KARPATHOS

The island history is spanned by its names, beginning with Homer's Krapathos through to the medieval Scarpanto to the modern Karpathos. Strabo asserts that the island was once so populous that it was named according to the number of its towns at any given time – e.g., Tripolis, Tetrapolis, Heptapolis and even Oktapolis. The best known of the villages of these days were Brikous Nisyros, south of Tristoma, Arkesia to the south-west (now Arkasa), and the old capital of the island, Poseidon, which was a little south of modern Pighadia.

Karpathos features less in myth than other Dodecanese islands but it was said to be the birthplace of the Titans, and Karpathos and Kasos both claim that the god Proteus reigned over them.

Perhaps because it stands between two much larger and bigger prizes, Crete and Rhodes, Karpathos has had a relatively peaceful past. In 1306 it passed from the Genoese Moresco family to the Venetian Cornaro family. In 1315 the Knights secured the island but stayed only two years and then gave the island back to Andrea Cornaro. In 1538 the Turks appeared, led by Barbarossa, the red-bearded pirate turned admiral who scoured the Aegean on behalf of the Turks and sent packing every Venetian lordling between Naxos and Karpathos.

EXCURSIONS ON KARPATHOS

Those who want to make the acquaintance of the villages of Karpathos must be prepared to climb high or settle for a bus or taxi. Of the more important villages only Pighadia and Mesochorio are below 500 feet. Volada (1,475 feet), Othos (2,295 feet), Piles (1,310 feet) and Spoa (1,150 feet) place themselves well out of the way of any but determined walkers. There are bus connections between Pighadia and Aperi (pop. 770), Volada (pop. 505), Othos (pop. 440), Piles (pop. 367), and from Pighadia to Menetes (pop. 740) and Arkasa (pop. 510). Another route links Pighadia with Piles, Mesochorio and Spoa. Three sample excursions are described below.

Pighadia to Piles via Aperi and Othos

Route Pighadia to Aperi is about 8 km. and it is a further 8 km. to Piles.
On Vronti Bay, 1·5 km. out of Pighadia, step aside to the right to visit the site of Aghia Fotini, only a few yards off the road. This early-Christian church of the fourth century A.D. is still being excavated and reveals itself as a small church graced with beautifully carved and preserved crosses on its fallen pillars, simple, elegant capitals and some stone and marble slabs bearing both formal and floral designs. Well worth the short detour.
Bus The bus from Pighadia to Piles returns the same day.

Aperi was the capital of the island once upon a time. Today it has 770 inhabitants, angular-stepped streets, a stream that crosses the village, and a fine view over the bay of Pighadia. It is also the seat of the Metropolitan of Karpathos and Kasos.

From Aperi the road climbs sharply to **Volada**, 1,475 feet above sea level. A valley links the two villages and the view up to Volada is very attractive. From Volada, a shoulder of the hill conceals Aperi and one can only look upwards to **Othos** with its white houses, its *Church of the Panaghia* with a spring issuing beneath it – very cooling to the feet on a hot day.

From Othos the road tilts downwards into Piles. En route there is a superb view across the sea to Kasos. **Piles** is a huddle of houses, the scene of a bustling festival on September 12th, and is the pivot village for travellers wishing to continue northwards to Spoa or turn south to complete a round trip via the hamlets of Finiki, Arkasa and Menetes.

Pighadia to Diafani and Olimpos

Route Inter-island vessels make occasional calls at Diafani on their passage from Rhodes to Crete and return. A *caïque* leaves Pighadia for Diafani once or twice a week and takes approximately 3 hours, returning the following day. A taxi ride or walk of 10 km. from Diafani brings you by a rough but motorable road to Olimpos.

For ardent walkers with time to spare and food in their knapsacks, an alternative route back might be the mule-track from Olimpos to Spoa. However, local advice is 'don't' : the track is reputed to be difficult and it is necessary to be sure which day the weekly bus from Spoa to Pighadia leaves, otherwise you may arrive at Spoa and find yourself still many kilometres from home.

Accommodation Three pensions at Diafani : *Belvedere, Diafani Pallas, Golden Beach.*

Olimpos (pop. 870) is easily the most rewarding village on the island. Its beginnings lie so far back in antiquity that experts can detect Doric words among the local dialect and the solidly built houses are fitted with locks and keys of wood that are similar in design to those of Homeric origin. Chimney-pots are as much a feature of domestic architecture as they are in the Cyclades: on Karpathos they are generally shaped like a fat vase and the decoration around the bowl is a series of circles or rectangles or zigzags. Balconies are of charming geometric designs in wood. Traditional costume is worn in Olimpos for no other reason than that it always has been worn. A long file of mills marches along the ridge of the hill behind the village.

Pighadia to Mesochorio and Spoa via Piles

Route There is a bus three times weekly to these villages but it does not return until the following day. Neither Mesochorio (37 km.) nor Spoa (42 km.) is accustomed to providing overnight accommodation ; best regard this excursion as a day-trip and that a taxi is necessary.

The route is included here because the coast north of Piles is so beautiful, whether you look out to sea or inland. Inland, the scenery is first of small, maritime pines and the foothills of Mt Kalolimno. Halfway to Mesochorio, the pines become larger and the peak of *Kalolimni* now towers above you, only slightly higher than that of *Profitis Ilias* a little to the north. The view out to sea may be diffused with sea mist or glittering and clear. There are some days of such pure light that you can see Crete in the far distance beyond Kasos.

Approximately 30 km. from Pighadia the road rides above the crescent of Lefkos beach and a further 4 km. downhill brings you to a water trough fed by a spring. Inland, four little domes of the *Monastery of Aghios Georgios* are grouped against a backcloth of pines and Mt Kalolimni. To the left is a track to Lefkos beach. I resisted the siren appeal of this bay on my outward journey but succumbed on my way back and swam alone and exultant in the marvellous water of the beautiful little beach. The detour is 6 km. in all, from the main route and back.

Just before Mesochorio there is a strongly built stone look-out lodge, a form of coastguard hut where watch is kept upon the tricks of the treacherous seas and reefs on this side of the island. The road does not enter **Mesochorio** but stops just above the village. On the rooftops in late summer you look down on grapes, figs and currants set out to dry. The village is neither distinguished nor particularly attractive but a stream gushes out of the paving of the *Church*, there are frescoes and some *Byzantine ruins*.

You must back-track some 2 km. before taking the fork to **Spoa**. A further 6 km. brings you to the village. On the way are a number of ruined *mills*, curved on one side to blunt the force of the wind, flat on the other (though, in my experience, Spoa seems to catch the wind from both east and west). Like Mesochorio, the road comes to an end about 10 yards before the village street begins. Below, on the eastern coast is the port of Spoa, the little harbour of **Aghios Nikolaos**.

Kasos

Getting to Kasos Once a week by inter-island steamer (see p. 37), also local boat from Rhodes.
Transport Taxi, mule, small boats.
Accommodation Private rooms only and few of those.
Beaches Ammoua, south-west of Phry, is sandy; other beaches lie between and on either side of Phry and Emborio.
Festivals See p. 55.

Kasos (pop. 1,400) lies 7 miles south-west of the heel of Karpathos and 30 miles east of Crete. It is approximately 17 km. long and 4 km. wide. The mountain range that extends the length of the island makes for an unfriendly, inaccessible south coast, and such villages as there are cluster around and above the small coastal town of Ophrys on the northern side. Inland from Ophrys is a fertile plain and beyond the plain the mountains tilt gradually upwards to the south-east till they reach their peak with Mt Priona (1,800 feet).

HISTORY OF KASOS

For centuries Karpathos was the big brother of Kasos, and the smaller island has many ties with Karpathian life and history. Phoenicians were the first to invade Kasos and it was they who, braving the turbulent, white-capped seas that break about the island, called it '*ikas*' or 'foam-girt'. In Classical times Poli became the capital. The present harbour of Emborio is built on old foundations.

The Genoese, Andrea Moresco, held the island from the end of the thirteenth century until the arrival of the Knights. After their brief sojourn, both Kasos and Karpathos were given to the Venetian Andrea Cornaro who held them until the coming of the Turks, two centuries later.

The eighteenth- and nineteenth-century history of Kasos is somewhat different from that of the majority of Dodecanese islands. Under the Turks, the poverty of Kasos was such that it became a forgotten island and at one point was probably uninhabited. For the following information I am indebted to Elias Kulukundis, an American-born Kasiot who returned to the island of his fathers in 1964 and has since written an absorbing book about it (*Journey to a Greek Island*). Mr Kulukundis relates how Claude Savary, the French philosopher, was forced to spend a storm-bound week on the island. Savary reacted in Gallic and single-minded fashion to the life of the island and his *Letters on Greece* published in 1788 seem to have reintroduced Kasos to the world. Here is his description of an evening on Kasos:

> About twenty young girls, dressed all in white, with flowing robes, and plaited locks, entered the apartment ... several of them were handsome, all healthy and lovely ... The uniform dress of these nymphs, the modesty which heightened their charms ... all contributed to make me almost imagine myself suddenly transported to the island of Calypso. They ... invited me to dance ... I followed where my partners led me, my mind

being less occupied with the dance than with the charming females who composed it.

The years of Kasos' greatest trials were fast approaching. During the War of Independence the Kasiots joined with the Cretans in their rebellion against the Turks and the then Sultan lost patience with the insurgent islanders. Some 2,500 Cretans had assembled in Kasos and by 1824 it become politically essential to crush Kasiot power and influence. By now the Egyptians had entered the war and they were deputed to attack Kasos. To read the full story of what happened, you cannot do better than refer to Mr Kulukundis' book. Briefly, however, the Egyptians sacked the island, killed the men and took some 2,000 women and children as slaves to Smyrna and Alexandria. The island was left smoking, razed and deserted.

But this dreadful acquaintance of Kasos with Egypt was to become happier in later years. About the middle of the nineteenth century Kasiots, desperate for work, emigrated to Egypt where they were employed on cutting the Suez Canal for de Lesseps. Later, many of these men moved to Port Said and gradually there developed a Greek community of wealthy pilots (Kulukundis points out that the first pilots to navigate ships through Suez *and* the Panama Canal were Kasiots). From the end of the nineteenth century to the first decade of the twentieth Kasiot ship-captains who still lived on the island astutely turned from sail to steam and made their fortunes. There are Kasiot shipping families living in London today.

EXCURSIONS ON KASOS

Ophrys (pop. 480 approximately) was built in 1840 to house Kasiots returning from the War of Independence. Ophrys is the old name for the town; today it is generally called **Phry**. On the other side of the bay from Phry is **Emborio**; its many abandoned houses are eloquent of the depopulation of Kasos. In the days when Kasos throve, however, the shipyard between Emborio and Phry brought wealth and employment to the island. **Polion** (literally, city) lies inland from Emborio and was the ancient capital of Kasos. Its present population is 114. There is a *Byzantine church* in the village and a *kastró* near by. **Aghia Marina** (pop. 540) is on the hills overlooking Phry. The fifth settlement is **Arvanitochori** (pop. 225), south-east of Aghia Marina. Its name means 'the village of the

Albanians' and this is probably where Albanian settlers – who migrated south to many Aegean islands – set up their capital some time after the sixteenth century. The village population today is about 220. **Panaghia**, a hamlet of 26 souls, is perched on a high track above the sea and near Emborio.

It is fairly easy walking from one to another of the five villages. Alternatively go by taxi. Also by *caïque* you can get to **Armithia** islet. This is off the north-west coast of Kasos and is one of the group Strabo called Casii. No one lives on Armithia today, but there are gypsum quarries on the south-west coast which used to provide employment for Kasiots.

Astypalaia

Getting to Astypalaia Once or twice a week by inter-island steamer from Piraeus which continues to Kos and Rhodes.
Transport Taxi, small boats.
Accommodation Two D-Class hotels and a small restaurant with rooms; some rooms in private houses.
Beaches The best beaches are on either side of the narrow isthmus between the two halves of the island.

Astypalaia (pop. 1,540) is some 18 km. wide and shaped like a butterfly, its two wings linked by a narrow isthmus of a body. The capital, Astypalaia or Skala, is on the western half of the island and though both halves are mountainous there are no very high peaks.

Of the many bays and coves, Livadhia Bay just south of Astypalaia and Maltezana Bay on the south coast of the other half of the island are of some importance. The latter gives particularly good shelter as it is protected by two islets, Glino and Khondro. North-west of the isthmus is Aghios Andreas Bay and the long island of Fokia. Cutting deep into the north-west coast of the western half is Vathy Bay.

In the past, Astypalaia was called 'the table of the gods' (*theón trapéza*) on account of its great fertility. It would not merit the term today, though some valleys are productive still.

The island has been called Astoupalia and Astropalia but the Venetian variant of Stampalia is the one best remembered, partly because the Italians revived it.

HISTORY OF ASTYPALAIA

This is the island the Knights never touched and foreign influence therefore is almost wholly Venetian. In its very early history the island was a colony of Epidauros and the Romans were accustomed to shelter their vessels in its bays. It was plundered by Barbarossa in the sixteenth century and was then held by the Turks. During the War of Independence Astypalaia broke free from the Turks for about seven years but was recaptured and remained Turkish until the coming of the Italians in 1912.

SKALA

The island capital includes the port of Skala at sea level and Chora on a hill to the south. A splendid row of *mills* surmounts the saddle below Chora and a *Venetian castle* rises grandly from the cluster of houses at the top of the hill. It was built by the Quirini family, rulers of the island from the thirteenth century to the early sixteenth century, and their stamp is everywhere. Some words of island dialect are of Venetian origin and to find so many outward signs of Venetian power you have to go to Naxos, seat of the Venetian Dukes of Naxos and of the Sanudo family. The *church of Our Lady of the Castle* (Evangelistria tou Kastro) was built above the entrance to the castle.

EXCURSIONS ON ASTYPALAIA

By foot or taxi from Skala to the eastern half of the island and *Maltezana Bay*; to the village of **Livadhi**; to the islet of **Ofidusa**, due west of Astypalaia.

Kastellorizzo

Getting to Kastellorizzo Local boat from Rhodes. (See p. 38.)
Accommodation A very few rooms.
Beaches Town beach called Nifti and another at Aghios Stephanos Point, about 5 km. from the harbour.
Information This smallest of Dodecanese islands has its own information centre in Athens; apply to the *Syllogos Kastellorizzo*, 71 Harilaou Trikoupi Street, Athens.

'We have occupied Castelrosso island,' wrote General Maitland Wilson to the C.I.G.S. on September 14th, 1943. (See *The Second*

World War, by Winston S. Churchill.) Chastel Roux, Castelrosso and now Kastellorizzo: all these French, Italian and Greek names spring from a folk-memory of the reddish stone of the original castle of the Knights. The oldest name of all is Megisti (literally 'largest' – in this instance, of a cluster of small islands off the Turkish coast). 'Megisti' is by no means a dead name; it is commonly and affectionately used throughout the Dodecanese and especially by Kastelloricians who have emigrated from its shores.

Kastellorizzo (pop. 475) is the farthest east and the smallest island of the Dodecanese. It is about 6·5 km. long by 3 km. wide; it lies 72 miles east of Rhodes and is only 1½ miles from the village of Kas on the mainland of Asia Minor.

HISTORY OF KASTELLORIZZO

For centuries the island capital was famed as a safe harbourage on the route to Beirut and consequently throve and was busy. It was also tempting to pirates and invaders: the Knights invested it as an outpost and the Grand Master Juan d'Hérédia built the first castle. In 1440 the Sultan of Egypt attacked the island, destroyed the fortress and put the Knights to flight. Ten years later Kastellorizzo became a possession of Naples and the castle was rebuilt. The Turks took over in 1512 and held the island for nearly four centuries with the exception of two brief periods when the Venetians became masters of Kastellorizzo, first in 1570 and again in 1659. During this last invasion the castle was finally reduced to the state it is in today (a wall and three towers survive). The Greeks got a foothold in 1828 but were ousted by the Turks five years later. The island was under heavy fire from the Turkish mainland during the First World War and, as General Maitland Wilson's memo shows, the island was part of the Allied plans for controlling the Aegean in the last war. (See also Leros, p. 222.)

The island is still uneasily aware that geographically it is related to Turkey rather than to Greece. It is this fact as well as the hardship of life on Kastellorizzo that accounts for the thousands of first-, second- and third-generation Kastelloricians in Australia and America. Wherever they come to rest they immediately set up an organization to help relieve the poverty of those staying behind. It is not unusual, either, to meet young Antipodean or American Greeks visiting their family island for the first time.

KASTELLORIZZO TOWN

The harbour is an open rectangle with a lighthouse on the point to the left as you enter the port. The waterfront and tiny town look neat and attractive with their Turkish wooden balconies and windows, but the nearer the boat draws to the jetty the clearer it becomes that, like a stage set, close acquaintance destroys conviction. The paint on the houses is peeling and blistered, the windows are often close-shuttered. Decay and departure are all about you and it is a great pity. Kastellorizzo was splendid once but no one these days – unless the Tourist Board comes to the rescue – is prepared to have faith enough in it to invest in the future.

To the right of the jetty two churches lie back a little from the harbour. One is relatively modern, the other is the *Cathedral of Aghios Konstantinos and Aghia Heleni*. Some granite pillars in the cathedral have been carried from a Temple of Apollo in Lycian Asia Minor. (There are various Lycian references on the island because the Dorians, who worshipped Lycian Apollo, were among the early colonizers.)

The remains of the *castle*, built on the site of a classical fortress, are set on a bluff above the *lighthouse*. You will probably be led there by a villager, up the Street of the Knights. On the way, step aside and climb the steep path to a rock-cut tomb with a Doric façade which is called the *Lycian tomb*.

The women of the village are shy and disinclined to be photographed wearing the magnificent silver discs which decorate the front of their white blouses. Understandably, they are disenchanted with a life where living demands such effort, where the island soil is so chalky and unproductive that they rely on the weekly boat for food. If a housewife is not down on the waterfront when the boat comes in then she has to wait another week for her flour or vegetables. Even water is hard to come by and some ancient catchment cisterns up on Mt Viglo are still used to catch winter rains today as they did in Classical times.

Excursion from Kastellorizzo town: Fokiali Cave

Boat A motor-boat from the harbour will take you there in about 45 minutes.

The cave of Fokiali ('the refuge of seals') is south-east of the harbour. It is larger than the Blue Grotto at Capri and reputed to rival it for colour. Wild doves swoop about the cave.

SELECTED BIBLIOGRAPHY

RHODES AND THE DODECANESE

Ernle Bradford, *The Companion Guide to the Greek Islands* (Collins, 1963).

Winston S. Churchill, *The Second World War*, vol. 5 (Cassell, 1952). The Aegean strategy of the Allies, with particular reference to Rhodes, Leros and Kos.

Lawrence Durrell, *Reflection son a Marine Venus* (Faber, 1953; also in paperback edition).

A. Gabriel, *La Cité de Rhodes* (Paris, 1921–23).

Christos Karousos, *Rhodes* ('Esperos' Editions, Athens, 1973). A study of the history, monuments and art of Rhodes by the one-time Director of the National Museum. Available in English.

Raymond Matton, *Rhodes* (Collection de l'Institut d'Athènes, 1966).

C. T. Newton, *Travels and discoveries in the Levant* (Paris, 1869). Admirably written travelogue by a vice-consul who was also an amateur archaeologist: chapters on Rhodes and Kalymnos.

A. Tarsouli, *Dodekanisa* (Athens, 1947). In Greek, 3 vols. The domestic and village arts of the Dodecanese. Hard to find, but the drawings alone are worth the trouble.

W. M. Thackeray, *Notes of a Journey from Cornhill to Grand Cairo* (Chapman & Hall, 1846, and Routledge & Sons, 1886).

Cecil Torr, *Rhodes in Ancient Times* (Cambridge, 1885).

Cecil Torr, *Rhodes in Modern Times* (Cambridge, 1887).

Michael Volonakis, *The Island of Rhodes and her eleven sisters* (Macmillan, 1922).

OTHER ISLANDS OF THE DODECANESE

Kalymnos. Charmian Clift, *Mermaid Singing* (Michael Joseph, 1958).

Patmos. The Revelation of St John.

Dr Charles Perry, *A View of the Levant* (London, 1743).

Tilos. Carola Matthews, *The Mad Pomegranate Tree* (Macmillan, 1968). Mostly about northern Greece and the Cyclades, but contains a personal account of this little-visited island.

Kasos. Elias Kulukundis, *Journey to a Greek Island* (Cassell, 1968).

GREECE: GENERAL

A. R. Burn, *The Penguin History of Greece* (Pelican Books, 1966).

Pierre Devambez, *Greek Painting*. The Contact History of Art (Weidenfeld & Nicolson, 1962).

Robert Graves, *The Greek Myths* (Penguin Books, 1955).

Homer, *The Iliad* (Penguin Classics, 1969).

Dr J. Lemprière, *Lemprière's Classical Dictionary of Proper Names in Ancient Authors* (Routledge & Kegan Paul, 1788 and 1963).

Robert Payne, *The Splendour of Greece* (Pelican Books, 1964).

Oleg Polunin and Anthony Huxley, *Flowers of the Mediterranean* (Chatto & Windus, 1965).

J. C. Stobart, *The Glory that was Greece* (Sidgwick & Jackson, 1st ed. 1911, revised 1933; also in paperback).

Joyce M. Stubbs, *The Home Book of Greek Cookery* (Faber, 1963).

William Younger, *Gods, Men and Wine* (Michael Joseph, on behalf of the Wine and Food Society, 1966).

GLOSSARY

acropolis	A citadel or highest part of a Greek city.
antis	'In antis' – a form of Greek temple in which two porch columns stand between the side walls of the central chamber or naos.
architrave	The lowest section of the entablature, sandwiched between the capital and the frieze.
black-figure painting	Greek vase painting of the seventh and sixth centuries B.C. The figures are painted in black against the ground of red fired clay.
cavea	The seating area of a theatre.
cella	The Latin word for the naos or sacred chamber of a Classical temple.
chrysobull	A document bearing a gold seal.
Corinthian	The last of the three great orders of Greek architecture: the capital is decorated with variations of the acanthus leaf. The Corinthian order was in use from Hellenistic times through to the Byzantine period.
Doric	The earliest of the three orders of Greek architecture, austere and simple. The column is thick and has no base, the capital is plain and the entablature is adorned with triglyphs and metopes.
entablature	The lintel between the capitals and the pediment or roof.
exedra	A semicircular (sometimes rectangular) open alcove.
fresco	Technique of wall painting in which paint is applied to fresh, wet plaster.
herm	A pillar surmounted with a bust of Hermes or a city dignitary: a phallus is often carved into the pillar.
hydria	A large vessel with three handles for carrying water.
hypocaust	The Roman technique of under-floor heating for public and domestic baths.
icon	A religious image, often painted, sometimes in mosaic. Generally portable, but see 'iconostasis'.
iconostasis	A screen bearing a number of icons: divides nave from sanctuary in Byzantine churches.

Ionic	The middle order of Greek architecture. The base is small, the pillar slim and voluted (see below).
kore	Literally, a young girl. Is commonly used to describe standing female sculptures of the Archaic period.
kouros	A young man. Term describing standing male figure of the Archaic period.
krater	A vessel for mixing wine and water.
kylix	A shallow cup on a base.
lunette	The half-moon shape of a light or air source above a door or window.
megaron	The central hall of a Mycenaean palace or house.
metope	The metope is placed between two triglyphs on a Doric frieze and is usually decorated with sculptures (e.g., the Elgin Marbles).
mihrab	Mosques often include this as part of their names: it means a niche and indicates the direction of Mecca.
Minoan	A name first used by Sir Arthur Evans to describe the Bronze Age in Crete – derived from the legendary King Minos.
naos	Greek name for the central and most holy part of a Classical temple. Usually contained the cult statue.
narthex	The porch or vestibule of a church, often with arch or colonnade.
necropolis	A burial ground.
nymphaion	The sanctuary of the Nymphs.
ogee	A moulding or arch with a double or S-shaped curve.
oinoechoe	A jug for pouring.
pediment	The familiar or pointed gable of Greek and Roman temples and other buildings.
pendentive	An architectural device enabling a dome to rest upon a square.
peripteral	Surrounded by a colonnade.
peristyle	A continuous series of outer columns surrounding a temple or court.
pronaos	The porch before the naos.
propylaea	A monumental entrance to a temple complex.
protogeometric	The early stages of Geometric art.

quadriga	A chariot drawn by four horses.
red-figure painting	The style of Greek vase painting that followed (about 520 B.C.) the black-figure period. The figures are drawn upon the red clay; the background is painted black.
stele	A gravestone, generally flat and carved.
stoa	A shady, colonnaded walk with a roof.
string-course	The horizontal moulding emphasizing or dividing an architectural design.
stylobate	The highest step of the base of a temple. The stylobate acts as a platform for the pillars.
temenos	A sacred enclosure; a sanctuary.
triglyph	The three projecting, vertical ridges on the frieze of a Doric temple. The triglyphs alternate with the metopes.
trireme	A three-oared Greek galley.
volute	The scroll or spiral decorating Ionic, Corinthian or Composite capitals.

INDEX